PURSUING GREATNESS

Empowering Teachers to Take Charge of Their Professional Growth

Pete Hall | Alisa Simeral | Bryan Goodwin

with Bj Stone and Bess Scott

MCREL
INTERNATIONAL
Denver, Colorado USA

McREL International

4601 DTC Boulevard, Suite 500

Denver, CO 80237 USA

Phone: 303.337.0990 | Fax: 303.337.3005

Website: www.mcrel.org | Email: info@mcrel.org | Store: store.mcrel.org

---

About McREL

McREL International helps educators flourish by turning research into solutions that transform teaching, learning, and leading. As a nonprofit, nonpartisan education research and development organization, McREL turns knowledge about what works in education into practical, effective guidance and training for teachers and education leaders across the U.S. and around the world.

All referenced trademarks are the property of the respective owners. All internet links mentioned in this book are correct as of the initial publication date.

Printed in the United States of America.

To order, visit store.mcrel.org

ISBN: 978-1-7326994-5-8

Library of Congress Control Number: 2019912620

Hall, P., Simeral, A., Goodwin, B., Stone, B., & Scott, B. (2019). *Pursuing greatness: Empowering teachers to take charge of their professional growth.* Denver, CO: McREL International.

Pursuing Greatness
Empowering Teachers to Take Charge of Their Professional Growth

Tools

Tools (continued)

Dedications

To Mrs. Mindy Hall and all the other great teachers out there, thank you for showing me that excellence comes from curiosity, passion, intentionality, and creativity. We only know what we know because of you.

—*Pete Hall*

To my father, Terry. You provided an upbringing filled with adventure, taught us how to see the world through different eyes, and instilled a desire to pursue greatness in all things. I am who I am today because of you. I love you Dad.

—*Alisa Simeral*

To my mother for insisting, "You can do anything if you set your mind to it."

—*Bryan Goodwin*

To Don and Tom: the two most important people in my life. You make living and learning magical!

—*Bj Stone*

To my sister, Katie, and daughter, Erin, extraordinary educators who change students' and colleagues' lives through their constant drive to learn and grow!

—*Bess Scott*

Prologue

 Becoming an expert, one problem at a time

More advice for teachers? Seriously? What more can be said that hasn't already been said?

Maybe that's what you're thinking.

Or maybe it's something more like, *I've got 101 problems, but reading your book ain't one.*

Fair enough.

But before you put this book back on the shelf, we want you to know it's *all about* solving your problems.

Don't worry. We're not going to pepper you with a bajillion things you must do to be a good teacher, nor make you feel guilty about all the things you're *not* doing.

Rather, we've written this whole book with you in mind—the challenges we know you face in your classroom. Whatever problem you're facing, other teachers have faced them too . . . and the cleverest ones have *solved* them. So, you can take solace in that.

You can also take solace that you don't need to read this book from cover to cover (unless that's how you roll). Rather, we encourage you to identify a challenge in your classroom—commonly referred to as a "problem of practice"—then read what researchers have figured out about how to solve it, and then do what real people (fellow teachers) have done to address the same challenges in their classrooms.

> **Definition: problem of practice (noun)**
>
> The particular element in your teaching and/or classroom responsibilities that nags at you, confounds you, and provides a challenge that you haven't yet been able to overcome.

Growing your expertise

Before you go flipping ahead through the pages of this book to find your problem of practice, though, we should share one more thing: We've written this book to not only show you how to solve your problems, but also help you understand *why* a particular strategy works, and help you reflect on what happens when you apply best practice in your classroom.

Why is that important? We want to help you embed these strategies deeply in your teaching so they become second nature. We also want to help you be a great teacher (or even greater one) by helping you to self-reflect on what is and isn't working in your classroom so you can keep becoming a better version of yourself. On top of that, we want to help you develop ever more *expertise* as a teacher, which entails developing mental models of *how* things work and *why*, so you're equipped with a whole set of *when-then* statements (*when* X happens, *then* I do Y) that you can use to diagnose and solve problems.

You'll likely find that this process is a little like climbing a mountain, in which cresting one hill brings a higher one into view. In the same way, overcoming one teaching challenge often reveals another. We've constructed this book, in fact, as a series of pathways with one challenge leading to the next. We don't do that to overwhelm you, but to help you develop those mental models for teaching: connecting dots among what otherwise might come across as a bunch of disparate tactics into some big, important ideas—that is, theories of action—that you can employ to lift student learning.

Also, we've constructed these pathways to inspire you, to show you how tackling common classroom problems one after another can bring you to a special place—to the top of the mountain, if you will—where you'll feel creative and innovative as you guide your students toward inquiry-based learning, helping them to stoke their fire inside to learn, and become passionate and persistent learners. A place where they can be deeply *curious*.

Ultimately, that's where we hope this journey, and solving one problem at a time, can lead you: to a place where learning is joyful, for both you and your students.

It'd be hypocritical, of course, to guide you toward inquiry-based learning without letting you engage in inquiry-based learning yourself. And really, that's what this book is all about—letting you take control of *your own* learning as a teacher. That's why we've designed it as something of an interactive quest, so you can select where you want to go next, finding your own opportunity for improvement and growth.

Don't travel alone

We also hope that you'll share this book with your colleagues, because your own learning is more likely to be fruitful and rewarding when you engage in cooperative professional learning (PL). We've known for a long time, of course, that drive-by professional development (PD) sessions don't really do much for teachers or their students. That's not to say teachers never get better; they do, all the time. In fact, contrary to what you may have heard, most teachers do grow as professionals and get better over the entire course of their careers (Goodwin & Slotnik, 2019).

What's more, education researchers have given us a pretty good handle on the "recipe" for talent development. It includes these ingredients:

1) Theory—learning *what* to do and *why* it's important.

2) Modeling—seeing *how* to do it.

3) Practice—applying a new strategy in an actual classroom setting.

4) Peer coaching—receiving feedback to improve the practice (Joyce & Showers, 2002).

We cannot overstate the impact of this fourth element, *peer coaching*. Without it, we only transfer about 5 percent of what we learn in PD sessions to our classrooms. Basically, we need critical friends to regularly observe our teaching and provide feedback to help us refine our practices and avoid backsliding into old habits. So, you'll find throughout this book questions to pose to your peers when you invite them to observe your classroom. We did that because most people are too nice to point out our shortcomings—unless we purposefully invite them to hit us between the eyes with them. When you say, for example, "I feel like my kids weren't all engaged with that lesson, so how might I have started that lesson better?" it's a lot easier for your peer to say, "Well, now that you mention it, there was one thing. . . ."

We didn't just make this stuff up

A quick word about the pathways themselves. Altogether, this book will help you solve 24 key problems of practice that you're likely to face (or may have already faced) in your classroom. You may wonder, why these 24 problems? (*After all, I have 101.*)

We chose them because they're not only common, they're also critical problems whose solutions will benefit your students most. How do we know that? We've drawn from an extensive review of decades of research that McREL has synthesized over the years and presented in two editions of the popular ASCD publication, *Classroom Instruction That Works* (Dean, Hubbell, Pitler, & Stone, 2012; Marzano, Pickering, & Pollock, 2001). Later, we added to this knowledge base—synthesizing research on teacher-student relationships, motivation, grading practices, and standards-based education—to create an even more robust view of what teachers do in the classroom, and shared our findings in *The 12 Touchstones of Good Teaching* (Goodwin & Hubbell, 2013). In all this work, we were cognizant of what education researcher John Hattie frequently refers to as the "hinge point" of research effect sizes; that is, we looked for practices with significant effect sizes—well beyond what we'd expect from ordinary effects for teachers. We used this work as a lens through which to view common classroom problems and focus on the ones most worthy of your attention.

In short, we want to help you solve the right problems. Sure, keeping your classroom plants alive may be a problem, but it's not an important one. Besides, if you saw our plants, you'd know we can't help you there.

So, what we aim to provide in this book is clarity about the most important problems you can solve in your classroom along with a sequence for solving them.

Our why

If we might be permitted to speak from the heart for a moment, we'd like to add this: We don't expect you to read this book just because of what we've written in these pages or how we've put it together. We believe both are strengths, but what's even more important to us is our *why*—the single, big compelling idea that drew all of us together to craft this labor of love.

It's an idea that is often ignored in conversations about teacher development: *curiosity*. We believe all students should have the opportunity to be curious—not just in a temporary or distractive way, but to become curious people whose lives are animated and enriched by questioning, exploring, and learning about others. As we've written elsewhere, curiosity has many powerful benefits—helping us become better students, demonstrate better job performance, experience better relationships, feel more fulfilled in life, become better leaders, and, believe it or not, live longer.

Creating classrooms where curiosity can flourish, though, requires teachers who have mastered the fundamentals and routines of teaching so well, and have so effectively internalized a broad repertoire of expert mental models about teaching, that they're able to focus less on *teaching* and more on student *learning*.

Hopefully at this point, some curiosity may have begun stirring inside you, making you want to read more to figure out how tackling one challenge after another can help you and your students experience a different kind of classroom. That's the other big idea animating this book: *teacher curiosity*. We want to help you make your classroom more rewarding and joyful, not just for your students, but for you. We hope that as you read this book, you'll experience curiosity and begin to wonder, *What if* I tried these ideas in my classroom? Would it really work?

Personalizing learning one step at a time, from the inside out

Finally, we don't believe expertise comes about through top-down direction or scripted programs. That's why this book offers neither. Rather, it's designed to inspire and guide you to follow your own journey of professional growth—and to help you work with your colleagues to do the same so that ultimately, together, you can create dynamic, personalized learning environments for students. It's worth noting that schools that have successfully created these environments say that it wasn't done with a snap of the fingers or by implementing a program. Rather, it was a messier, more organic process akin to *innovating together*. People in these schools describe their efforts as "failing forward" in rapid, iterative cycles—operating with an experimental mindset that says mistakes are OK, but errors (repeated mistakes) should be avoided (Halverson et al., 2015). These efforts almost always start with small, incremental steps, laying a foundation with the basics and then building on that foundation, together, to develop more expert practice and innovation:

❖ Often, as a first order of business, they translate standards-based curriculum into learning progressions.

❖ Next, they work together to develop the ability to quickly size up and support student learning.

❖ Then, through trial and error, they become more comfortable with loosening their grip on instruction and handing the reins over to students—understanding that it's far easier to differentiate *learning* than instruction.

Use this book as a guide for personalizing your professional learning—not as a step-by-step process like those migraine-inducing instructions for ready-to-assemble furniture, but rather as more of a road map to help you reflect, with your colleagues, where you are on your journey. In doing so, we hope this book makes a unique contribution to conversations about personalized learning by recognizing that it isn't something we wake up one morning and decide to do. Like all good things, it takes time—the culmination of a variety of teaching practices delivered with such mastery, precision, and creativity that students can take ownership and control of their own learning. With sustained commitment to professional reflection and collegial feedback, you can get there.

So, if you're ready to begin (or continue) your journey, we are, too.

Chapter 1

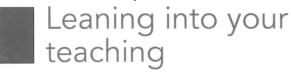

Leaning into your teaching

Think about the best teacher you've ever seen in action—a person who models excellence in the profession, their classroom a beacon of learning. Students are engaged, lessons provide rigorous challenges, and there's palpable synergy between students and teacher. Teaching and learning pass over, under, around, and through each other, with students instructing the teacher about learning—what causes confusion, what examples are meaningful—and the teacher inspiring, facilitating, and guiding students' growth.

As you consider this individual, ask yourself these questions: What top three characteristics would you use to describe this excellence in the classroom? What sets this teacher apart from other educators? What distinguishes this teacher as "excellent?" Perhaps you'd use the words passionate, organized, or well-planned. Or maybe warm and caring, patient, and funny. What about "sets high expectations" or "has a deep knowledge of content?" How about "is flexible," "strong in classroom management," or "develops a strong rapport with students?"

If we pause for a moment to gain our bearings, we realize our list can't be limited to just three descriptors; instead we could easily fill a whole book listing the qualities, characteristics, and attributes that describe this educator extraordinaire.

Another pause reveals a subsequent truth: Put two of these "excellent" teachers side by side and they would look undeniably different. While they may resemble each other in some general ways, the specific characteristics we use to describe one may very well not describe the other at all.

For years, the secret to great teaching has seemed more like alchemy than science, with research only complicating the matter. Take a quick glance at the studies on teacher quality over the past several decades and you'll have a long list of lists—each report offering its own rendition of what it takes to be categorized as "excellent." Combine all the characteristics that you read about, and we're right back to where we started: with enough qualities and attributes to fill a book.

What, then, is the difference between excellence and mediocrity? Is there one big factor that distinguishes great teachers from the others? Maybe the answer is just below the surface. As renowned education thinker John Dewey (1933) proposed many years ago, we do not learn from experience itself, but rather, from *reflecting* on experience. Excellent teachers think differently than their peers. They think differently about their students, which leads them to build stronger rapport and cultivate a strong classroom climate. They think differently about curriculum and content—leading them to make deeper learning connections for their students. They think differently about teaching strategies—leading them to engage students in more effective ways. In short, what distinguishes excellent teachers from others is how they think, what they think about, and the frequency, accuracy, and depth of their thinking.

Reflection broadly defined

A Latin term, the word *reflection* dates to the mid-1300s with the meaning to "bend back." A mirror bends back the light, letting us see ourselves. Mental reflection, simply put, is shifting our perspective by "looking back" and examining ourselves with the purpose of learning, developing, and growing. Dewey defined it as *thinking about thinking*. Reflection requires us to develop a deep understanding of our own thought processes. It furthers our learning and inspires provocative thought and action. In *The Reflective Practitioner* (1983), Donald Schön states, "Reflective practice is a dialogue of thinking and doing through which I become more skillful" (p.31). And the only real prerequisites for engaging in this level of introspection are gusto and curiosity (there's that word again!).

Reframing professional learning: Both an individual and collective shift

Ask your colleagues to define professional development and you'll get a plethora of answers, most lamenting that it is something done "to" us, outside of any teacher's control. A 2015 report published by a nonprofit, The New Teacher Project (TNTP), found that teachers spend 19 school days each year in professional development sessions mandated by their district. A research study conducted through a partnership of the Bill & Melinda Gates Foundation and the Boston Consulting Group in 2014 found that of the 68 hours teachers spend each year on professional learning activities, workshops are the most common delivery format, with an average of 20 hours spent in mandated district-provided trainings. Overall, nearly one in five teachers (18 percent) say they've never had a say in their own professional development, likening their experiences to hapless sheep being herded through the chutes, following blindly the course chosen by others.

Startling statistics, to be sure; and while we're all nodding our heads in agreement remembering our own grueling PD experiences, we'd like to offer a revolutionary and insightful new idea. What would happen if the control shifted to *us*, if we could take charge of our learning and development as teachers, reclaiming the shepherd's cane and determining our own destiny instead?

A literal definition of professional development, of course, is *developing as professionals*. Authentic professional development occurs when *we* as teachers unlearn, relearn, and learn some more, when *we* unpack the thinking that drives our doing, when *we* deepen our reflective habits to shift and grow as practitioners. Herein lies our assertion: *We* are in charge of our own professional growth. Let that sink in for a moment.

While we might like to think that the workshops we attend will magically solve all our problems and transform us into perfect educators, it just isn't so. The only person who holds the power of self-development is you. Our co-author Bryan wrote that "We can't force anyone to learn anything; knowledge rarely enters anyone's head involuntarily. To learn something, we must *want* to learn it" (Goodwin, 2015, p. 3). He was writing about students, but that statement applies to teachers as well. Unless some form of professional curiosity guides our own learning, we're unlikely to reflect on our own practice, deepen our knowledge, challenge our own thinking, and hone our skills.

Teachers have opportunities to engage in active learning every day—when we're checking for student understanding during a lesson, reflecting with colleagues on student progress in a team meeting, sitting in a district-mandated workshop, or grading papers late at night. These moments all offer an opportunity to shift and develop our thinking, and to shift the ownership of professional learning from someone else and back to ourselves. It bears repeating: The power of professional learning lies in *your* hands (and in your mind).

Reflecting before, during, and after action

For many practitioners, reflection may seem like just another task on a to-do list. A lesson is taught, then reflection happens when time permits at the end of the day, or we quickly reflect on the previous day while we're preparing our plans for the day ahead. True reflection, though, ought to be something we do as a matter of habit, all day, every day. To use an anatomically imprecise but apt metaphor, if we only go to the gym occasionally, we can't expect our bodies to transform into a flawless physique. Likewise, if we only engage in occasional reflection, we can't expect to reach high levels of professional practice. When we engage in reflection before, during, and after action, we sharpen our thinking and move beyond mere competence toward expertise.

Strengthening the muscle to develop refined habits of thought

Reflective thinking is something of a flywheel—it spins slowly at first, then picks up speed as we become increasingly reflective in our practice. Before long, we've built up enough momentum that the whole process becomes our habitual way of thinking. We find ourselves regularly "going meta"—becoming more aware of our thinking—and asking ourselves, *Am I thinking about this right?*

So, what does this look like?

Regardless of the challenge they may face, reflective teachers use a series of intentional thoughts. Co-authors Pete and Alisa first surfaced this predictable pattern of thinking—one that leads to growth, improvement, and excellence—and coined it the Reflective Cycle (Hall & Simeral, 2015; Hall & Simeral, 2017).

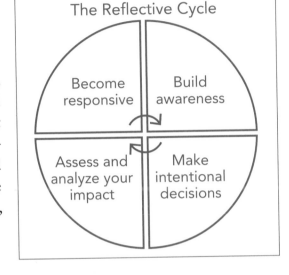

What do reflective practitioners do?

❖ **They build awareness.** This starts by making observations, tuning into what's going on in their environment and detecting problems. You won't find them hip-deep in just *doing* stuff in their classrooms; instead, they're on a constant mission to collect data—little bits of information that arrive in many forms—about their students, their content, and their pedagogy. Going deeper, reflective practitioners examine their instructional reality to seek the full picture of what's happening in front of, behind, and around them. When they run into a problem of practice, rather than bemoaning their challenges, they search for root causes and access the many resources at their disposal to size up the situation and create a plan of attack. By first asking the reflective question *Why is this happening?* they're better able to ask and answer the more pragmatic question, *How do I . . . ?*

❖ **They make intentional decisions.** Based on their observations and their diagnosis of the problem at hand, reflective teachers think—and then act—with intentionality. In short, they connect knowledge with action. They can explain the logic of the actions they're taking; that is, they know *why* they're doing *what* they're doing. As a result, they can offer an if-then statement or testable hypothesis for their actions: *If I do X, then Y should happen.*

❖ **They assess and analyze their impact.** After taking action, reflective teachers return to their if-then hypotheses to consider how well they applied a solution and the results of their actions. That is, they ask themselves *Did I do X correctly?* followed by *Did Y happen?*

❖ **They become responsive.** Analysis of their efforts leads reflective teachers to consolidate their learning by *routinizing* a new strategy (adding it to their repertoire if it works), *refining* it (finding ways to make it work even better), or *reconsidering* it (abandoning it if it didn't produce the desired result despite being done well).

❖ **They repeat this pattern.** With increasing frequency, accuracy, and depth, reflective practitioners engage in the four thought processes of the Reflective Cycle over and over. By creating and refining their habits of thought, they essentially strengthen their reflective muscle, leading them ever closer to attaining the goal(s) they've set for themselves and their students. Following the pattern, in short, allows us to think our way to success.

Talking about failure to find success

There's success, and then there's failure. Yes, failure—a taboo word in our line of work, one that evokes fear in the best of us. It's seen as an ending, as proof that your efforts didn't yield the results you wanted, that your ideas weren't good enough. Yet the truth is that failure is a key part of *trying*.

We don't have to look very hard to find successful people who have "failed" along the way. These folks encountered obstacles and relied on grit, perseverance, *sticktoitiveness*, or whatever you want to call it to overcome those struggles. Curiosity, inquisitiveness, and a willingness to try new things are the driving factors to self-reflection; and these don't come in a tidy box with a *mistake-free* logo stamped on the side. "A man of genius makes no mistakes. His errors are volitional and are the portals of discovery," wrote novelist James Joyce (1922).

Our quest to engage in authentic reflection must include the willingness to talk about, analyze, and learn from each mistake and struggle. Ultimately, our ability to grow as reflective practitioners will come down to our willingness to be transparent about these things and to embrace that the key to success lies in the power—yes, we said *power*—of failure. So, as you explore the learning in these pages, please keep this in mind: You're not learning if you're not failing—and reflecting candidly and honestly on your failures with your colleagues. ❧

Chapter 2

How do I use this book to develop my expertise?

We wrote this book assuming that you want to get better at your profession. And judging by the fact that you've made it to chapter two, that appears to be true. You desire better outcomes for all your students. You long to become a great teacher. You have your sights set on expertise. You're driven by excellence, as opposed to mediocrity. You understand that your professional growth is important, and you see problems of practice not as annoying nuisances but rather as hills to climb on your way to scaling the mountain.

Why do Y? Two big ideas

Before we travel too far down this path without a map, allow us to offer our theory of action in writing this book; you may even recognize it as our thesis statement.

First, we believe research and best practice are useful and important, yet we often get them backwards or incomplete. That is, instead of explaining to people, *Hey, if you're having X problem, try doing Y*, many writers and researchers present their best practices and research findings as simply *do Y*—with no further explanation about *why* doing Y is important.

Such guidance is sometimes useful, but it doesn't do much to help people become more intentional or reflective about their practice; instead, they wind up with a toolkit full of strategies and are left to their own devices to figure out when to use which tool. As a result, we often see people using a teaching strategy—cooperative learning, for example—without much understanding of what problem they're trying to solve with that strategy. Worse, they may use the right strategy at the wrong time: Using cooperative learning for direct instruction, for example, is akin to using pliers to put a nail in a board. So, with this book, we're flipping all that around and starting with problems of practice, then offering research-based best practices for what to do about them.

| Big Idea #1 | There is tremendous power in self-reflection to build your capacity as an effective educator. |

How you *think* about your challenges drives how you *act*. Thus, developing your self-reflective habits will help you refine your craft. Drawing upon co-authors Pete and Alisa's exploration of the connection between our *thinking* and our *doing*, published in a series of books—including *Building Teachers' Capacity for Success* (Hall & Simeral, 2008), *Teach, Reflect, Learn* (Hall & Simeral, 2015), *The Principal Influence* (Hall, Childs-Bowen, Cunningham-Morris, Pajardo, & Simeral, 2016), and *Creating a Culture of Reflective Practice* (Hall & Simeral, 2017)—we believe that the straightest route to long-term professional growth lies in the habits of self-reflection. Of course, that begs the question: What things should you reflect about? Where should you focus your reflective energy to best meet your students' needs? Those questions bring us to our second big idea.

| Big Idea #2 | There are some classroom practices that yield a greater impact on student learning—and are more likely to help you solve your current problem of practice—than others. |

Classroom challenges are opportunities to get better, and you'd like to give your students a better learning experience. As a dedicated teacher, you know that while kids may challenge you, they *need you* to help them. As a lifelong learner, you believe "the truth is out there"—that you can find solutions to your challenges and that, often, the best shortcut to those solutions lies in research and best practice. Sure, you could cast about for months or even years to figure out what works, or you could just stand on the shoulders of those who have already figured this stuff out. That's why we've grounded this book in extensive research on effective teaching practices combined with practical guidance to help you figure out *how* to use those best practices to get optimal results and the opportunity to *think about* those practices.

These two ideas come together into the prevailing theory of action for this book:

| Theory of Action | IF we start with key problems of practice, use research-based best practices to solve them, and reflect on our practice as teachers, THEN we will become more expert in our practice, better able to meet our students' needs, and engaged in career-long professional growth that will allow us to become amazing, unstoppable teachers in whose classrooms learning will flourish. |

We can all improve our practice. By developing consistent habits of mind that focus on diagnosing and solving problems, and continuously engaging in reflection, you can shorten your learning curve and exponentially expand your ability to change students' lives. In the chapters that follow, we'll help you expand your technical expertise, problem-solving acumen, and ability to "go meta" with your practices by stepping back and looking at them objectively to spot opportunities for improvement and become increasingly precise in your professional practices.

What are you curious about?

We've written this book with you in mind—to give you a path for your personalized professional learning. We've laid the path out—several of them, actually—for you. Your job is to begin the journey.

Here's our advice: Start by setting a goal. It doesn't need to be lofty or grandiose, but it does need to be an important step you'd like to take in your professional learning, one that reflects your most pressing problem of practice. What are your challenges? What are you most curious about? How would you like to grow as a professional educator? Ideally, these things would connect: "I wonder how I might solve the problem of _____." You might, for example, complete this statement: *A year from now, I'd most like to be able to say, "Wow, I got a lot better at _____!"*

Most of us set annual professional growth goals anyway, so let's take a moment to reflect on what really drives your interest and captures your fancy with regards to your own professional performance. Because professional development is really in our own hands (and heads), let's own it.

Helping you to develop know-how

You may recall that our aim in this book is to help you solve *the right problems*. So, we've drawn from an extensive review of decades of research that McREL has synthesized over the years and looked for the things that jump off the page of studies to say, *These are really important. Doing these right will address most of your classroom challenges.* Doing so generated the six *pathways* listed below.

1. Nurturing a positive learning environment.
2. Challenging students to commit to mastery.
3. Designing engaging learning.
4. Motivating with feedback.
5. Assessing for learning.
6. Creating dynamic group learning.

We've arranged the problems of practice presented in this book into these six pathways for two reasons. First, you'll find that many of the solutions we offer to the problems of practice tend to be additive—that is, one set of solutions builds on the next. Second, we want to help you do what experts do—connect dots into larger mental constructs which researchers sometimes call mental models or mental schema but we'll just call *know-how*.

It's the interweaving of research and cognitive science about teaching and learning (the *know* part) with practical classroom strategies teachers use to create effective classrooms (the *how* part).

In practice, you'll find that these pathways tend to interconnect and complement one another and that, in the end, great teaching is really a stew of lots of things. However, we know that while our brains may be able to *tend to* multiple things at once, we can only *focus on* one at a time. So, for the sake of clarity, simplicity, and more focused learning, we've separated the ingredients of the stew into these six pathways knowing that eventually, you'll get to all six (and are likely already addressing some parts of all six right now).

When you begin this journey, you may want to share this note with your supervisor.

Note to my administrator	Dear administrator,
	I'm interested in my own professional growth. This year, I'm going to begin by addressing a critical problem of teacher practice by applying a research-based best practice in my classroom, chosen from the list of six pathways in *Pursuing Greatness: Empowering Teachers to Take Charge of Their Professional Growth*. I'm going to learn how to allocate my mental energy and reflect more frequently, accurately, and deeply about this practice, and my performance and results shall improve. Please know that this work takes time, support, and concentration. As I grow and learn, I'll be trying new strategies, assessing their impact, and making modifications to better meet my students' needs. From you, I'll need feedback, advice, and coaching support—in both my technical work and my reflective journey.
	Thank you in advance!

Understanding the journey

As noted in *The 12 Touchstones of Good Teaching* (Goodwin & Hubbell, 2013), we can boil decades of research on effective teaching down to three imperatives (must-do's) that great teachers follow: 1) they challenge students by setting a high bar for learning and helping students meet those expectations, 2) they support students emotionally and academically, and 3) they are intentional with their practices; that is, they understand the *why* behind *what* they're doing. This third imperative—linking thinking to acting—serves as the common thread of this book. That's because it's difficult, if not impossible, to grow as a professional if you're not being deliberate and intentional about it! You'll find the language of intentionality sprinkled throughout this text in the reflective questions, and soon, in your own thinking. Ultimately, we hope to help you to strengthen that little voice in your head that provides you with a running color commentary on what you're doing: *Something doesn't feel right . . . what is it? What's really going on here? How'd that go? Did I do it right? What could I do better?*

We've constructed each pathway to include a series of *refinement phases*. You might think of them as waypoints on your journey toward expertise. Each phase reflects what we know from numerous studies about how people develop their talents—be it in sports, the arts, science, or professional knowledge (Bloom, 1985). Consider, for a moment, any talent you've developed or something you've become an expert in doing. If you were to trace back how you developed that talent and expertise (as researchers have done), you'd likely find that you moved through the following four phases:

1. Master the fundamentals (be *consistent*)

The first phase of talent development is often a period of exploration and joy as you learn the fundamentals of the field—whether it's mastering shading and perspective in art, learning chords on a guitar, or making flip turns at a neighborhood swimming pool. This initial "romance" phase is followed by the "digging in" phase—our initial, painstaking efforts yield rapid improvements; we learn to draw more convincingly, to play more chords on the guitar, or shed seconds off our swim times. During this phase, we can shorten our learning curve by imitating others—be it other master artists, musicians, or Olympic swimmers.

Teachers are no different. Our initial *how do I* questions often involve the mechanics of lesson planning, lesson delivery, classroom management, or student-teacher interactions. And we can grow quickly by borrowing from other, more expert teachers—their lesson plans, classroom management tricks, and classroom personas. Our initial efforts here may feel slow and faltering at first, so it's good to have a coach to encourage us to stick with them. If we can do that, and grow more consistent in applying the fundamentals, they start to become more automatic and we feel ourselves growing in leaps and bounds. Our initial anxieties about being able to cut it as teachers begin to fade and we find ourselves thinking, *OK, I've got this.* These can be heady times, but a professional pitfall can be lurking right around the corner.

In this first phase of developing our talents, we focus, necessarily, on our *own* practices—doing the right things right, as it were. As a result, our classrooms tend to be *teacher-owned* and *student-experienced*. We are often so consumed with what *we* must do, that we may not be thinking much about what's going on inside our students' minds. At best, we may focus on their outward expressions of learning, like whether they're on task, without giving much thought to whether they have bought into or truly understand the task. That's normal. And there's nothing horribly wrong with that—unless we get stuck there.

2. Move beyond ourselves (learn to *connect*)

In any field, becoming good enough often keeps us from getting better. Anders Ericsson, who studied professional athletes, found that it only takes about 40–50 hours of deliberate practice for us to become *pretty good* at something—after a few weekends on the driving or putting range, for example, we can avoid embarrassing ourselves when we play a round of golf with our buddies (Ericsson & Pool, 2016). The same could be said for playing the guitar, painting a still life, or baking a cobbler. We reach a point where we often don't have to think that much anymore about what we're doing. And therein lies the problem. We're good but we're not great. Moving beyond this stage requires looking beyond ourselves (or back on ourselves) to see what we could keep doing better. In sports, it's often a matter of looking at what other players are doing. In the arts, it's considering how others respond to our artistry. When it comes to teaching, we begin to consider how students are responding to what we're doing.

So, in this next phase, like a basketball player who must redirect her attention from what *she's* doing (dribbling without traveling) to what *others* are doing (who's open for a pass and who's trying to steal the ball), as teachers we need to redirect the mental bandwidth we recently freed up by becoming more fluent and automatic with our practices to consider how our students are responding. Thus, our *how do I* questions begin to shift toward connecting students with the purpose and goals of their learning so they can take a more active role in it. This phase requires a significant change: We redirect our instruction to help students activate their prior knowledge, to collaborate in meaningful ways, and fuel their curiosity. It's no longer about *teaching* as much as it is about our *students*—it's this "aha" moment that defines this phase. In short, we consider how to create *teacher-directed*, *student-connected* classrooms.

3. Translate knowledge into expertise (learn to *differentiate*)

When we focus on what's happening for our students, we recognize an obvious fact: They are all really different; they come into our classrooms with different interests, abilities, and social-emotional skills. So, at this point, our *how do I* questions begin to focus increasingly on creating classrooms that meet the needs of all students—those who are ready to accelerate their learning and those who need more time, those who are dialed into learning and those who are checked out, and those who are emotionally ready to learn and those who have unmet needs. During this phase, we grow our talents not just as practitioners (applying the tools of the trade, as it were) but as experts (bringing know-how to address the needs of all students). Because we have multiple ways of looking at challenges, we don't get stuck on a single interpretation of events (like the Far Side cartoon of an airline pilot looking out his cockpit, spotting a mountain goat, and remarking to his copilot, "Say, what's a mountain goat doing way up here in a cloud bank?"). Instead, we draw upon a broad base of knowledge to check and recheck our assumptions and adapt what we're doing to the situation at hand.

When individual students struggle, expert teachers use a variety of mental models to diagnose the problem. Are students not yet reading with automaticity? Do they lack background knowledge? Or do they have a fixed mindset about new, challenging content? Rather than concluding a student cannot learn, expert teachers ask themselves: *How do I* help him learn? During this phase of development, teachers focus more squarely on student learning—they understand how learning happens and seek to engage all students in active learning. But they recognize that students must choose to learn; teachers are there to facilitate the process. As a result, they create classrooms that are *student-engaged* and *teacher-facilitated*.

4. Become creative—and let go (*empower* students)

The final phase of talent development reflects creativity. Ultimately, having multiple mental models (know-how) at our disposal creates a seedbed for creativity and innovation to begin sprouting in our professional practice. It's what allows jazz musicians to improvise—they follow the same chord progressions as the original tune, but can throw in extra notes, often spontaneously, because they've internalized another set of routines—jazz scales—and simply listen for what sounds good. What creativity often boils down to is knowing the rules so well that we see when and how to break them. Painters such as Picasso or Monet created wildly inventive works of art by breaking contemporary conventions of perspective and detail.

Great teachers reach a similar plane. They develop innovative ways to help students learn. Some "break the rules" by, for example, flipping what's normally done in class with independent learning for students. Others set aside the textbook and help students consult primary sources to develop accounts of historical events or engage in rigorous, natural studies of local biomes. Others find ways to help students connect learning with their own passions and interests. Ultimately, they help students *own* their learning, which requires doing something a bit scary: letting go of control over student learning. That doesn't mean they leave students entirely to their own devices. Teachers still *guide* the process—ensuring, for example, that student projects stay on track, address essential questions, and demonstrate deep learning. In short, they create classrooms that are *student-owned*, yet *teacher-guided*.

We see and admire these great teachers and may assume that they're just naturally talented. What we know about talent development, though, is that reaching this pinnacle of teaching requires deep understanding and appreciation of the fundamentals as well as expert know-how to check for student understanding and guide learning. Creative teachers build on these things to create student-centered learning that's nonetheless grounded in high expectations for students and solid pedagogy.

Embarking on your journey

What all of this adds up to is a talent development journey that looks something like this.

Figure 1. The four refinement phases within each pathway.

Be consistent *Teacher-owned,* *Student-experienced*	Be connected *Teacher-directed,* *Student-connected*	Differentiate *Student-engaged,* *Teacher-facilitated*	Empower *Student-owned,* *Teacher-guided*

You may notice that the overall progression of your technical application of any given teaching approach (from the *teacher-owned, student-experienced* phase all the way to the *student-owned, teacher-guided* phase) looks something like the gradual release of responsibility model originally shared by mother birds in their nests and popularized by Doug Fisher and Nancy Frey (2013) in their handbook, *Better Learning Through Structured Teaching*. You're also likely to find that your rate of growth from one refinement phase to the next in any given strategy or set of strategies will be determined by the frequency, accuracy, and depth of your reflections about that skill. Because we're here to help you grow as reflective practitioners, we'll provide you with many guiding questions to drive your reflective growth in each phase of development along these six pathways.

How are the chapters organized?

We begin each chapter with a short description of a pathway and why it deserves our attention. Each pathway is then subdivided into four problems of practice—*How do I?* questions—that reflect the *refinement phases* that can guide your thinking and growth as you move from *consistency* to *connecting* to *differentiating* to *empowering*.

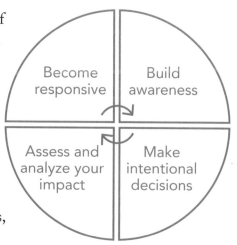

In each of these sections, we'll guide you through the Reflective Cycle, helping you to engage in the habits of thinking of highly reflective—and, thus, highly effective—educators.

Apply directly to classroom. Apply directly to classroom. Apply directly to classroom.

That's not a typo, just a paraphrase from the annoying (but effective) commercials for a headache remedy. We hope it's how you'll use this book—take what's in these pages and immediately apply it in your classroom. It might even alleviate your professional headaches. In all seriousness, we don't imagine that you'll read this book cover to cover or blaze through all these reflective cycles in a matter of days, weeks, or even months. Rather, it will likely take you weeks if not a few months to work through each problem of practice. So, give yourself time to refine your practice, hone your skills, and "lock in" the new strategies until they become a natural part of your repertoire and who you are as a teacher.

Be sure to engage in an honest self-assessment of where you are as a teacher. While it can be tempting to skip right to the "fun" stuff (empowering learners in your classroom in creative ways), in practice, no one leaps right to creativity without first doing the work of engaging fully in the phases of talent development. Sure, there are lots of people who *try* to be creative without taking the necessary steps to grow their talents, but that rarely goes well—resulting in a hot mess of unlistenable music, tortuous performance art, or a snowboard trick that lands on a blooper video. Similarly, we've probably all seen teachers' misguided attempts to leap to creativity with a "fun" project that's not grounded in the fundamentals of curriculum and instruction design, or that reflects limited understanding of what students ought to learn and how.

Take your time . . . and travel with a friend

If becoming an expert teacher sounds daunting, take heart. You'll be there soon enough. But you can't expect to jump right from playing Putt-Putt golf to Pebble Beach, or from the bunny hill to a double-black diamond.

Think of it this way: If you make unbelievable gains in your professional practice, adding strategies to your instructional arsenal with confidence and regularity, great! If your students begin learning at absurdly high rates because of your focused energy, great! If not so much, still great! Just remember to look for little mile markers of progress along the way—a student who's more engaged, a few more lessons where things go swimmingly, feedback that provides "aha" moments for kids, etc. There's no rush; greatness takes time, patience, and a great deal of concerted mental energy. Trust the process, embrace the lessons you're learning along the way, and feel free to retrace your steps. The direction, pace, and pathways you choose are all up to you, the professional educator.

One final point worth repeating: Be sure to ask for help. Researchers have, in fact, found that coaching—namely, receiving critical feedback from peers—is the key to developing your talents (Joyce & Showers, 2002). Feedback is the breakfast of champions—that's equally true for you and your students. As scary as it might sound, inviting others to observe you as you teach, to review your lesson plans, and serve as a sounding board for your ideas, will help you to develop your expertise even more quickly. So, you may want to share this note with some "critical friends."

Note to my colleagues	Dear colleagues, I am so excited to share with you my professional growth goal! I'll be working earnestly toward the strengthening of my practice, all the while challenging my thinking and beliefs about the purpose, implementation, and results of my chosen skill. As I travel this path, I invite you to share my learning, to support my efforts, to focus my thinking, and to celebrate my growth. Improving my practice—and helping more and more students attain high levels of learning—is of great interest to me, and this is a road I've chosen to pursue. It may take me some time to grow as much as I'd like, and I'm OK with that. Help me stay the course! Thank you very much.

Let's get started

So, are you ready to start your journey? If so, find the page on the chart below that best reflects a problem of practice on your mind now and flip to it. Bon voyage! ✻

Phase ⇨	Be consistent	Be connected	Differentiate	Empower
Nurturing a positive learning environment	How do I ensure my classroom is an emotionally safe place to learn? Turn to p. 19	How do I connect with students? Turn to p. 26	How do I provide emotional support to students without exhausting myself? Turn to p. 33	How do I create a classroom culture where students care about and support one another? Turn to p. 42
Challenging students to commit to mastery	How do I cover all this content? Turn to p. 55	How do I challenge students with rigor? Turn to p. 62	How do I challenge every student when they have different abilities? Turn to p. 68	How do I help students challenge themselves to learn at high levels? Turn to p. 74
Designing engaging learning	How do I keep students focused and on task? Turn to p. 85	How do I make learning interesting to students? Turn to p. 92	How do I get every student to engage in learning activities? Turn to p. 99	How do I help students be curious, persistent, and independent learners? Turn to p. 106
Motivating with feedback	How do I guide students to do better? Turn to p. 116	How do I help students become more receptive to feedback? Turn to p. 123	How do I tailor feedback so it's meaningful for every student? Turn to p. 130	How do I help students give one another effective feedback? Turn to p. 136
Assessing for learning	How do I know whether students are learning? Turn to p. 147	How do I use assessments to adjust teaching and learning if students don't get it? Turn to p. 154	How do I use assessments to make thinking visible and encourage critical thinking? Turn to p. 164	How do I help students self-assess and guide their own learning? Turn to p. 171
Creating dynamic group learning	How do I manage unwanted behavior so students can learn? Turn to p. 183	How do I get students to participate actively in group work? Turn to p. 190	How do I match cooperative groups to individual needs? Turn to p. 197	How do I create opportunities for students to support one another in deep learning? Turn to p. 205

Chapter 3

Nurturing a positive learning environment

We've probably all heard the adage "No one cares how much you know until they know how much you care." Research on schools and the science of learning supports this aphorism. Relationships are so important to learning, we might think of them as the fourth "R"—a key component of, if not a necessary condition for, learning. That's because, as Yale University professor Dr. James Comer (1995) put it, "No significant learning occurs without a significant relationship."

You've likely turned to this page because you understand the importance of relationships. Perhaps you've already experienced the power of connecting with students to motivate and inspire them. That said, you've probably also seen that these connections don't always develop easily. In fact, with some students, we may feel that despite our best efforts, that personal connection remains just barely outside our reach. The bond isn't cultivated, our attempts aren't successful, or they keep pushing us away. On this pathway, you'll learn some best practices for connecting with students—even the ones who are difficult to reach.

You may also have observed Abraham Maslow's hierarchy of needs (1954) at work in your classroom. That is, you've seen that learning (i.e., "self-actualization") sits atop their pyramid of needs; thus, it does not occur easily until students' other, more pressing needs are met, including their physiological (e.g., food, sleep), safety (e.g., physical, emotional), and interpersonal needs (belonging and self-esteem). Clearly, students' interactions with one another influence their learning, which leaves you wondering how to create a classroom where students support each other. Moreover, you may have seen that a growing body of research is illuminating the unfortunate, negative effects of adverse childhood experiences and psychological trauma on learning—as well as the tremendous power of social-emotional competencies to promote learning. Here again, we return to the "fourth R," as relationships are critical to building students' social-emotional competencies and providing students who have experienced psychological trauma with a safe place to learn.

As mental health expert Kristin Souers and Pete Hall (a co-author of this book) note, relationships are a "prerequisite skill that students must have in order to be learning-ready" (Souers & Hall, 2018).

This pathway emphasizes the importance of emotional safety and the power of relationships—the relationship between you and your students as well as relationships among students themselves. As we'll see, many students live in a sort of relationship desert—void of meaningful connections with others, including adults. On this pathway, you'll learn to turn your classroom into an oasis of trust, respect, and emotional safety, which is at the heart of what we do as educators. After all, we teach kids, not curricula. We don't teach content, we teach our students. We're in the human being business. It's all about relationships.

Take charge of your own professional growth

To help you consider how to create a relationship-based environment that encourages authentic collaboration and excites your students about deep learning, we'll start with *your own curiosity*—questions you're likely to ask about your classroom. You may have found yourself asking one (or all) of the questions below. To help you meet your pressing needs and address your current problem of practice, we've placed a page number next to each so you can flip ahead and engage in some self-guided exploration:

- ❖ How do I ensure my classroom is an emotionally safe place to learn? (p. 19)
- ❖ How do I connect with students? (p. 26)
- ❖ How do I provide emotional support to students without exhausting myself? (p. 33)
- ❖ How do I create a classroom culture where students care about and support one another? (p. 42)

How do I ensure my classroom is an emotionally safe place to learn?

Be consistent *Teacher-owned, Student-experienced*	Be connected *Teacher-directed, Student-connected*	Differentiate *Student-engaged, Teacher-facilitated*	Empower *Student-owned, Teacher-guided*

Welcome to the first phase of the "Nurturing a positive learning environment" pathway. Not surprisingly, the focus here is on your actions as a teacher: what you are doing, what is expected of you, and what it will take for you to be successful. This pattern of thinking is typical of the *teacher-owned, student-experienced* phase, and as you proceed through the Reflective Cycle and expand your reflective vision, you'll begin to become more *consistent* in your approaches, allowing you to better meet your students' needs.

Build awareness: Observe

How do I ensure my classroom is an emotionally safe place to learn? To begin our journey, let's consider what research says about creating classroom environments where students feel safe and respected. We'll start by considering where learning happens for students: Their minds.

- ❖ **Students need to feel emotionally safe before they can learn.** Cognitive science shows that our brains filter out most of what's in our external environments, sort of like a spam filter on your email inbox. These mental filters follow something of a pecking order; they tend to pay attention, first, to stimuli that carry emotional weight, followed by novel stimuli—what's new and interesting. This pecking order likely helped our ancestors navigate a hostile environment, cueing them into threats and changing conditions ("That's the same tree as yesterday, except today, there's a lion under it. Good thing I noticed"). Although we modern humans generally find ourselves in less hostile environments, our brains retain the same pecking order, which means if we're emotionally distraught (or giddy with excitement), we're likely to find it difficult to pay attention to much else. Our kids are no different, of course. And many of them have a lot going on in their personal lives. So, when they enter our classrooms, their feelings (and thus, minds) are often elsewhere. If, however, they can associate positive emotions with our classrooms, they're more apt to learn because their brains tell them, in effect, "You're safe here. Focus on learning."

- ❖ **Student emotional safety has a significant impact on success.** Student surveys reveal that 50 percent admitted to bullying other students within the past year, and 47 percent said they had been "bullied, teased, or taunted in a way that seriously upset" them (Josephson Institute, 2010). Such bullying takes a heavy toll on students emotionally and academically; a study of 2,300 middle school children found victimized students had much lower grade point averages than non-victimized students (Juvonen, Wang, & Espinoza, 2010).

❖ **Teachers' personalities influence student success.** It's not surprising that a meta-analysis of 119 studies with effect sizes for more than 300,000 students (Cornelius-White, 2007) found that the two teacher traits most strongly linked to student success were *empathy* and *warmth*. In addition, interviews with students reveal they respond better to learning environments in which teachers show they care. In the words of one student, "If a teacher is nice to you, you have more of a motive to learn" (Marsh, 2012, p. 162). Studies have also shown that when kindergarten students with behavioral, attention, academic, or social problems are in the classroom of a teacher who offers strong emotional supports (e.g., cueing into their emotions and creating a positive classroom climate), those behaviors effectively disappear by the end of the school year, prompting researchers to conclude that "having teachers who attend to their social and emotional needs may be as or more important to academic development than specific instructional practices" (Hamre & Pianta, 2005, p. 962).

❖ **Students often don't feel emotionally supported in school.** Sadly, many students do not experience much empathy and warmth at school. Surveys of middle and high school students find that only about half feel like valued members of their school community, believe teachers care about them as individuals, or enjoy coming to school. Even fewer (42%) agreed students in their school are supportive of one another (Quaglia Institute, 2011).

So, what can you do to make sure students feel safe and respected in your classroom? Certainly, classroom rules and an orderly environment are important to emotional safety—you'll find a discussion of strategies for both in the first phase on the "Dynamic group learning" pathway (see p. 181). On this pathway, though, we'll focus more on the other side of this coin: emotional safety and relationship quality. Here are a few strategies drawn from research to help students feel emotionally ready to learn in your classroom:

❖ **Project positive emotions.** This may be the most important thing you can do as a teacher. When interviewed, students say that when teachers bring personality and friendliness to the classroom, they feel more comfortable, engaged, and eager to learn (Marsh, 2012). This doesn't mean you should be best buds with students. Nor does it mean you have to be giddy, disingenuous, or sappy—but simply positive, setting a tone that says you're glad to be in your classroom and you're glad your students are there, too. You may find it helpful to consider what you want your "classroom persona" to be—a personality that likely differs from the one you display around friends and family but nonetheless shows genuine kindness and respect for students while remaining the authority figure in your classroom. It's OK to reveal some of yourself to your students by sharing personal anecdotes as well as engaging in "spontaneous laughter and exclamations of excitement" and being "confident enough to do silly and memorable things," which researchers note generally support higher levels of learning (Hamre & Pianta, 2005, p. 957). In short, as we were once told by our mentors, be yourself—but yourself on a good day.

❖ **Tune in to student emotions.** Even as you strive to keep your emotions even-keeled and positive, it's important to "read the room," dialing into the emotions of your students. Indeed, one of the teacher traits University of Virginia researchers found to be positively associated with better student achievement was something they called "teacher sensitivity," which they defined as teachers being aware of students' "needs, moods, interests, and capabilities" and interacting with students accordingly (Hamre & Pianta, 2005, p. 957). Conversely, they found teachers' lack of emotional connection to students linked to lower achievement.

❖ **Help students tune in to their own emotions.** A small but growing body of research has found positive effects of mindfulness programs—efforts to teach students to use meditation, reflection, self-talk, and other techniques to embrace the moment, ruminate less on the past, and worry less about the future—on a variety of outcomes, including student attention, behavior, anxiety, and self-control (Meiklejohn et al., 2012). Similarly, a meta-analysis of 213 studies of programs that aim to directly teach students to recognize and manage their emotions, set and achieve goals, appreciate others' perspectives, and develop positive relationships found they improved students' social skills, attitudes, behavior, and academic performance—equivalent to an 11-percentile-point gain in achievement (Durlak, Weissberg, Dymnicki, Taylor, & Schellinger, 2011). If morning yoga isn't your thing, take heart: Many of the most effective interventions were as simple as a brief meditation or "quiet time" during which students unplugged from their worries and focused on learning.

Make intentional decisions: Be deliberate in planning

As you look around your classroom, what do you see? *Students* or *humans*? It's a subtle but significant distinction. Now that you've begun to view your students as human beings—fellow travelers, if you will—you more deeply understand the need to build strong relationships and create an emotionally safe environment where learning can truly flourish. As noted earlier, when we orient our minds to something, we're more likely to make gains and experience growth. The tools on the following pages— "Morning Meetings" and "Mix 'n Mingle"—will help you to wrap your head around some of these ideas and shorten your learning curve as you apply them in your classroom.

Become responsive | Build awareness

Assess and analyze your impact | Make intentional decisions

Morning Meetings

Why do it: Learning only occurs when kids feel safe and emotionally ready to learn. Providing a few structured, intentional minutes to relate to students on a human level, ask what's on their minds, tune into their moods, listen to their emotions or interests, and surface problems that they face helps them to prepare for and focus on learning.

How to do it: There are dozens of models of *Morning Meetings* out there, and we're not trying to get fancy by creating something unusual or unheard of here. Try some of the ideas below or find something online that satisfies the general idea: to get the students to be real with you.

Sometimes, students will share the highlights, lowlights, and question marks with us voluntarily. It may simply need a prompt like, "So what's going on today, my cherubs?"

Here are some additional prompts you might use or modify:

- What was the first thing you thought about this morning?
- How much TV should kids your age watch?
- What is your earliest memory as a child?
- Are you a morning person or a night owl?
- Does anyone have a chance of beating the Red Sox this season?
- What can we do today to make this classroom a better place?

When to do it: While there's no rule that the Morning Meeting has to happen in the morning, it's usually advisable to begin the day or the class period with this opportunity to connect and communicate. Use the first couple of minutes of each day (elementary folks) or each class period (secondary folks) to settle in, talk informally, and touch base with each other.

While doing it: Be sure to engage in active listening. If you notice some tension in the air, you may have to name it to tame it. "I've noticed some anxiety today. Do y'all feel that? Let's huddle up and talk about it for a minute."

Mix 'n Mingle

Why do it: When students feel connected to one another, they experience the effects of the neurochemical oxytocin—sometimes called the "hug drug." We often develop these connections through simple dialogue that helps us get to know one another. This tool accelerates relationship-building in your classroom.

How to do it: Instead of asking a question and waiting for students to raise their hands, prompt the students to think about their response while they stand up and walk around the classroom. You might even play some soothing music in the background to facilitate the process. When you pause the music, or when you announce it, students stop and engage in some discussion with whoever is closest to them at that moment. After sufficient discussion time, you ask for volunteers to share their responses. This process is repeated for however many questions you select.

When to do it: You can employ this tool in many phases of the learning cycle—for example, to launch a lesson by engaging students to consider prior knowledge and curiosity questions about a new topic, during a lesson to help them process what they're learning, or at the end of a lesson to help them summarize their learning.

While doing it: Notice if students are looking for partners they feel the most comfortable with and make adjustments as necessary. Ask them to approach three people they've not spoken with in the last week, for example.

Assess and analyze your impact: Notice learning

At this point, you've likely had a few (or many) "aha" moments along the way and your thinking has begun to shift. At first, these new practices may feel a bit forced or mechanical, but if you can commit to sticking with them for a few weeks, they should start to feel a bit more natural, like breaking in a new shoe. This is a good time to reflect on your comfort level with creating emotionally safe places for students. If you had initial doubts about these strategies, what do you think about them now? Are they coming more naturally to you? Also, this is a good time

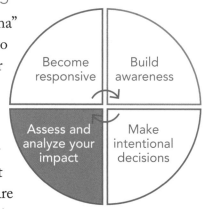

to refer back to your initial question: *How do I ensure my classroom is an emotionally safe place to learn?* How has your teaching changed? How has student learning changed? Use the prompts below to guide your reflections about both:

Reflect on Teaching	Reflect on Learning
• What classroom routines are most helpful in getting students ready to learn?	• How would students describe your learning environment? Friendly? Supportive? Competitive?
• What are your favorite (or most natural) strategies for building relationships with students? Do some work better than others? Why do you think this is so?	• How might you collect evidence to know how students feel about learning, the class, and you?
• Have you had interactions with students that didn't go well? If so, what might you say or do differently next time?	• When you have robust morning conversations, what are the questions or prompts that generated them? How did they come about?
• How would you describe your classroom persona? How would a colleague observing your classroom describe it?	• How comfortable are students talking about their feelings?

Become responsive: Make changes

While working through this phase, you've likely made some important shifts in your practice and you can sense yourself growing as a reflective practitioner. Hopefully, you've also noticed some positive changes in your students as you've focused more on creating an emotionally supportive learning environment. You ought to be proud of these accomplishments. Productive struggle leads to productive outcomes, and you've allocated your mental energy to productively struggling with many elements of relationship-building. We call this *effort optimism*—the belief that our hard work, concentrated efforts, and intentional focus will yield positive outcomes. Still, you may see room for you (and your students) to grow. Here are some questions that you might want to bring to a trusted colleague—a "critical friend" or an instructional coach or mentor—to reflect on what's improved and what your next steps might be:

- ❖ How do individual relationships with students contribute to a positive learning environment?

- ❖ What sort of events/interactions/incidents derail your work?

- ❖ How do you talk with your students about the need for creating that safe learning environment?

It's time to heed that ageless advice, "Look back to look ahead." The question you sought to answer at the beginning of this pathway was, *How do I ensure my classroom is an emotionally safe place to learn?* Now think how you'd answer it. Here are three simple ways to return to your problem of practice and deepen your reflective capacity:

- ❖ Jot some notes down in a learning journal or another place where you might be able to archive your thinking and access ideas, musings, questions, and other ponderings later.

- ❖ Find a trusted colleague or two to engage in a dialogue with you. Exchange thoughts, suggestions, critical feedback, and celebrations together.

- ❖ Engage your administrator, instructional coach, department chair, or another member of your support network in a discussion about this question, your journey thus far, and any shifts in perspective you've noticed.

Your reflections, of course, may surface new professional challenges and questions for you. For example, you may find you've "clicked" with some students, but not others. Or you may see some students pushing you away, struggling with their emotions, or in need of interpersonal connections, which leads you to wonder, *How do I connect with students?* If so, turn to the next page and take it on.

✔ Or, if you find yourself with another nagging question, turn to the grid on p. 16, find that question, and turn to the page where we help you address it.

How do I connect with students?

Be consistent	**Be connected**	Differentiate	Empower
Teacher-owned, Student-experienced	*Teacher-directed, Student-connected*	*Student-engaged, Teacher-facilitated*	*Student-owned, Teacher-guided*

Welcome to the second phase of the "Nurturing a positive learning environment" pathway. As you've sought to ensure your classroom is a safe, predictable, and consistent place for learning, you've likely found that you're connecting better with some students than others. That's natural. Some students are charming, funny, or personable, while others may be more aloof, temperamental, or taciturn. Others may have a personality that matches your own, so it's easier to relate to them. That happens. Yet you want to avoid playing favorites or neglecting students, even those who challenge you. What's happening at this point is you're becoming increasingly *connected* to your students. You're observing cause-and-effect between your behaviors and their emotional, mental, and social well-being. Your classroom is becoming *teacher-directed* and *student-connected*.

 If you're joining us from another pathway, or if you're skipping ahead to this problem of practice without reading the previous phase in its entirety, we suggest you skim through or review the previous section just to get your bearings.

Build awareness: Note cause-and-effect relationships

How do I connect with students? Likely, you have colleagues or know teachers who are veritable child whisperers. Kids hang out in their classroom at lunch time or after school, or follow them across the schoolyard like the Pied Piper. You may wonder, what do they do to nurture such strong, positive relationships with students? How exactly do they connect with reluctant students? Students with particular needs? Marginalized students? Outliers? If you haven't done so already, we'd suggest you seek out these colleagues and learn from them as many new strategies

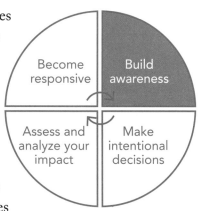

and approaches as you can. That's called professional wisdom. Another form of professional wisdom is called research—which, when you think about it, was really just someone with a clipboard asking the same question as you: What makes some teachers more effective than others? Here are a few big ideas we can draw from researchers' findings on student-teacher relationships:

❖ **Better student-teacher relationships support better behavior and learning.** No surprise here. Still, it's good to know that "hard science" provides evidence for the power of the "soft side" of teaching. For example, studies of kindergarten students with behavioral problems found that if their teachers develop strong relationships with them, they demonstrate better behavior and higher achievement in later grades (Hamre & Pianta, 2005); conversely, if their teachers fail to develop strong relationships with them, their academic and behavioral issues worsen.

❖ **Connecting with teachers supports student engagement in school.** Studies have found that middle school students with highly supportive teachers (who show students they care about them as individuals) are nearly three times more likely to be engaged in school—exerting effort on schoolwork, paying attention in class, and taking academic performance seriously. Conversely, those with unsupportive teachers were 68 percent more likely to be disengaged in school (Klem & Connell, 2004).

So, how *exactly* do these effective teachers connect with students? Studies have shown that for starters, they bring some natural dispositions to the classroom, including concern for students, intuition, and perceptiveness (Wadlington & Wadlington, 2011). That said, they also engage in some straightforward behaviors you can use to connect with students. Here's a starter list:

❖ **Interact with every student every day.** In the crush of daily events, it's easy to overlook connecting with individual students. Yet it's important to greet every student as they come into your classroom and to call on students directly rather than waiting for them to volunteer a response during classroom discussions. That's because if classroom interactions are left to chance, studies show one-fifth of students fill about 80 percent of the air time and roughly a third (29%) have no meaningful interaction with teachers (Jones, 1990). For younger students, you might write their names on craft sticks and randomly draw them from a jar; for older students, you can keep a tally of your interactions with a simple check-mark system or app.

❖ **Set aside time for interaction.** In addition to ensuring that whole class instruction doesn't become a small group conversation with many bystanders, it's important to set aside frequent opportunities to interact with individual students (e.g., during independent working time). Students report they welcome these opportunities for one-on-one coaching and interaction; when interviewed about favorite teachers, they often single out those who are willing to make "time for personal questions and one-to-one conversations. They come around to check that I understand the work and explain it to me" (Marsh, 2012, p. 162).

❖ **Learn at least one thing that matters to each student.** Marsh also reported that students say they appreciate teachers who "say things that show that they know and understand me." As one put it, "I like it when teachers get interested in what you do besides the lesson." You can do this with writing prompts, show and tells, weekly activity logs, student presentations, and information forms that invite students to share their interests with you.

- ❖ **Converse at "eye level."** Students also report having strong relationships with teachers who "talk to them outside of lessons" and "ask how I am and ask about my personal interests." Moreover, they appreciate it when teachers "listen to what I have to say. . . . By asking us our opinions, they seem to value ours as much as they value their own." So, as it turns out, asking higher-order (e.g., comparison, analysis, interpretation) questions brings the added benefits of encouraging critical thinking and showing students you respect them as thinkers and individuals.

- ❖ **Make use of nonverbal cues.** Like a picture, a smile, wink, fist-bump, or thumbs up can speak a thousand words—and go a long way toward building connections with students. Conversely, failing to make eye contact with individual students may send the wrong message that they are unimportant to us.

Make intentional decisions: Plan, then implement

Yes, connecting with individual students takes work. And some teachers may tell you it's not in the job description (e.g., "My job is to teach, and kids' job is to learn"). Yet, as we've seen, students learn more from teachers with whom they feel a personal bond. Or as the late, great Rita Pierson put it more bluntly in her wonderful 2013 TED Talk about building relationships with students, "Kids don't learn from people they don't like." Whether or not some of these bonding strategies come naturally to you, the truth is in order to cultivate and incorporate them

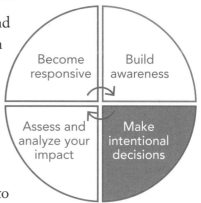

into your regular routines, you've got to allocate some of your mental energy into planning to do so with *intentionality*. The tools on the following pages, "Learn 'Em" (from Souers & Hall, 2016) and "Conferring," offer some strategies you can use to develop strong, positive connections with students and ensure relationship-building remains front and center in your classroom. As you implement these tools, you'll find it important to observe their impact on student learning, which is, after all, the essence of the *connected* phase of this pathway.

Learn 'Em

Why do it: You may have a caseload of up to 150 students and wonder how you could possibly manage that many relationships. Well, just like every journey begins with the first step, every array of relationships begins with the first relationship. So start with one. In the *Learn 'Em* strategy, you build your knowledge of each and every one of your students (one at a time is fine)—what makes them tick, what they do outside of school, how they learn. There will come times in the year when you'll need to refer to these cards as you attempt to connect with a particular student.

How to do it: We suggest you begin building your collection of information by recording answers to some of the questions below on an index card for each of your students:

- What is s/he interested in?
- What are his/her hobbies?
- What are his/her most/least favorite subjects?
- What does s/he want to be when s/he grows up?
- What are his/her goals?
- What makes him/her laugh?
- What makes him/her sad?
- What words would you use to describe him/her?
- Who are his/her friends?
- What is his/her family like?
- Who is his/her adult champion at school?

Feel free to add questions as you see fit, and use your index cards as working documents.

When to do it: Kick off your year by asking students to tell you about themselves on these cards. File them by class. Revisit them and add info as you learn more. Set aside a few minutes each week to glance through the cards to add or revisit the information.

While doing it: As you collect cards and gather information for the purpose of relationship-building, you'll find cards with a lot of white space. That just indicates that you need to spend more time talking with, listening to, and noticing things about those students—as learners and as human beings. And eventually, as you truly *learn* your students, you'll find you depend on those "cheat sheets" less often.

Conferring

Why do it: Nothing affirms the purpose of education more than an eye-to-eye, one-to-one conversation between a teacher and a student. When you sit down with a young person and focus all your attention on him or her, you have the opportunity to clarify your expectations, describe your observations, listen to the student's explanations, and discuss avenues for improvement.

How to do it: There are two keys to success in *conferring* chats: frequency and focus. Select a student that you're having difficulty connecting with or you notice is having difficulty connecting with others. Reach out to the students with whom you haven't connected yet. The idea is to identify students who you notice struggle with—and/or thrive off of—relationships.

If you were to sit down with a student individually and talk about the football scores or the weather, that child would infer that those topics are the most important thing (and there's a time and place for these conversations, too). So, of course, these conversations need to be focused on student learning, student work, student goals, the value of education, and/or whatever pressing topic finds itself at the top of the priority pile. Demonstrating your investment in each student's education, trajectory, and future pays dividends—it shows your values and it illustrates your genuine care for that young person's life. That's what relationships are built upon.

When to do it: Depending on the needs of each student, you might have a special sit-down once a week, once a month, or once a quarter. Such conferences needn't be extremely lengthy, either. Three minutes might suffice, or it might require 15 minutes to truly get at the heart of the dialogue. What matters is that you make time to have the conversation when it's needed. Often, while students are working independently or in groups, finishing up a project, or are otherwise meaningfully occupied, you have the opportunity to invite a student to chat.

While doing it: Notice how your students respond when you connect with them in this manner.

Assess and analyze your impact: Recognize the results of your actions

As you've focused your mental energy on ways to effectively engage students in cooperative groupings, you'll notice your attention turning to the direct impact of your efforts. So when you assess the impact of your actions, reflect on your guiding question for this phase: *How do I connect with students?*

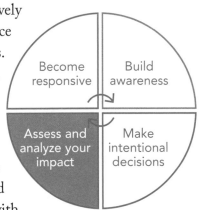

Think about the intentionality with which you are building strong relationships with your students. You're probably learning more about them as individuals and as learners. Your index cards are likely filling up with information and you're noticing which students you know more about than others—and which students you still have a lot of questions about. Do you find that you can leverage your deeper relationships with students to help them get back on track, improve a behavior, put more effort into their work, answer a question, comply with a request? Have you noticed changes in their learning? Have you noticed preferences in how individual students learn? Remember the cause-and-effect connections in your classroom: *When I do X, students respond with Y* or *If I want students to do Y, then I'll do X.* The questions below are designed to help you further hone and shape your mental models by engaging in self-reflection and dialogue with your colleagues.

Reflect on Teaching	Reflect on Learning
• When you put effort into connecting with a student, how did it go? • If you've connected with students, what actions did you take to make those connections? • How do you show students you respect them? What steps are you taking to do this intentionally? • How do you show students you care about them? What steps are you taking to do this intentionally?	• Which students are most successful in your class? How would you characterize your connections with these students? • Which students are least successful in your class? How would you characterize your connections with these students? • Are some students more receptive than others? Why do you think this is so? • Are you still struggling to connect with some students? Do they have anyone in the class (or the building) with whom they connect? What plan do you have for connecting with them?

Become responsive: Respond to the needs you see

As you reflect on your class(es), you probably can pick out students with whom you have stronger working relationships; you know some of them better than others. As you completed the *Learn 'Em* strategy, for example, you may have found that for some students, you completely filled an index card with information about them while your cards for other students were still blank. That doesn't mean you're a bad teacher; just that you have more work to do to connect with all students. Remember the question that prompted this investigation: *How do I connect with students?* Show yourself some professional grace and allow yourself the time needed to build those relationships—after all, this can be deeply emotional work, and that's not going to happen overnight. The good news, though, is you've likely got some existing strong relationships with some students that point to some go-to strategies you could use more often. Here are some questions you might ask yourself—and your colleagues—to reflect on what's improved for you and your students and what steps to take next.

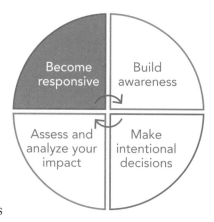

- ❖ What strategies have helped you to connect with students very effectively?
- ❖ What strategies have been less effective? Why weren't they effective? How might you adapt them?
- ❖ What strategies do your colleagues use to connect with students that you could attempt? What might that look liske in your classroom?

At the same time, even as you build better connections with students, new questions may arise. For example, you may find some students have built walls around themselves, making it difficult for you to connect with them. You may also realize that they've created these walls as a defensive mechanism, perhaps due to traumatic experiences or psychological stress in their lives. You want to connect with them but aren't exactly sure how. Or maybe you've begun connecting with students and are now finding yourself emotionally spent. If so, you may want to tackle the problem of practice on the next page, *How do I provide emotional support to students without exhausting myself?*

 Or, if you find yourself with another nagging question, turn to the grid on p. 16, find that question, and turn to the page where we help you address it.

How do I provide emotional support to students without exhausting myself?

Be consistent *Teacher-owned Student-experienced*	Be connected *Teacher-directed, Student-connected*	**Differentiate** **Student-engaged, Teacher-facilitated**	Empower *Student-owned, Teacher-guided*

Welcome to the third phase of the "Nurturing a positive learning environment" pathway. Prepare yourself to experience all sorts of reflections, anxieties, and emotions. These often occur as you move into the *differentiate* phase of this (and every other) pathway, a point at which you increasingly begin to consider individual students and their needs—finding ways to draw them out of their shells as you seek to make your classroom *student-engaged* and *teacher-facilitated*. You now see yourself as not only responsible for ensuring the learning and progress of every child, but as a viable influence in their success.

 If you're joining us from another pathway, welcome! Before diving headlong into this challenge, though, we suggest you review the previous phase of this pathway to get your bearings.

Build awareness: Zoom in on the details

How do I provide emotional support to students without exhausting myself? As you've developed more connections with students, you may have found some resist your efforts to connect with them. They may be withdrawn. Or hostile. Either way, the impact is the same; there's a wall around them. It's also likely that as you've gotten to know some students better, you've learned their home environments may be full of chaos or uncertainty or lacking stable relationships; thus, you may wonder if your inability to connect with certain students reflects the aphorism, "Sometimes you put walls up not to keep people out, but to see who cares enough to break them down." So, you're looking for ways to connect with students despite these barriers.

At the same time, though, as you come to fully understand the challenges your students face, you may find yourself emotionally drained. Perhaps you lie awake at night worrying about many of them—if they're (physically and emotionally) safe, fed, or doing harm to themselves or others. That's a lot of baggage to carry, of course, and can leave you feeling helpless and exhausted. At times, you may want to put a wall around yourself, which may leave you feeling even more guilty that you cannot endure the psychological pain your students experience every day.

At this point in the pathway, we're diving into deep, complex stuff—including psychology and brain science. So, let's explore what may be happening with some of your students as well as for you as you seek to connect with them, starting with these data. A major study of more than 100,000 students in the U.S. (Bethell, Newacheck, Hawes, & Halfon, 2014) found that nearly half (48%) of children under the age of 17 have endured at least one adverse childhood experience (including exposure to violence or emotional, physical or sexual abuse; deprivation, neglect, or social discrimination; family discord or divorce; parental substance abuse, mental health problems, death, or incarceration) and nearly a quarter (22.6%) had experienced two or more of these experiences—even more (30.5%) if they were over the age of 12. We also know from this research that children with exposure to two or more adverse experiences were 2.67 times as likely to repeat a grade in school, 8 times as likely to have behavior problems in school, and 4.4 times as likely to engage in bullying behavior.

Brain scans of people with chronic stress, like that associated with adverse childhood experiences, show they often have a smaller hippocampus (the part of the brain responsible for creating long-term memories), increased activity in their amygdala (which triggers flight-or-fight responses), and decreased activity in their medial prefrontal cortex, which helps to tamp down anxiety (Bremner, 2006). As a result, children in emotional or psychological trauma tend to be in a state of constant high alert, which it makes it difficult for them to focus on learning or regulate their behavior (Streeck-Fischer & van der Kolk, 2000). Moreover, students experiencing psychological trauma tend to be less likely to demonstrate emotional resilience (i.e., an ability to "stay calm and in control when faced with a challenge") than those with no adverse experiences (Bethell et al., 2014).

All of this has important implications for educators. For children who have experienced psychological trauma, classroom rules and consequences may remind them of abuse. Moreover, these students may fall into a downward spiral of bad behavior (or "cycle of trauma") in which they exhibit anti-social behavior (students who have experienced trauma can be violent), are punished for it, and thus become "retraumatized," further exacerbating the trauma and continuing the cycle (Streeck-Fischer & van der Kolk, 2000).

So, what can you do for students who appear in need of additional emotional supports? Here are a few guiding principles from research.

❖ **Help them to build resilience.** Among children with two or more adverse childhood experiences, those who demonstrate resilience are 1.55 times likelier to be engaged in school (Langley, Gonzalez, Sugar, Solis, & Jaycox, 2015). So, helping students develop self-regulation skills by, for example, directly teaching them coping techniques like relaxation, courage thinking, social problem-solving, and conflict resolution, can help them counteract the negative effects of adverse childhood experiences.

❖ **Empower them to do the right thing.** Children who have experienced trauma often seek to control their environment to protect themselves, so if they feel out of control, their behavior can deteriorate fast. If you need to correct or redirect their behavior, it's important to do so in a respectful way that gives them agency, reminding them they're in control of their actions.

❖ **Provide them with "unconditional positive regard."** This concept, drawn from therapy, doesn't mean ignoring or tolerating bad behavior, but assuming that students, like all human beings, have an innate desire to engage in pro-social behavior, and that when you respect their need for self-determination, those behaviors are more apt to emerge. In practice, it may mean going high when they go low. For example, if they say, "I hate you," you could say, "I'm sorry to hear you say that. I care about you and am here to help you succeed."

❖ **Go beyond the *what* to consider the *why* of student behavior.** It's easier to engage in unconditional positive regard when you consider not only what students are doing (e.g., being defiant), but why they're doing it (e.g., their father recently moved out). Often, students' attempts to meet their unmet needs (relational, control, emotional, or physical) are disruptive and inappropriate. Rather than get caught up in *how* they're acting, you can focus on the unmet need and attempt interventions based on that (Souers & Hall, 2018):

- Relational need: Pull the student aside and engage in a quick "how are you doing?" conversation.
- Control need: Offer choice for proceeding—academically or behaviorally.
- Emotional need: Allow for self-selected "brain breaks" with regulation tools.
- Physical need: Provide a snack, for instance.

❖ **Help students make it right.** When students engage in antisocial behavior, they hurt others as well as themselves—often because they don't know how to undo the damage they've done to a relationship with you or their peers. You can teach students this simple (yet better) approach to apologies: 1) state what they did, 2) how it affected the relationship, 3) what their goal is, 4) what they'll do in the future, and 5) ask for forgiveness. And if you ever make a mistake, model the same process (e.g., "I've lost my temper and raised my voice at you all. That probably was scary for some of you, and I'm really sorry because I want us all to feel safe in this class. In the future, I'll take a couple deep breaths to calm down when I'm feeling frustrated. Will you forgive me?").

❖ **Practice compassion (not empathy).** This may sound like an odd parsing of words, yet we know from brain science that we human beings have an amazing capacity to experience others' emotions; we fire nearly the same neural networks when we ourselves experience pain as when we see others in pain (Singer & Klimecki, 2014).

In short, we actually *feel* their pain, which can prompt us to rush to their aid. Yet if we feel others' pain too intensely or for too long, it can create empathic distress or burnout. In fact, studies have found that the longer students stay in medical school, the less empathy they feel, with the biggest drop-off occurring when they begin working with, and experiencing firsthand, the pain and suffering of real patients (Neumann et al., 2011). A better response is *compassion*—being concerned for others' well-being and wanting to help them, yet not necessarily mirroring their emotions. In short, compassion is feeling *for*, not feeling *with*, other people (Singer & Klimecki, 2014). As it turns out, we're more likely to help others when we feel compassion versus empathy (Batson, 2009). Practicing unconditional positive regard and considering the *why* behind the *what* of student behavior are intellectual exercises that can provide us with some emotional distance to avoid distress, while still remaining supportive to students.

Make intentional decisions: Develop a clear vision

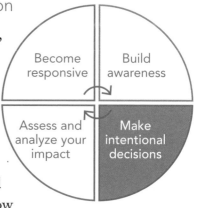

So, how do you apply all of these ideas to your classroom, including the strategies from previous sections? The first step, as you've likely acknowledged, is that since your classroom is a dynamic place and you've got students with all sorts of needs and relationships that change from day to day, you've got to think larger than interaction-to-interaction. The mural you're painting, if you will, is less a series of individual images than it is a collage and a blending of one magical theme. Your reflections are now leading you in the direction of truly connecting the dots, of incorporating multiple approaches and various strategies that address many needs simultaneously. And here at this phase, our guidance will be a little less prescriptive and a little more cerebral. That's because you're beginning to develop expert mental models (*If I see students doing or needing X, then I do Y*) and tailored approaches to instruction based on your assessments of student emotional and psychological needs. It's important to note, though, that you shouldn't go it alone, especially with students whom you suspect may have deep emotional scars from adverse childhood experiences. The following strategies, then—"Name the Emotion" and "Restorative Circles"—are offered not as comprehensive therapy for students, but rather, as ways that you can ensure your classroom is responsive to their needs—what we might call a trauma-invested, *differentiated* classroom.

Name the Emotion

Why do it: Tuning into and labeling emotions can help students understand their feelings and help them to feel more in control of their situations. When feelings are labeled and honored through a class activity like this, it not only empowers individuals but also facilitates better interaction between peers.

How to do it: At the beginning of the day/period, use sticky notes to ask students to write down how they're feeling and why. They have the option of sharing them with the whole class, telling a partner, or keeping it to themselves before passing them in to you. You may want to briefly talk about what it means to honor another's emotions and/or feelings as you collect the notes. Another option is to read the notes to the class in an anonymous manner and talk about ways to support one another.

Variations of this approach could include (optionally) wearing color-coded wristbands, pointing to particular images (emojis, for instance) that match their emotions, or role-playing particular emotions to help students see and understand their feelings.

When to do it: This activity is often used at the beginning of a day or class period. However, it can be utilized any time you notice students who may be more emotional or have something on their minds.

While doing it: Observe student interactions. Which students choose to share openly? Are there any that keep their emotions more private? How might you follow up with them one-on-one?

Restorative Circles

Why do it: This is a technique for proactively building the skills and relationships students need to tackle challenges that arise in their lives. It helps teach the processing of thoughts and feelings and can replace punitive forms of discipline.

How to do it:

Set up:

a. Arrange the classroom so that students are sitting in a circle. Identify a "talking stick"—an item that can easily be passed from student to student. Only students holding the "talking stick" may speak. You may opt instead for calling on raised hands.

b. As a group, develop agreements that will guide discussion. The guidelines should provide a standard for both speaking and listening. For example:

   》 *I will speak from the heart and talk about what is true to myself based on my experiences.*

   》 *I will listen from my heart and refuse to make judgments or assumptions about the speaker.*

c. In Restorative Circles, there is always a "Circle Keeper." Most of the time this is the teacher, but it can also be a student. The Circle Keeper asks questions and invites everyone to respond.

d. Determine the focus of the circle for the day and select the types of questions you'll use: "Check-in" questions that will build community and deepen relationships or "Restorative" questions that will allow for dialogue around a conflict or problem.

Check-in Prompts/Questions	Restorative Prompts/Questions
✓ Share a happy childhood memory.	✓ Share the thoughts and emotions you had during the incident.
✓ How would your best friend describe you?	✓ Who was affected by what happened and how?
✓ Who do you respect? Why?	✓ What about this has been the hardest for you?
✓ What would you not want to change about your life? Why?	✓ What needs to be done to make things as right as possible?
✓ Describe a person who is a good friend or ally. What characteristics and qualities do they have?	

Engage in Discussion:

a. The Circle Keeper poses a question and hands the talking stick to a student. This student is the only speaker. Interruptions are not allowed. When finished, the student may pass the stick to the student sitting next to him/her or place it on the floor in the middle of the circle for another student to pick up.

b. The Circle Keeper's job is to guide discussion, not lead it. You don't determine who is right and wrong. Instead, you keep the discussion on track and ensure that everyone has a voice. If a student continues to talk without passing the stick, jump in and suggest that the speaker pass the stick to hear what others have to say.

c. All students should be encouraged to speak, but some may choose to pass. The talking stick may come back to a student who has already spoken. Students should be encouraged to speak about their experiences and make connections between the discussion content and their lives.

d. At the end of the discussion, ask students to thank one another for both speaking and listening.

When to do it: Restorative Circles are most effective when they're an integral part of school or classroom culture. When introducing this tool, plan to incorporate it into the weekly/semiweekly routine.

While doing it: Sit in the circle with students and be present. Model what it looks like to listen without judgment and participate in the discussion.

Assess and analyze your impact: Transfer the vision

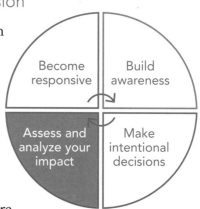

For a while now, you've been working to connect with hard-to-reach students, which has likely led you to more deeply consider their feelings—as well as help them process and regulate their own emotions. Now, as you assess and analyze the impact of your actions up to this point, we remind you to keep your guiding question in mind: *How do I provide emotional support to students without exhausting myself?*

Along this phase of the pathway, you've likely become more adept at understanding your students' emotions and watching for signs that some may need more support than others. It's also healthy to recognize that you may need your own support network to help you stay objective—*feeling for* versus *feeling with* your students to avoid empathic distress (something teachers have long been famous for). As you well know, experts don't go it alone; indeed, they consult with one another to diagnose and solve problems. With a "critical friend," use the following reflective questions (and then create your own to add to the list) to help you to develop your expert mental models and challenge each other's thinking:

Reflect on Teaching	Reflect on Learning
How have you changed your approach to relationship-building? What are the results?	Are students becoming more resilient in your classroom? How do you know?
Have you been able to feel for students without feeling empathic burnout? How so?	What emotions do students feel in your classroom? Has that changed? How so?
Have you been able to help students process and regulate their own emotions? How so?	What unwanted behaviors do students demonstrate? Why do you believe they demonstrate those behaviors?

Become responsive: Respond in the moment

The third phase in this pathway marks a seismic shift in your thinking, as well as your actions. As you've pursued the question that launched this pathway—*How do I provide emotional support to students without exhausting myself?*—you have become quite knowledgeable. You've built considerable awareness about the importance of relationships, personal psychology, and emotional safety in learning, and you've grown more thoughtful about the myriad ways to build those relationships and support

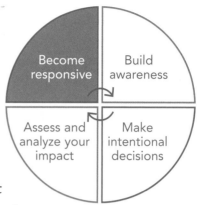

students' emotional needs. You're now ready to embrace a new level of performance. You're no longer simply interested in mechanical relationship-building exercises; indeed, for you the new challenge is how to make those relationships meaningful, authentic, and universal in your classroom. The more intentionally you have been thinking about building relationships in your classroom, the more they've taken place. And now, the more deliberate you are about tending to them, the more they'll continue to flourish. Take a moment and reflect on your professional growth from the beginning of this pathway until now, and challenge yourself (and a trusted colleague, instructional coach, or administrator) with a few bonus reflective questions:

- ❖ Why, exactly, are individual relationships important? What is the connection between the teacher-student relationship and student success? Can you summarize this element in a succinct, powerful manner?

- ❖ What changes occur when a student feels that connection with an adult? What if that adult isn't you, but a different staff member? Does that impact learning in your classroom?

- ❖ What strategies do you employ to practice self-care? How do you fill your own bucket to stave off burnout and emotional exhaustion? What can you do to remind yourself to practice those strategies?

Of course, as you've developed stronger relationships with individual students, you've likely found that for many students, their relationships with other students are often at the heart of their anxiety or feelings of limited self-worth. Some may feel excluded or ostracized by their peers. Others may feel bullied. So, you may now be ready to tackle the problem on the next page, *How do I create a classroom culture where students care about and support one another?*

Or, if you find yourself with another nagging question, turn to the grid on p. 16, find that question, and turn to the page where we help you address it.

How do I create a classroom culture where students care about and support one another?

Be consistent *Teacher-owned, Student-experienced*	Be connected *Teacher-directed, Student-connected*	Differentiate *Student-engaged, Teacher-facilitated*	**Empower** *Student-owned, Teacher-guided*

Welcome to the fourth phase of the "Nurturing a positive learning environment" pathway. Here, you'll begin to *empower* students to create a safe, supportive classroom culture in a *student-owned, teacher-guided* environment. This is no subtle shift, either. Building your students' capacity to own their environment requires steady, significant development of your own capacity—both as a master of the technical elements of teaching and as a reflective practitioner. Getting to this point requires building on the foundation of everything you've learned, the acute awareness you've built, the many steps you've taken with great intentionality, and your ability to gauge your impact and make course corrections.

 If you're joining us from another pathway, we encourage you to review the previous three phases in this pathway to ensure you're ready to address this challenge.

Build awareness: Bring all the variables together

How do I create a classroom culture where students care about and support one another? As your practices have become more sophisticated, and your students more frequently engaged in cooperative group learning, you may find yourself wondering what it would take for them to go one step further—namely, developing a supportive classroom culture. In short, you want students to own their classroom culture, understanding how their relationships can create a mutually beneficial environment

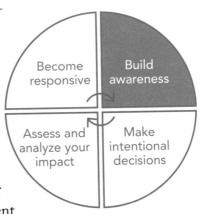

where they can take positive action to ensure everyone feels safe and supported. Notice we used the plural "they" and "their" in that description, and that's quite intentional: It's a collective ownership, whereby students' relationships and interpersonal connections have them embracing a Three Musketeers philosophy: *All for one and one for all.*

Student ownership of the classroom environment is often a distinguishing characteristic of the most effective teachers. As you've shifted your thinking from a *teacher* focus to a *student* focus, you've likely shared with your students that you want them to think about what they're *learning* instead of just what they're *doing*. This ownership allows for curiosity, investment, passion, partnerships, transfer of learning, and committed communities to flourish. Many teachers are frightened by this prospect. Give up ownership of the classroom? It's *my* room!

Those are *my* students! *My* materials! The fun part of acknowledging and acting on this shift is the fundamental reality: It's *their* learning and *their* success that really matters, so let's help it be *theirs*.

Let's explore some big ideas from research that offer some guiding principles for creating a culture of learning in your classroom, where students value learning and show empathy to one another.

❖ **Peers influence student learning.** As kids mature, they become increasingly attuned to their peers. An interesting series of experiments in the 1960s called "conformity studies" suggested that age 9 or 10 was a critical point at which children become more susceptible to peer influence, even to the point of, for example, giving obviously wrong answers to simple questions to fit in with their peers. In one study, Paul Torrance (1967) gave students from different grades a difficult word problem and a full day to solve it, allowing them to consult with peers, teachers, or parents for the answer. Nearly half of third graders (30–50%) sought help from adults while just 20 percent asked peers for help. Among fourth graders it was the exact opposite: Less than 20 percent consulted adults and nearly half consulted peers. In short, fourth grade appears to be when young people feel an increasing need to fit in socially.

❖ **As students grow older, they experience greater social anxiety.** As students enter adolescence, peer influence often translates into social anxiety—which stays with most people well into their mid-20s. David Eagleman and his graduate assistant Ricky Savjani discovered as much when they monitored the stress responses of teenagers and adults while sitting atop a stool in a shop display window. Not surprisingly, all participants registered increased levels of stress with strangers staring at them, yet for teenagers, their emotional response appeared to "go into overdrive: the teens were much more anxious—some to the point of trembling—while being watched" (Eagleman, 2015, p. 16). Why? Brain studies show that a portion of the brain that involves thinking about oneself grows throughout childhood, peaking at about age 15. For teens, thinking about themselves is a high priority, which means social situations are freighted with more emotional weight than they are for adults, who have grown more accustomed to a sense of self and are thus less anxious about strangers staring at them.

❖ **Stereotype threat is a real and often powerful negative influence on student learning.** Studies have also shown that for many minority students, social anxieties often take the form of what's called "stereotype threat." This is especially true as they enter adolescence—a time when they begin developing a personal identity, absorbing messages about race and confronting negative stereotypes. Studies of more than 500 African-American middle school students, for example, found a strong, negative link (r = -.25) between performance on standardized tests and the extent to which students had internalized negative stereotypes about their own ethnic group's academic abilities (Okeke, Howard, Kurtz-Costes, & Rowley, 2009). In a now famous study, Princeton researchers (Alter, Aronson, Darley, Rodriguez, & Ruble, 2010) found that minority children performed worse on an end-of-grade exam when asked to report their ethnicity prior to the test than afterward (getting 38% vs 59% of questions right).

What does all of this mean for your students? Students are apt to worry intensely about what others think of them—far more so than adults. So, that means before they can speak freely in class, make mistakes, and fumble around for the right words to express themselves, they need reassurance your classroom is a safe place—that their peers won't judge or make fun of them. In short, they need a positive classroom culture that embraces everyone. How can you create such a culture? Here are a few guiding principles from research:

❖ **Teach and encourage a growth mindset.** In a now famous experiment, Stanford psychologist Carol Dweck and her colleagues (2006) randomly divided students into two groups and directed teachers in the first group to consistently praise students for their *ability* ("Wow. You got eight right. That's a really good score. You must be really smart at this"). Teachers in the second group were told to praise students for their *effort* ("Wow. You got eight right. That's a really good score. You must have worked really hard at this"). Afterward, researchers found that students praised for their *ability* (smarts) developed a "fixed mindset"—they saw school success as a fixed trait, unrelated to effort. As a result, they were less willing to take on challenging tasks, fearing if they tried and failed, they'd no longer be seen as smart or special. On the other hand, students praised for *effort* were not just willing to take on challenges, but actually enjoyed them. Dweck concluded that great teachers operate from, and convey, a "growth mindset" for students, reinforcing the link between effort and success, and the power of productive struggle to make our minds stronger.

❖ **Model a growth mindset by inviting feedback about your teaching.** Great teachers also model a growth mindset by showing they, too, are willing to listen to feedback and always looking for ways to get better. One way you can do this is by inviting feedback on your own teaching. As one student put it, "I like it when teachers . . . ask your opinions on what you are doing and how they can make it better because they care what you think about their lesson" (Marsh, 2012, p. 162).

❖ **Help students reflect on their own positive attributes.** This simple intervention nearly wiped out the negative effects of stereotype threat and improved outcomes for all students: At the start of a semester-long course, students spent 15 minutes writing about the role of their own personal values (e.g., religion or family relationships) in their lives to boost their feelings of self-worth (Cohen, Garcia, Apfel, & Master, 2006). This exercise appeared to have powerful effects on student outcomes: It halved the number of African-American students earning a D or less, reduced achievement gaps 40 percent, and reversed previous performance declines. The takeaway: Having students reflect on their own positive attributes can unleash "hidden, yet powerful psychological forces" (Yeager & Walton, 2011, p. 274) and "lead to large gains in student achievement and sharply reduce achievement gaps" by helping them see their own potential as learners and human beings. Rita Pierson (2013), in her TED talk, recounted how she helped her class of impoverished students boost their self-esteem. "I told all my students, 'You were *chosen* to be in my class because I am the best teacher and you are the best students. They put us all together so we could show everybody else how to do it.'" To reinforce the message, she gave them a saying: "I *am* somebody. I was somebody when I came here. I'll be a *better somebody* when I leave. I am powerful, and I am strong. I *deserve* the education that I get here."

❖ **Encourage a sense of together-we-can.** As students embrace these ideas, it's easier to help them see—and reinforce—the potential in their peers. By filling your classroom walls and teacher talk with statements that reinforce the power of effort, the value of feedback, and learning from mistakes, you can help students begin to use these statements with one another. At the same time, it's important to avoid ranking students so they understand they're supporting one another, not competing. Yes, the world is competitive, but the competition lies outside, not inside the classroom.

Make intentional decisions: Move beyond strategy to design

So, how do you bring all of these ideas together in your classroom? The ability to do this—both consistently and consistently *well*—is often referred to as the art of teaching. You're way past the focus on *what* you are going to do to address this challenge; indeed, you're now thinking about *how* all of these strategies and approaches blend together to create an assessment design. *Empowering* students in such a classroom environment does not happen by accident, and it's no coincidence that your growth as a reflective practitioner has accompanied—in fact preceded—this shift in practice. Because of the complexity and uniqueness of your situation (no one has ever faced exactly what you're facing before, with exactly the students you have), you're in uncharted territory, as it were. How cool is that? But it also means there's no step-by-step guide that we (or anyone) can offer. Instead, we can offer guiding principles designed to support students' metacognition (thinking about their own learning) and help them become increasingly independent in self-assessing and self-correcting their learning. The following two tools—"Classroom Environment Audit" and "Ask/Offer"—can help you to continue this journey with confidence.

Classroom Environment Audit

Why do it: A classroom audit is a student-driven, nonjudgmental assessment of the classroom environment. It involves students "reading" the messages conveyed on the classroom walls, the arrangement of furniture, and the books on the shelves with an eye on diversity, student empowerment, and equity. The audit also includes descriptions of interactions between teacher and students, and among students. When asking students to explore issues of tolerance and identity, we must ensure that our classroom environment is a safe place from students' perspectives, not just our own. When we ask students to conduct a classroom audit, we give them ownership of their space and create an opportunity to see things through their eyes.

How to do it:

Set up:

Create a clear plan with students for describing the classroom learning environment. Identify "look-fors" and discuss how to identify feelings associated with the learning space. Create a note-taker similar to the one started for you below.

Criteria	No	Yes	Some	Description	Feelings Associated
Does the furniture arrangement allow for ALL students to collaborate and learn from one another?					
Does the seating arrangement provide for integrated and equitable learning?					
Is the furniture arranged in a way that is aesthetically calming and conducive to learning for ALL students?					
Is the classroom free of clutter?					
Are the messages on the walls inviting and show that differences are embraced?					
Are the instructional materials multicultural and unbiased regarding gender, race, national origin, and disability?					

Criteria	No	Yes	Some	Description	Feelings Associated
Are classroom tasks distributed equitably without regard to gender, race, national origin, or disability?					
Are classroom expectations identified and developed by all classroom stakeholders?					
Does the teacher promote cooperation and integration of students through activities which help students work together?					
Does the teacher direct the discussion to enable all students to participate?					
Are teacher-to-student interactions equitable, without regard to gender, race, national origin, or disability?					
Do students show respect for ALL peers through praise, questioning, and feedback?					
Are student-to-student interactions equitable, without regard to gender, race, national origin, or disability?					

Implementation:

The audit works best when students are paired. This allows for discussion and analysis. Give students a week to complete the audit, focusing on 2–4 criteria daily. Allow for discussion and encourage using evidence to support claims.

Analysis:

When finished, compile the results and go over each criterion with the class. Mark each with one of the following designations: *"We've got it going on,"* *"Needs some refinement,"* or *"How do we make this happen?"* Determine next steps, involve students in the process, and sit back and watch your classroom transform.

When to do it: A student-driven classroom audit is a powerful strategy that supports the development of a student-centered learning environment. Use this strategy at various intervals throughout the school year.

While doing it: Step back, be open-minded, and allow students to explore their learning environment. Chances are, they've never been asked to do this before. Notice the results. What happens when students are given ownership?

Ask/Offer

Why do it: We all have strengths, and we all have weaknesses. More often than not, in any particular classroom you'll find those strengths and weaknesses offset one another. So one person may struggle in something while a classmate excels. What would happen if we were to begin pairing students intentionally to maximize their strengths and support each other? This tool helps students to create an authentic peer support network.

How to do it: In the Ask/Offer strategy, students pose (on chart paper, an online form, or aloud in a morning meeting) requests for support: some extra tutoring, guidance in a skill, time to help with a project, whatever the need may be. If a classmate can help, a match is made. Meanwhile, students acknowledge their own expertise and strengths, and they avail their services (using the same venue as the Asks) to classmates that might take advantage of this offer.

When to do it: This process can be done formally on a regular basis, or informally on an as-needed basis—or, by using an online platform to house the asks and offers, it can be a living document. By creating an environment in which you value and recognize the benefits of teamwork, partnerships, and collaboration, your students will begin to take the reins and seek out ways to help (and get help from) each other.

While doing it: Check in with the students routinely and note the students taking advantage of this powerful resource. No doubt, there will be students who need to utilize it but aren't. Encourage the use of this resource often. Ask students to speak about their experiences and share how peers were able to support them.

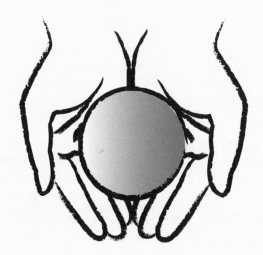

Assess and analyze the impact of your actions: Assess with purpose

At this phase in the pathway, you're using your deep knowledge and skills to help students take ownership of their learning journeys. Some may observe the culture of your learning environment and consider such empowerment in your classroom to be innovative and creative divergence. As a committed, reflective practitioner, you're well aware that you've reached a place in your professional development that is only possible because of your consistent, intentional focus on growing, learning, gauging, and tinkering with your practices to better 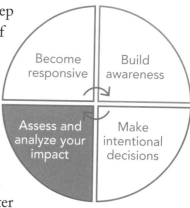 meet individual students' needs. You know the most important part of any classroom isn't what you're doing as a teacher, but rather, what's going on in students' minds; thus, you want to design a positive learning environment that adds real value to student learning—helping them to learn and do things together they couldn't do independently. Your initial question is truly guiding your inquiry: *How do I create a classroom culture where students care about and support one another?* Do the strategies and structures you've designed for students support deep learning? With that in mind, gather some colleagues, administrators, coaches, and your teammates and lead a discussion based on the following questions (and feel free to add your own):

Reflect on Teaching	Reflect on Learning
• What strategies have been most effective in building a positive classroom culture? Why? What contributes to that success?	• When does your classroom feel most like a team? When is that feeling lacking? Why is this?
• When you aren't getting the results you were hoping for, why not? What is interfering with that process?	• How are you including student voice in the governance and day-to-day operations of your classroom?
• How are you celebrating the elements of your classroom environment that you value? To what extent do students have a say in these celebrations?	• How are you gathering information and input from your students about the strength and authenticity of their relationships and connections? What are you doing with these data?
• How does addressing the whole child impact students' motivation, collaboration, and performance in the classroom? How can you tell?	

Become responsive: Trust your intuition

The wonderful work you're doing to build community and empower your students in your classroom ought not to be confined solely to your class. Have you considered expanding your "win to the nth degree" philosophy— the idea that wins build upon each other ad infinitum— to your entire grade level, department, team, and/or faculty? What might this look like? How might you open that conversation? There is a lot of research out there on teacher-leadership. The truth is, as you know, you

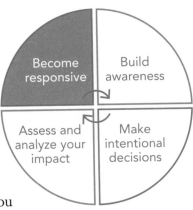

needn't be cast in an official role (team leader, department chair, committee president, or the like) to influence your peers and your work environment in a profoundly positive way. Sharing articles, inviting colleagues into your classroom, hosting a Friday-morning coffee-talk session before school, launching an action-research project, volunteering to lead a book study, and simply engaging your colleagues in dialogue about problems of practice, burning questions, and the state of affairs can change the climate of your school or department. That's leadership.

❖ How would you describe your classroom community? How would each of your students describe it? Have you asked them? What might you do with the information you collect?

❖ What processes are in place for you to monitor the tenor of your learning environment? How might students take the reins?

❖ How do you truly know if the structures and environment you're establishing lead to deeper student learning outcomes? How might you connect those dots?

You're probably wishing there were more phases in this pathway, right? Well, we agree, and we want to acknowledge a couple of realities: First, you've really grown as a thinker and a practitioner as you've built relationships within your interdependent, positive learning environment. Second, though you've progressed through this chapter, there really is no end to this work. You can always grow, you can always improve, and you can always learn and refine your approaches. Yes, there's a lot to celebrate, and yes, there's still a lot on the horizon.

Final thoughts on nurturing a positive learning environment

As you've come to the end of the "Nurturing a positive learning environment" pathway, it's important to take stock of your journey, appreciate the phases you've mastered, and note the growth you've made. In short, this is a wonderful time to appraise your professional development.

First, let's look at the pathway from the 10,000-foot level:

Be consistent	Be connected	Differentiate	Empower
Teacher-owned, Student-experienced	*Teacher-directed, Student-connected*	*Student-engaged, Teacher-facilitated*	*Student-owned, Teacher-guided*

You've made significant strides in transforming your classroom from one that's inherently *teacher-owned* (and student-experienced) to one that is becoming more *student-owned* (and teacher-guided). Through a systematic process of identifying key questions that either confound or interest you (or both), you've investigated and addressed four critical problems of practice related to the "Nurturing a positive learning environment" pathway. Along the way, you repeated a very predictable, very deliberate pattern of reflective steps that a) built your self-reflective capacity and b) enhanced your professional acumen. That pattern, the Reflective Cycle, really ought to be second nature to you by now:

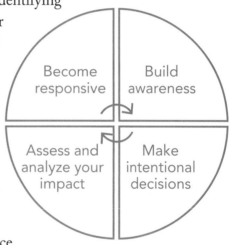

1. Build awareness about the problem of practice by asking key questions and conducting research to learn more.

2. Make intentional decisions about implementing strategies, based on the research and your desired goal.

3. Assess and analyze the impact of your actions to determine the effectiveness of particular strategies over a period of time.

4. Become responsive to the changing needs you notice in order to better meet your (and, more specifically, your *students'*) needs.

5. Repeat, repeat, repeat, and repeat again and again and again.

Remember the theory of action that drives this combination of approaches:

Theory of Action	IF we start with key problems of practice, use research-based best practices to solve them, and reflect on our practice as teachers, THEN we will become more expert in our practice, better able to meet our students' needs, and engaged in career-long professional growth that will allow us to become amazing, unstoppable teachers in whose classrooms learning will flourish.

Though you've come to the end of this particular pathway, you're far too astute to believe the journey is over. Learning is cyclical—a progression that leads you ever upwards, not unlike a spiral staircase—and you realize there will be times that you need to backtrack, regroup, and revisit some of the foundational elements of this pathway to solidify and enhance your effectiveness. And of course there's more yet to learn, different approaches to implement, and all sorts of new ways of looking at—and solving—your newfound problems of practice. Indeed, the growth you've made is more than just about creating a safe, positive learning environment; in addition, you're becoming masterful at the art of growing as a reflective practitioner and transferring your learning into the classroom.

And as you've certainly noticed, building strong relationships and cultivating a classroom of interdependent, collaborative students is just part of a robust, powerful, successful schooling experience for students. Now your task is to weave the other refinement pathways into your work in a seamless expression of excellence, ensuring that all students thrive and flourish.

 Or, if you find yourself with another nagging question, turn to the grid on p. 16, find that question, and turn to the page where we help you address it.

Chapter 4

Challenging students to commit to mastery

Years ago, in a famous experiment, Robert Rosenthal and Lenore Jacobson tricked some teachers into thinking that a handful of students in each of their classes were on the brink of rapid academic growth when, in reality, the students were no different than other students. Nonetheless, by the end of the year-long experiment, they demonstrated higher IQs than their peers—an apparent effect of their teachers' expectations (Rosenthal & Jacobson, 1992). Since this study, additional research has shown that students often learn up (or down) to our expectations. And several studies have shown that setting big goals for ourselves can serve as a self-fulfilling prophecy, goading us to work harder and achieve more (Locke & Latham, 2006).

You've likely seen the power of these two big ideas (high expectations and goal setting) in your own life; maybe you had a teacher or a coach who helped you to dream big—to reach for something you initially didn't believe you could achieve. Perhaps you were even drawn into teaching to do the same thing for others, helping them to set and achieve challenging goals. You've probably realized by now, though, that high expectations aren't like Dumbo's magic feather; they don't magically help students soar. Rather, you must share your expectations for students and show them how to reach them. It's at this point, though, that the daily realities of classrooms can leave us wondering how, exactly, we're supposed to turn our good intentions and aspirations for students into reality.

Take charge of your own professional growth

To help you consider how to use goal-setting and high expectations to inspire your students towards deep learning, we'll start with *your own curiosity*—questions you're likely to ask about your classroom. You may have found yourself asking one (or all) of the questions listed below. To help you meet your pressing needs and address your current problem of practice, we've placed a page number next to each so you can flip ahead and engage in some self-guided exploration:

- ❖ How do I cover all this content? (p. 55)
- ❖ How do I challenge students with rigor? (p. 62)
- ❖ How do I challenge every student when they have different abilities? (p. 68)
- ❖ How do I help students challenge themselves to learn at high levels? (p. 74)

How do I cover all this content?

Welcome to the first phase of the "Challenging students to commit to mastery" pathway. Not surprisingly, the focus here is on your actions as a teacher: what you are doing, what is expected of you, and what it will take for you to be successful. This pattern of thinking is typical of the *teacher-owned, student-experienced* phase, and as you proceed through the Reflective Cycle and expand your reflective vision, you'll begin to become more *consistent* in your approaches, allowing you to better meet your students' needs.

Build awareness: Observe

How do I cover all this content? If you're like many teachers, on your first day in your new classroom, someone may have handed you a curriculum guide, pacing chart, standards document, or textbook and said, "Here. Teach this." Before long, you may have found yourself falling behind—six weeks into the school year and still on week three of your pacing guide—or on pace, but feeling like you've been waterskiing over stuff you should've been scuba-diving into, which leaves you wondering, *How can I possibly cover all this stuff in one year?*

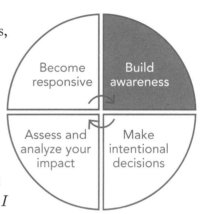

First, you probably can't; nor do you need to. Seriously. Let's examine what's going on here. Great teachers, as they say, don't *cover* content, they *uncover* it. They start by digging deeply into standards to extract key vocabulary terms, concepts, skills, and themes students need to learn. They determine which standards (or aspects of standards) are just worth being familiar with, which describe what all learners should know or be able to do, and which articulate enduring understandings. It's tedious, but worth it. Why? For starters, by figuring out the core elements of what you want students to learn, you may find many overlaps—the same concept or skill addressed in multiple standards—as well as larger themes, which lend themselves to more interesting units. Thus, you don't need to teach each standard as a standalone unit or lesson (e.g., "Let's analyze how complex characters develop over the course of a text") but rather, use them to stay grounded in what students ought to do as they, say, read *Of Mice and Men*.

Second, by figuring out the core elements of what you want students to learn, you won't fall prey to the belief that "if it is in the textbook, it has to be taught." Great teachers look for "big ideas" across the curriculum, content, and standards. They teach for meaning rather than coverage. No research supports the idea that a coverage mode of instruction increases achievement on external tests. If anything, research suggests that focusing on fewer topics and core understandings is likelier to increase student achievement (Schmidt, McKnight, & Raizen, 1997).

Unpacking standards not only streamlines and focuses your instruction, but also serves another purpose: helping students set and achieve learning goals. Brain science tells us that when we anticipate achieving a goal, our brains fill with the same chemical, dopamine, as when we eat chocolate, finish grading a stack of papers, or win a prize at the county fair (Sapolsky, 2017). In short, setting and achieving goals feels good and forms a positive addiction. However, we must help students break up larger tasks—like doing long division, understanding mitosis and meiosis, or analyzing *Beowulf*—into smaller bite-size learning objectives, so they can experience quick wins (and shots of dopamine) which, in turn, provide the motivation to take on greater challenges.

Make intentional decisions: Be deliberate in planning

To address the challenge of needing to cover content, it helps to understand that your goals are to 1) unpack what students really need to learn and 2) set learning goals. After all, in order to achieve mastery, we've got to be clear on *what* the students will master—and then describe exactly what mastery looks like, sounds like, and produces in the classroom. The two tools that follow—"Zoom In" and "Zoom Out"—will assist with that, while providing an opportunity to calibrate and remove any content that doesn't need covering.

Zoom In

Why do it: Objectives provide clarity for teachers and students. They focus on both teaching and learning.

How to do it:

1. Begin with the district content-area curriculum and associated standards.
2. Investigate the curriculum/standards that apply to the lesson being designed to determine the declarative and procedural knowledge and the level of rigor.
3. Write the UNDERSTAND portion of the learning objective first (declarative).
4. Using the UNDERSTAND statement, next determine the facts, details, steps, and/or vocabulary for the KNOW portion of the objective (declarative).
5. Using the information from the declarative portions of the objective (KNOW and UNDERSTAND) determine how students will demonstrate their knowledge through the BE ABLE TO DO portion of the objective (procedural).

Here are a few examples:

By the end of the lesson we will:

1. Know all colors are made from red, yellow, and blue (primary colors).
2. Understand that mixing the primary colors in certain proportions creates all other colors (secondary and tertiary colors).
3. Be able to create color wheels of secondary and tertiary colors.

Secondary example:

By the end of the learning session we will:

1. KNOW that the rights American women had in the 1920's differ from the rights they have in the present day.
2. UNDERSTAND that the rights people have impact their ability to engage fully in society.
3. BE ABLE TO compare the rights of women in the 1920's with those of today through the lens of social equality.

The use of *we will* makes the learning environment more inclusive and states that the teacher is an active learner—no one is a completed project—everyone is a learner.

When to do it: Map objectives prior to every unit; share learning objectives with each lesson.

While doing it: Notice your clarity of thought during a lesson as you keep the lesson objective in the forefront of your mind. How does it impact your teaching? At the same time, notice how students respond when they have a clear understanding of the lesson objective. How does it impact their learning?

Adapted from *Classroom Instruction That Works* (Dean, Hubbell, Pitler, and Stone, 2012). © McREL. Used with permission.

Zoom Out

Why do it: To clarify what students must learn through backward planning, by identifying areas of alignment and making connections across standards, content, and curriculum.

How to do it: Either by yourself or with a trusted partner (or with your entire grade-level or department team):

1. Identify the end result. What should your students know, understand, and be able to do? In this first step, we ask you to grab all your national, state, provincial, and/or district standards, as well as all pacing and curriculum guides. Because there is typically more content than can be reasonably addressed within a school year, we must look for connections across these resources and make choices to prioritize goals and streamline learning.

2. Read through each of these resources, make connections, and write down a list of long-term performance goals—what you want students to do by the end of the year. Write these goals as headings on separate pieces of paper. Underneath each heading, you'll later add standards and curriculum that "feed" into each of the goals.

3. Now it's time to connect the long-term goals and create several essential questions that address the big ideas for the year. These questions will provide a backbone to your weekly/daily plans and engage learners in "meaning making." For more information on the development of essential questions, check out *Understanding by Design* by Grant Wiggins and Jay McTighe (ASCD, 2005).

4. Determine how students will show mastery: How will you know if students have achieved the desired results? How will you evaluate student performance? Determine which task will provide understanding as outlined by *Understanding by Design* and determine which task will provide the clearest window into learning for each of your learning goals. When someone truly understands, they:

    a. Can explain concepts, principles, and processes by putting them in their own words, teaching them to others, justifying answers, and sharing their reasoning.

    b. Can interpret by making sense of data, text, and experience through images, analogies, stories, and models.

    c. Can apply by using and adapting what they know in new contexts.

    d. Demonstrate perspective by seeing the new picture.

5. Create your plan: Map out how you'll lead students to reach the goals you've set. To do so, logically group and order the learning goals you identified in the first step and make connections to any pacing guides you may be using. Add details, such as curriculum resources, learning activities, and smaller formative assessments. Schedule the learning goals on a year-long calendar so that the pacing supports learning.

6. Now it's time to zoom in and develop smaller units of study. The next task will guide you through that process.

7. Tailor your plan: Once the plan is in place, continually return to calibrate and adjust as needed.

When to do it: The ideal goal is to begin each year with this task; however, this can be done at any point in your school year.

While doing it: Pay close attention to your thoughts as you seek to find and build connections across all the resources in front of you. Notice how many connections can be made when starting with the end in mind. Notice the amount of connections you can make between your resources. Keep a journal of questions that arise and reach out to colleagues to find answers. What "aha" did you have as you engaged in this task?

Assess and analyze your impact: Notice learning

At this point, you've likely had a few (or many) "aha" moments along the way and your thinking has begun to shift. Along with those changes in your reflective process, you've begun to plan and do things differently in your classroom. This ought to result in you gaining some clarity on exactly what you expect students to master and what comprises an effective learning objective. Keep your initial question in mind: *How do I cover all this content?* It's here that we ask you to pause and notice a few essential things that have happened. How has your teaching changed? How has student learning changed? Use the prompts below to guide your reflections about both.

Reflect on Teaching	Reflect on Learning
• What specific themes or "big ideas" did you uncover in the Zoom Out task? • Which standards did you identify as essential for students to go deeply into? Which did you determine don't need as much emphasis? How did you make these decisions? • Name one specific way that focusing on a "big idea" has changed your thinking when you plan.	• Do students describe objectives as what they're doing . . . or what they're learning? • Throughout a lesson, randomly ask students to explain the purpose of that particular lesson and describe the big idea that is at the heart of the content they are studying. What does their response tell you? • Can all of your students describe the connections among their learning activities, the objectives, the target standards, and the big idea? How might you lead them in doing this?

Become responsive: Make changes

With the answers to the reflective prompts above fresh in your mind, we now ask you to return to the plans you created (and the activities that accompanied them) to determine your next steps. This is the process of growing your reflective muscle in order to handle tougher and tougher cognitive challenges—and act on them in a way that helps you to be more intentional in your planning. Not surprisingly, you'll have some successes and some struggles along this path, because rarely does anything go as planned the first time (or, for that matter, the first couple of dozen times).

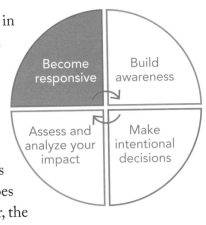

Here are some questions that you might want to bring to a trusted colleague—a "critical friend" or an instructional coach or mentor—to reflect on what's improved and what your next steps might be:

❖ Which content is absolutely necessary to cover and needs to be prioritized in your planning?

❖ Which standards need to be taught to mastery, and which are simply introductions?

❖ How might you introduce an objective a week or two before you teach it to mastery?

❖ Which learning objectives can you make even more student-friendly?

It's time to heed that ageless advice, "Look back to look ahead." The question you sought to answer at the beginning of this pathway was, *How do I cover all this content?* Now think how you'd answer it. Here are three simple ways to return to your problem of practice and deepen your reflective capacity:

❖ Jot some notes down in a learning journal or another place where you might be able to archive your thinking and access ideas, musings, questions, and other ponderings later.

❖ Find a trusted colleague or two to engage in a dialogue with you. Exchange thoughts, suggestions, critical feedback, and celebrations together.

❖ Engage your administrator, instructional coach, department chair, or another member of your support network in a discussion about this question, your journey thus far, and any shifts in perspective you've noticed.

Backward planning and using objectives to guide learning are powerful strategies that can ensure the coverage of necessary content, but you may find that your new clarity of focus may surface other problems and raise different questions. For example, you may be concerned that students understand their *objectives*, but don't see how they add up to a larger *goal* (mastering a standard), nor do they understand what it looks like to master important knowledge and skills. If so, you may want to tackle the problem on the next page: *How do I challenge students with rigor?*

 Or, if you find yourself with another nagging question, turn to the grid on p. 16, find that question, and turn to the page where we help you address it.

How do I challenge students with rigor?

| Be consistent *Teacher-owned, Student-experienced* | **Be connected** *Teacher-directed, Student-connected* | Differentiate *Student-engaged, Teacher-facilitated* | Empower *Student-owned, Teacher-guided* |

Welcome to the second phase of the "Challenging students to commit to mastery" pathway. In this phase, you'll still be directing learning, but you'll find your attention shifting from what you're *teaching* to what students are *learning* and how they're responding to your actions as a teacher. Your practice is truly becoming more *connected* as the cause-and-effect relationships between your actions and your students' performance are revealed. And as you become more intentional about weaving rigorous learning opportunities into your class, you'll begin to take note of how this impacts student learning outcomes—mastery of learning objectives—in a profound way. Your classroom is becoming *teacher-directed* and *student-connected*.

 If you're joining us from another pathway, or if you're skipping ahead to this problem of practice without reading the previous phase in its entirety, we suggest you skim through or review the previous section just to get your bearings.

Build awareness: Note cause-and-effect relationships

How do I challenge students with rigor? As your teaching becomes more focused and your students become clearer about what they're expected to learn, you'll likely face a new challenge: determining how good is good enough. You've probably heard a lot about the need for rigor. After all, that's the whole point of high standards: to set a high bar for learning, not merely in terms of breadth (learning a lot of content) but perhaps more importantly, in terms of depth (demonstrating deep knowledge or a high level of skill). So, you may be asking yourself, *How do I know where to set the bar?*

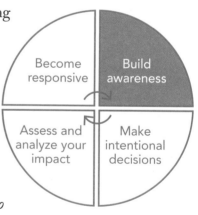

To help address these nagging questions, you might want to first define for yourself, *What is "rigor"?* Does rigor mean piling more work on students? Grading harder? Moving faster? Or does it reflect a less-is-more approach—encouraging deep thinking and complex application? In asking this question, you've begun to wade into something of a philosophical schism among educators, with one side saying students ought to learn a bunch of *stuff* (state capitals, multiplication tables, parts of a cell, the literary canon) and another side saying that with so much information at our fingertips, we should focus on helping students *learn*

to learn and develop critical thinking skills. So, which side is right? In our humble (and research-informed) opinion, we say: Neither.

As it turns out, deep learning is a matter of applying knowledge, which requires attaining both *declarative* knowledge (facts) and *procedural* knowledge (skills). Studies show, for example, that, unlike novices, experts are better able to categorize a problem (find the hypotenuse), identify the right strategy to solve it (Pythagorean theorem), apply the strategy ($3^2 + 4^2 = 25$; $\sqrt{25} = 5$), evaluate the answer and their problem-solving strategies, repeat the cycle if the first strategy doesn't solve the problem, and store the correct solution for later use. Sound familiar? It should. It's basically the same sequence of steps you're using in this book. Rigorous learning, then, is about helping students grasp concepts and think about them. Stated differently, to be critical thinkers, we need things to *think about*.

Make intentional decisions: Plan, then implement

Once you've oriented yourself to the challenge of rigor by reflecting on and defining what rigorous learning means to you, you're ready to bring it to life in your classroom. The following tools, "Talk the Talk" and "Go Deeper," will help to ensure you're providing students with adequate rigor in their learning by helping them to master both declarative knowledge and procedural skills so that ultimately, they're able to apply knowledge. To maximize the effectiveness of these tools, you'll want to hone your focus into implementing these strategies by observing their impact on student learning—the essence of the *connected* phase of this pathway.

Talk the Talk

Why do it: "Words are the pegs on which to hang ideas," so we must help students learn and *use* subject-specific vocabulary with precision in the classroom.

How to do it:

1. List all the vocabulary terms you identified when you unpacked standards.

2. Present students with a brief explanation of each new concept or term.

3. Provide students with a nonlinguistic depiction of the new concept or term (a mental image, diagram, or symbol/icon).

4. Ask students to generate their own definition or explanation of the term or concept.

5. Ask students to create their own nonlinguistic representation of the term or concept.

6. Design learning tasks and classroom discussions that require students to use the subject-specific vocabulary terms to *explain their thinking*, like this:

   > **Teacher:** *How do we calculate the area of this box?*
   >
   > **Student:** *We times all the sides.*
   >
   > **Teacher:** *Times all the sides? Does. Not. Compute.*
   >
   > **Student:** *Sorry. We multiply height by width and depth.*
   >
   > **Teacher:** *Exactly.*

7. Insist on precise use of vocabulary when students use the terms in class, like this:

   > **Student:** *Shakespeare uses the analogy of a summer's day to describe his lover.*
   >
   > **Teacher:** *Analogy? Is that the correct term?*
   >
   > **Student:** *Oh, no wait. It's a metaphor.*
   >
   > **Teacher:** *Why?*
   >
   > **Student:** *Because a metaphor compares A to B. An analogy says A is to B like C is to D.*

When to do it: With every unit and when introducing a new concept or idea. Don't assume students have prior knowledge of key terms they need to grasp concepts and big ideas. And even if they come to class with that background knowledge, a good review of the vocabulary always helps!

While doing it: Pay attention to your consistency with this task. How do you intentionally look for opportunities to implement this tool?

Go Deeper

Why do it: Students are more apt to remember what they think about, so learning tasks should encourage students to think about what they're learning.

How to do it:

1. From your backward planning with standards and curriculum, list the *declarative* and *procedural* knowledge students must learn in a unit/lesson.

2. Identify the level of cognitive demand required by the *declarative* or *procedural* knowledge as shown in the graphic below.

Recall/Understand
- Students can perform basic addition and subtraction.
- Students can list the basic elements of plot structure.

Apply
- Students solve addition and subtraction word problems.
- Students identify elements of plot structure in a story.

Analyze and evaluate
- Students critique mathematical reasoning of classmates.
- Students analyze the use of literacy devices in a story.

Create and synthesize
- Students create a mathematical model for a situation.
- Students integrate literacy devices into creative writing.

3. Design a learning task that engages students in the appropriate level of cognitive challenge, ideally moving them beyond merely recall/understanding learning and into deeper thinking.

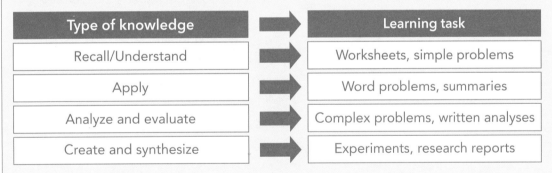

Type of knowledge		Learning task
Recall/Understand	→	Worksheets, simple problems
Apply	→	Word problems, summaries
Analyze and evaluate	→	Complex problems, written analyses
Create and synthesize	→	Experiments, research reports

4. You can enhance the depth of thinking for any learning task by asking students to follow an explanation of their thinking with a "because" (e.g., "I believe this is the right answer *because* . . . .")

When to do it: When planning and implementing each lesson.

While doing it: Notice how students articulate their thinking in both verbal and written form. What does this tell you about their learning?

Assess and analyze your impact: Recognize the results of your actions

As you've focused your mental energy on ways to effectively engage students in cooperative groupings, you'll notice your attention turning to the direct impact of your efforts. So when you assess the impact of your actions, reflect on your guiding question for this phase: *How do I challenge students with rigor?*

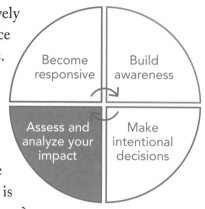

Most likely, your lessons and assignments are a bit more rigorous now. And as a result, you're probably seeing some changes in student learning outcomes. To what extent is this true for you, and—very importantly—how do you know?

The mental processes you're engaged in reflect how experts think, honing and shaping their mental models by continually examining and reexamining assumptions about cause and effect: *If I want X to happen, I should do Y. If X didn't happen, is it because I didn't do Y well or because Y wasn't the right solution?* The questions below are designed to help you to further hone and shape your mental models by engaging in self-reflection and dialogue with your colleagues.

Reflect on Teaching	Reflect on Learning
• How consistently do you provide students with direct instruction of subject-specific vocabulary?	• What percentage of students demonstrate the ability to explain key facts, concepts, and big ideas?
• How many of your learning tasks engage students in *deep thinking* as opposed to lower-level recall & recognition?	• What percentage of students demonstrate the ability to explain their thinking and/or defend their answers?
• Name one specific way that focusing on a "big idea" has changed your thinking when you plan.	• Have students shown a better grasp of subject-specific language on classroom assessments since you've shifted your instruction?
	• What's a good example of student work that reflects *deep learning*? Does it incorporate subject-specific vocabulary and clear, logical thinking? If so, ask yourself: What specific actions did you take that led to this level of learning?

Become responsive: Respond to the needs you see

Let's face it: the word *rigor* can be freighted with negative connotations, like strictness, rigidity, or death (i.e., *rigor mortis*). Our view of rigor, though, is something more engaging, nimble, and lively. It's giving kids a cognitive challenge that motivates them. So, hopefully, as you've amped up the rigor in your classroom, you've also seen higher levels of energy, enthusiasm, and engagement among your students. You may also see some ways you could improve the level of academic discourse in your classroom and cognitive challenge of classroom learning

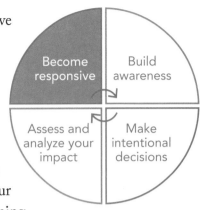

activities. After all, that was the question that launched you down this path: *How do I challenge students with rigor?* To that end, here are some questions you might ask yourself—and your colleagues—to reflect on what's improved for you and your students and what steps to take next.

❖ Do you have any learning tasks that *don't* help students to think deeply? How might you add rigor to them?

❖ Which students need help engaging in cognitively demanding learning? How might you provide this support?

❖ Which students need help using subject-specific language? How might you prompt them?

Even with these refinements, you're likely to find that everything's far from perfect in your classroom. Quite likely, in fact, as you've raised the bar for students, you've begun to surface some new, heretofore unseen problems for you and your students. For example, you may worry that not all students are ready to engage in deep learning—after all, you've got students who bring a wide array of abilities and prior learning to your classroom. If so, you may want to tackle the problem on the next page, *How do I challenge every student when they have different abilities?*

Or, if you find yourself with another nagging question, turn to the grid on p. 16, find that question, and turn to the page where we help you address it.

How do I challenge every student when they have different abilities?

| Be consistent
*Teacher-owned
Student-experienced* | Be connected
*Teacher-directed,
Student-connected* | **Differentiate**
*Student-engaged,
Teacher-facilitated* | Empower
*Student-owned,
Teacher-guided* |

Welcome to the third phase of the "Challenging students to commit to mastery" pathway. Here, you may feel the ground shifting beneath your feet as you increasingly focus on working to ensure students of different abilities can master challenging content, which requires you to *differentiate* learning for them, and in turn, shift your thinking away from focusing solely on what *you* must do in the classroom—that is, your teaching—to what must happen in students' minds for them to achieve mastery—that is, student learning. This important shift happens in every pathway as we move into the *differentiated* (or *student-engaged, teacher-facilitated*) phase.

> ✓ If you're joining us from another pathway, welcome! Before diving headlong into this challenge, though, we suggest you review the previous phase of this pathway to get your bearings.

Build Awareness: Zoom in on the details

How do I challenge every student when they have different abilities? Many teachers feel frustrated by the challenge of needing to teach students of differing abilities. Often, they may feel they're not allowed to express these frustrations for fear of sounding like they don't believe all students can learn. So, at the risk of stating the obvious, we'll come right out and say what you already know: You're teaching students with differing levels of ability, prior knowledge, and motivation. There, we said it: Students have different abilities. We might also add that

they have different interests, too. Some like horses. Some like tinkering with old cars. Some like writing books. Now that we've got that out there in the open, we can tackle the obvious, follow-on question: How do I find the right level of challenge for all students?

In a way, you don't. Your job is not to find a single level of difficulty that is "just right" for all students. Rather, it's to set a minimum bar for learning—the level of learning that every student must master before moving on to what comes next.

Wait . . . what? A *minimum bar* for learning? Does my principal/superintendent/school board know that you just said that? Won't that dumb down learning?

Well, no, not if it's a *minimum* bar—and a bar worth achieving. In fact, if we set the bar too high, there's nowhere for accelerated learners to go. As Robyn Jackson (2018) writes, we want to define the floor, not the ceiling for learning, so students can exceed our expectations.

Here, it's also helpful to note the difference between a *learning* versus a *performance* goal. As researcher Carol Dweck has noted (2006), performance goals are about looking smart (or at least not dumb) and getting a desired grade. Learning goals, on the other hand, are about gaining new skills and understanding new things. A performance goal would be, *I want to get an A*, while a learning goal would be, *I want to become a better writer*. Dweck's research has shown that when students set learning goals instead of performance goals, they're more motivated to embrace struggle and push themselves to *learn* (not simply get a grade).

You must know *what* individual students need and *how* to support their learning. To do this, you'll need a deep understanding of your content, including how students' current learning connects with prior and future learning, what level of performance reflects mastery, and what common misconceptions students may have. Second, you'll want to understand your students as individual learners: where they are with their learning, what engages them, what they should expect of themselves, and so on. Third, and perhaps most difficult: You may need to begin to change your own paradigm as a teacher—seeing yourself less as the deliverer of instruction and more as a facilitator of learning.

Make intentional decisions: Develop a clear vision

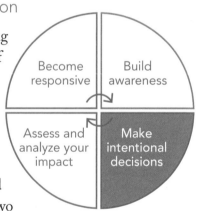

The next two tools will help you connect these dots, offering some practical guidance for addressing this problem of practice. At this phase, our guidance will be a little less prescriptive and a little more cerebral. That's because from this point on, the refinements to your practice will increasingly reflect branching decision trees of if-then responses (*If I see students doing or needing X, then I do Y*). As you do this, you'll begin to think more and more like an expert, using what you learned in the first two phases of this pathway to support individual student needs.

Because experts use terms with precision, let's take a moment to define what we mean by *mastery*, a term that often gets tossed around and can wind up meaning different things to different people. We define mastery as the *level of fluency required for students to take and apply ideas and skills to new problems*. In other words, simply memorizing the dates of Civil War battles doesn't reflect mastery. What would? Using subject-specific language to discuss an essential question like, *How are wars driven by economic and cultural conflicts?* and being able to analyze other historical events. The tools on the following pages—"EMC²" and "BYOG"—will help you ensure all students are challenged in your *differentiated* classroom, regardless of their academic levels and varying skills.

EMC² (Expect Mastery, encourage Cognitive Challenge)

Why do it: Students will be more motivated to learn if they see how to meet (and exceed) expectations, so it's important to clarify what *mastery* looks like and let students know we *expect* them to *achieve* mastery even as we *encourage* them to exceed expectations.

How to do it:

1. Go back to the unpacking work you did earlier to identify the *declarative* and *procedural* knowledge contained in standards—the concepts and skills you expect students must learn.

2. For each concept/understanding, identify what proficiency looks like. How will you and your students know when they have fully grasped a concept or consistently applied a skill?

3. Now identify what *inadequate, incomplete,* or *inconsistent* learning looks like. You may find it useful to identify the misconceptions or skills gaps that could impede future learning.

4. Next, describe *excellence.* It may be useful to consider cognitive challenge. For example, if you've defined mastery as demonstrating *application,* excellence might reflect use of the same skill for *analysis,* cross-unit (or curricular) *synthesis,* or *creativity.* (Note: We're *not* saying you *should* set your bar for mastery at *application*; we leave that up to your expert opinion.)

5. Once levels are defined, convert your definitions into a rubric that helps students see what incompleteness, mastery, and excellence look like. Here's an example:

Incomplete	Mastery	Excellence
Knows and understands terms like "theme" and "motives" but cannot consistently identify them in a story or novel.	Identifies character motives and story themes in a short story or novel.	Uses specific examples to critique a writer's use of dialogue and narrative to develop characters and advance plot or theme.

6. Finally (and most important) share this rubric with your students to give them a clear vision of what mastery and excellence look like. You should discuss and create examples together. Over time, you may find you can include students in the task of setting expectations.

When to do it: Prior to planning every unit and lesson.

While doing it: Notice how this task stretches your thinking and strengthens your vision of proficiency. In what ways does this task change the way you teach?

BYOG (Bring Your Own Goals)

Why do it: Like adults, students are more motivated (and likely to exceed expectations) when they can set their own goals for mastery, rather than being given their goals.

How to do it: Here are some guiding principles for helping students set their own learning goals.

- **Learning goals are powerful when fueled by curiosity.** When students are learning *declarative knowledge*, you can tap into their curiosity by using a simple **K-W-L chart** that helps students define what they already **K**now about a concept (or big idea/ essential question), what they **W**onder, and what they hope to **L**earn.

- **We're more likely to achieve goals when we choose them.** Prior to every unit or learning episode, give students the rubrics created with the EMC² tool, then invite them to decide *for themselves* the depth of learning (to or beyond mastery) they'll demonstrate. You've already set a high bar for mastery, so getting all students to that point will be great, although you'll likely want to encourage them to stretch themselves.

- **Goals are most powerful when we write them down and commit to them.** Your students may already use "I can" or "I will" statements. That's great. Remind them that these goals aren't for *your* benefit, but *theirs*—the goals represent a commitment students make to themselves to master important content and skills (e.g., *"I will be able to understand the quadratic formula and apply it to interesting things in my life, like Angry Birds"*). That means you'll also want to give students opportunities to revisit their goals.

- **Goals should spur effort.** Many students don't recognize the link between effort and success, so we often must help them make this connection. One way to do this is with a *performance contract* through which students set a goal and then identify what they'll do (e.g., pay attention in class, quiz themselves after each section in their reading) to achieve those goals. Students are also more likely to achieve goals if they anticipate what might get them off-track and what they'll do if that happens.

- Here's an example of how to pull these ideas into a single goal-setting template.

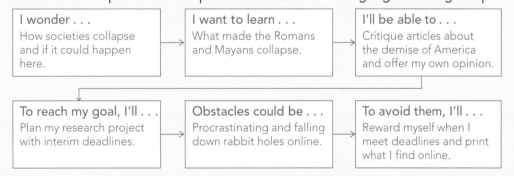

When to do it: Students can set "mini" learning goals every day, yet they benefit from setting and tracking progress toward long-term goals. So, you might start with helping them set short-term goals and move them toward long-term goals as they become more adept with setting and achieving goals.

While doing it: How does your understanding of your students shift as you engage in these tasks? What questions do they surface? Write these "ahas" in a journal.

Assess and analyze your impact: Transfer the vision

You've been working hard to implement strategies that ensure all students master important content and engage in deep thinking, while allowing accelerated learners to go even deeper with their learning. And now, as you assess and analyze the impact of your actions up to this point, we remind you to keep your guiding question in mind: *How do I challenge every student when they have different abilities?*

At this point in your journey, you're really thinking like an expert, relying on knowledge of both your content and your students' learning progress to help them set goals that stretch them. This phase also requires you to weave together many big ideas and complex techniques, so it's likely to be messy, especially at first. As you well know, experts don't go it alone; indeed, they consult with one another to diagnose and solve problems. With a "critical friend," use the following reflective questions (and then create your own to add to the list) to help you to develop your expert mental models and challenge each other's thinking:

Reflect on Teaching	Reflect on Learning
• How clear is your vision for student mastery in each lesson? How could you guide students to that same level of understanding?	• What differences do you see in students' performance and engagement when they set their own goals?
• What habits must you develop to facilitate student success? How might you involve students more in setting rigorous goals?	• Does letting students choose their level of challenge improve their motivation? How many of them have set goals beyond mastery? Why is that?
• How do your instructions and student interactions change when you become more focused on helping them achieve their learning goals?	• Do performance contracts improve motivation and performance? For which students? For the others, what might you try to impact their engagement and efforts?

Become responsive: Respond in the moment

The third phase in this pathway marks a seismic shift in your thinking, as well as your actions. As you've pursued the question that launched this pathway—*How do I challenge every student when they have different abilities?*—you've begun to see new student behaviors taking root. For example, they may be asking questions that reflect a desire to achieve mastery, not simply a grade. You may also be seeing students developing a growth mindset, embracing productive struggle because they understand that's when learning occurs. You've likely been

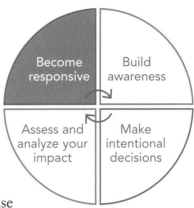

engaged in some productive struggle yourself: Some lessons, learning tasks, or approaches to goal-setting may have fallen flat. Take note of those. You could even share your observations with your students so they see that even adults make mistakes—and learn from them. Take a moment and reflect on your professional growth from the beginning of this pathway until now, and challenge yourself (and a trusted colleague, instructional coach, or administrator) with a few bonus reflective questions:

❖ For each of your students, do you know what motivates them and inspires them to pursue deep learning? How do you know? How did you learn this?

❖ How does the shift from *teaching students* to *facilitating learning* impact your interactions with students during a lesson? A unit? An entire course or school year? Why is that?

❖ How would you define the difference between *differentiated instruction* and *differentiated learning*? Ask a couple trusted colleagues for their thoughts and compare notes.

As you strive to help every student operate in their own individual "Goldilocks" zone, where learning is neither too challenging nor too easy, your mind is whirring. And it may surface a new set of challenges. For example, you may feel like a honeybee buzzing around your classroom, constantly checking in on every student and nudging them forward—perhaps because you're not yet confident that they could push themselves without your constant attention and intervention. You may be wondering what it would take—or if it's even possible—to get students to commit to and *own* their individual learning goals. If so, you may wish to turn to the next page to consider, *How do I help students challenge themselves to learn at high levels?*

Or, if you find yourself with another nagging question, turn to the grid on p. 16, find that question, and turn to the page where we help you address it.

How do I help students challenge themselves to learn at high levels?

Be consistent	Be connected	Differentiate	**Empower**
Teacher-owned, Student-experienced	*Teacher-directed, Student-connected*	*Student-engaged, Teacher-facilitated*	*Student-owned, Teacher-guided*

Welcome to the fourth phase of the "Challenging students to commit to mastery" pathway. Here, you'll begin to *empower* students to pursue deep learning in a *student-owned, teacher-guided* environment. This is no subtle shift, either. Building your students' capacity to own their self-directed learning energy requires steady, significant development of your own capacity—both as a master of the technical elements of teaching and as a reflective practitioner. Getting to this point requires building on the foundation of everything you've learned, the acute awareness you've built, the many steps you've taken with great intentionality, and your ability to gauge your impact and make midcourse corrections as necessary.

 If you're joining us from another pathway, we encourage you to review the previous three phases in this pathway to ensure you're ready to address this challenge.

Build awareness: Bring all the variables together

How do I help students challenge themselves to learn at high levels? We've all heard that teachers should not be a "sage on the stage" but a "guide by the side." It sounds nice, of course. Yet how to make this happen in classrooms often remains ill-defined, leaving this expression sounding like a platitude. At this point in your refinement journey, however, you're close to making this a reality. You and your students are clear about *what* they should learn, *why* they should learn what they're learning, and *how* to get there; moreover, students are increasingly engaged in the learning process. Yet you feel there's still something missing: you'd love to see your students take true ownership of their learning—not simply for a grade, but because they *want* to learn. You may find yourself wondering, *If students didn't have to come to my class, would they?*

First, let's recognize this is a good problem to have. Many teachers never reach this rarefied air of wanting their students to become passionate and persistent learners. Likely, it's because of everything you've done so far in your classroom that you now see this as a problem. Certainly, you could stop here, and no one would fault you for it. Yet if you want to take the next step to become an *amazing* teacher, there are two additional areas of expertise you can develop to become more creative and innovative in your practice: helping students to develop their own questions for learning, and to engage in positive self-talk to guide their own progress toward meeting learning goals. These practices reflect three big ideas from research:

- ❖ The success of project-based learning hinges on the presence of a *driving question*; instead of just doing work, projects should help students solve big problems or resolve big questions (Barron et al., 1998).

- ❖ Giving students choice in their learning drives motivation and deeper learning, though too many choices can demotivate them if they expend too much mental energy fretting over which option to pursue (Patall, Cooper, & Robinson, 2008).

- ❖ Positive self-questioning is the key to deep learning. Self-questioning is the voice in our heads that helps size up what we've learned and do not yet fully comprehend. Studies, in fact, show students are more apt to retain learning when they quiz themselves on what they've read. The good news is that we can teach these self-questioning strategies to students. When we do, they demonstrate significantly higher levels of learning and achievement—the equivalent of almost two letter grades (King, 1991).

Make intentional decisions: Move beyond strategy to design

So, how do you bring all of these ideas together in your classroom? The ability to do this—both consistently and consistently *well*—is often referred to as the art of teaching. You're way past the focus on *what* you are going to do to address this challenge; indeed, you're now thinking about *how* all of these strategies and approaches blend together to create an assessment design. *Empowering* students in such a classroom environment does not happen by accident, and it's no coincidence that your growth as a reflective practitioner has accompanied—in fact preceded—this shift in practice.

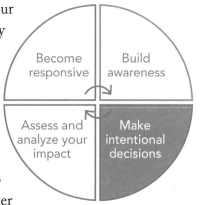

Because of the complexity and uniqueness of your situation (no one has ever faced exactly what you're facing before, with exactly the students you have), you're in uncharted territory, as it were. How cool is that? But it also means there's no step-by-step guide that we (nor anyone) can offer. Accordingly, the advice we offer here are really guiding principles designed to support students' metacognition (thinking about their own learning) and to help them become increasingly independent in self-assessing and self-correcting their learning. The following two tools—"Burning Questions" and "Inner Voice"—can help you to continue this journey with confidence.

Burning Questions

Why do it: Burning questions tap into the power of student choice, curiosity, and cognitive challenge, helping to motivate students to push themselves to engage in deep learning.

How to do it: Keep these key ideas in mind when helping students develop burning questions to drive their own learning.

- **Start with what matters.** Your job as a teacher, of course, is to help students match their interests with the content they should learn, so you should consider how pursuing burning questions will help them develop valuable declarative and procedural knowledge. The hard work you've done to unpack standards will pay off because standards typically call for students to develop critical thinking skills, not to regurgitate some specific bit of knowledge.

- **Keep the questions open-ended and challenging.** To drive deep learning, burning questions should be open-ended and not easily answered; if you can get an answer to your question from Google or Siri, it's not exactly burning. Answering a burning question instead should require students to gain significant new knowledge and skills (e.g., "Can I teach my dog to read—that is, to connect abstract symbols with rewards?").

- **Help students connect their personal interests to learning.** One student's burning question is rarely another's. It all comes down to personal interest, the real "sweet spot" of learning—closing a gap in *our own curiosity*. The more you know about your students, the more you can help them connect their interests to deep learning. There's no pre-approved list of burning questions we can offer you or you can offer your students. Rather, they must be developed through dialogue with students, piquing their interest, and helping them find personal interest in the content of your classroom.

- **Scaffold the process.** Initially at least, you may need to help students identify their burning questions. Because students can feel overwhelmed by too many choices, simply turning them loose to research a topic of their choice may backfire. Thus, you may find it more effective to give students a few choices of topics you know are fertile ground for exploration, while allowing those students who already have a burning question to pursue those interests.

When to do it: Initially, you might use burning questions to drive a once-a-year or once-a-semester research or complex-problem-solving project. Over time, as both you and your students grow more comfortable with student-directed learning, you may find ways to frame every unit around a burning question, helping students connect the concepts and skills they're learning to a compelling, personal question.

While doing it: Grab a nearby Bloom's Taxonomy chart and notice the depth of questions your students are seeking to answer. Encourage them to form questions that drive toward synthesis and evaluation. When we teach our students the art of question-asking, we set them up for true learning success.

Inner Voice

Why do it: Self-questioning is a powerful memory aid. The ability to self-assess progress toward mastery learning is what differentiates successful learners from unsuccessful ones.

How to do it: Here are a few key ideas and guiding principles for helping students nurture an "inner voice" to guide their own learning. You may need to explicitly model the thinking you ask students to do.

- **Help students pause and reflect.** Prior to reading a text, teach students to ask themselves these questions:
  - *Why* am I reading this?
  - What do I *already know* about it?
  - What am I *curious* to learn?

  Afterward, teach them to ask themselves these questions:
  - *What* did I learn?
  - What *surprised* me?
  - How do I *feel* about what I've learned?

- **Help students keep their self-talk positive.** If students feel pessimistic or that they have no influence over their achievement, their self-talk will likely be negative. You can help students have positive self-talk by understanding the strength training paradox: *Failure leads to success.* The whole point of weight lifting is to tax a muscle until it fails, triggering it to rebuild stronger. So, too, cognitive struggle—failure to grasp something—builds new neural pathways and reinforces existing ones, making our brains "stronger." Remind students of this when learning gets tough. You can also give the "voices in their heads" these go-to phrases:
  - I can do this.
  - Struggle makes my brain stronger.
  - If I can't figure something out, I should try a different learning strategy.

- **Help students engage in deliberate practice.** The best athletes, musicians, or performers don't practice *longer*, they practice *smarter*—they devote more practice time to what they do not already do well. Students can apply this same principle to their learning by asking themselves these questions:
  - What have I *not yet* mastered?
  - What do I *need to do* to master it?

When to do it: Teaching self-questioning can be done relatively quickly. After a few sessions of directly teaching these techniques, students will begin to internalize them. Afterward, occasional reminders will suffice.

While doing it: Before practice sessions (e.g., homework assignments) encourage students to focus on what's most challenging instead of what's easy. If they're doing math problems, for example, encourage them to skip over problems they already do well to devote most of their practice sessions to problems or computations that *don't* come as easily to them.

Assess and analyze the impact of your actions: Assess with purpose

At this phase in the pathway, you're using your deep knowledge and skills to help students take ownership of their learning journeys. Some may observe your motivational techniques and consider such empowerment in your classroom to be innovative and creative divergence. As a committed, reflective practitioner, you're well aware that you've reached a place in your professional development that is only possible because of your consistent, intentional focus on growing, learning, gauging, and tinkering with your practices to better meet individual students' needs. You know the most important part of any classroom isn't what you're doing as a teacher, but rather, what's going on in students' minds; thus, you want to design captivating mental experiences that add real value to student learning—helping them to learn and do things together they couldn't do independently. Your initial question is truly guiding your inquiry: *How do I help students challenge themselves to learn at high levels?* Do the strategies and structures you've designed for students support deep learning? With that in mind, gather some colleagues, administrators, coaches, and your teammates and lead a discussion based on the following questions (and feel free to add your own):

Reflect on Teaching	Reflect on Learning
• Is your guidance for students' self-learning clear? How can you seek feedback from your students to refine your practices?	• Does self-guided learning promote deeper learning than more traditional learning? Why or why not?
• Review student work from 3-4 self-guided learning activities. What level of learning does it reflect? How does this knowledge inform your teaching?	• Gauge motivation. How do students rate their engagement in learning? What does this mean for your role as "guide on the side?"
• In what ways are engagement, effort, and attitude toward learning shifting for each individual student in your class? What are some ways to share and extend your learning with colleagues?	• Do students' self-assessments match your assessments of their learning? Why or why not? How might you achieve a tighter alignment?
	• What happens if you don't grade homework and instead empower students to engage in self-guided practice?

Become responsive: Trust your intuition

At this point in the pathway, you may find yourself reflecting on the myriad ways you could revise and refine your approaches to better meet your students' individual needs. Perhaps they need more scaffolding to identify burning questions that propel effective learning and avoid "dead end" projects. Similarly, you may find you need to scaffold self-questioning strategies by asking students to reflect on, and write down, questions they have. Or you may find that students are too hard on

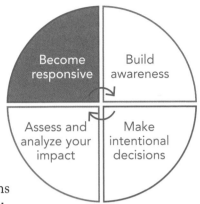

themselves (or not hard enough) and determine you should spend more time helping them to develop positive self-talk or reviewing expectations for mastery. Such adjustments are reasonable—a part of the creative process, if you will. A simple guideline is: If you think you can do better, then you probably can. Trust your inner voice. At this point, your reflective capacity has developed to a point where you're attuned to your students' needs and how to address them, both in the moment and from a grander perspective. And if you'd like to couple your inner voice with that of your trusted colleagues, we invite you to reflect on the following questions together, challenging each other's thinking to continue to refine your practice:

- ❖ Do you need to give students more support to generate powerful, burning questions?
- ❖ Were students' projects aligned with standards? If not, how might you redirect them?
- ❖ Do you need to adjust the frequency of self-directed learning activities and projects?
- ❖ What new systems do you need to track and report all of this?

You're probably wishing there were more phases in this pathway, right? Well, we agree, and we want to acknowledge a couple of realities: First, you've really grown as a thinker and a practitioner as you've challenged your students to *own* their learning journeys. Second, though you've progressed through this chapter, there really is no end to this work. You can always grow, you can always improve, and you can always learn and refine your approaches. Yes, there's a lot to celebrate, and yes, there's still a lot on the horizon.

Final thoughts on challenging your students

As you've come to the end of the "Challenging students to commit to mastery" pathway, it's important to take stock of your journey, appreciate the phases you've mastered, and note the growth you've made. In short, this is a wonderful time to appraise your professional development.

First, let's look at the pathway from the 10,000-foot level:

Be consistent *Teacher-owned, Student-experienced*	Be connected *Teacher-directed, Student-connected*	Differentiate *Student-engaged, Teacher-facilitated*	Empower *Student-owned, Teacher-guided*

You've made significant strides in transforming your classroom from one that's inherently *teacher-owned* (and student-experienced) to one that is becoming more *student-owned* (and teacher-guided). Through a systematic process of identifying key questions that either confound or interest you (or both), you've investigated and addressed four critical problems of practice all related to the "Challenging students to commit to mastery" pathway. Along the way, you repeated a very predictable, very deliberate pattern of reflective steps that a) built your self-reflective capacity and b) enhanced your professional acumen. That pattern, the Reflective Cycle, really ought to be second nature to you by now:

❖ Build awareness about the problem of practice by asking key questions and conducting research to learn more.

❖ Make intentional decisions about implementing strategies, based on the research and your desired goal.

❖ Assess and analyze the impact of your actions to determine the effectiveness of particular strategies over a period of time.

❖ Become responsive to the changing needs you notice in order to better meet your (and, more specifically, your *students'*) needs.

❖ Repeat, repeat, repeat, and repeat again and again and again.

Remember the Theory of Action that drives this combination of approaches:

Theory of Action	IF we start with key problems of practice, use research-based best practices to solve them, and reflect on our practice as teachers, THEN we will become more expert in our practice, better able to meet our students' needs, and engaged in career-long professional growth that will allow us to become amazing, unstoppable teachers in whose classrooms learning will flourish.

Though you've come to the end of this particular pathway, you're far too astute to believe the journey is over. Learning is cyclical—a progression that leads you ever upwards, not unlike a spiral staircase—and you realize there will be times that you need to backtrack, regroup, and revisit some of the foundational elements of this pathway to solidify and enhance your effectiveness. And of course there's more yet to learn, different approaches to implement, and all sorts of new ways of looking at—and solving—your newfound problems of practice. Indeed, the growth you've made is more than just about lessons filled with rigor and student motivation; in addition, you're becoming masterful at the art of growing as a reflective practitioner and transferring your learning into the classroom.

And as you've certainly noticed, creating rigorous learning opportunities and helping students to own their learning is just part of a robust, powerful, successful schooling experience for students. Now your task is to weave the other refinement pathways into your work in a seamless expression of excellence, ensuring that all students thrive and flourish. ❋

Or, if you find yourself with another nagging question, turn to the grid on p. 16, find that question, and turn to the page where we help you address it.

Chapter 5
Designing engaging learning

We've probably all gotten a chuckle out of Ben Stein's deadpan lecture to a group of slack-jawed high school students with vacant looks in the iconic 1980s film, *Ferris Bueller's Day Off*. On one hand, we may relate to our own school days of listening to class lectures while bored out of our minds. On the other hand, as teachers, we may laugh sheepishly as the on-screen images remind us of dazed expressions we've seen on the faces of our own students as we deliver lessons.

Of course, sometimes our own classroom challenges don't feel so funny. At times, we may feel we're at our wit's end—we've run out of ways to encourage, browbeat, and cajole students who seem to have exasperatingly short attention spans to stay focused on their learning. As a result, we may find ourselves becoming increasingly frustrated and impatient with their inability to attend to learning or constant disruptions as they veer off task. Or perhaps we feel hopeless and despondent; we want to get our kids to care as much as we do about their own learning, yet don't know where to start. Nothing seems to get through to them.

Take heart: on this pathway, you'll learn how to create increasingly dynamic learning opportunities for students that engage them in deep learning and encourage their motivation to learn—two of the most important things you can do as a teacher.

Take charge of your own professional growth

To help you consider how to create and deliver engaging lessons that fuel your students' curiosity and inspire them toward deep learning, we'll start with *your own curiosity*—the questions you're likely to ask about your classroom.

You may have found yourself asking one (or all) of the questions below. To help you meet your pressing needs and address your current problem of practice, we've placed a page number next to each so you can flip ahead and engage in some self-guided exploration:

- ❖ How do I keep students focused and on task? (p. 85)
- ❖ How do I make learning interesting to students? (p. 92)
- ❖ How do I get every student to engage in learning activities? (p. 99)
- ❖ How do I help students be curious, persistent, and independent learners? (p. 106)

How do I keep students focused and on task?

| Be consistent
Teacher-owned,
Student-experienced | Be connected
Teacher-directed,
Student-connected | Differentiate
Student-engaged,
Teacher-facilitated | Empower
Student-owned,
Teacher-guided |

Welcome to the first phase of the "Designing engaging learning" pathway. Not surprisingly, the focus here is on your actions as a teacher: what you are doing, what is expected of you, and what it will take for you to be successful. This pattern of thinking is typical of the *teacher-owned, student-experienced* phase, and as you proceed through the Reflective Cycle and expand your reflective vision, you'll begin to become more *consistent* in your approaches, allowing you to better meet your students' needs.

Build awareness: Observe

How do I keep students focused and on task? At some point in our careers as teachers (actually at every point) we struggle with getting kids to pay attention. That's likely because in many ways, as cognitive scientist John Medina explains in his book *Brain Rules* (2008), our brains did not evolve in classrooms, but rather, outdoors, where our survival depended on our ability to detect hidden dangers, food opportunities, and changing conditions in the world around us. As a result, our brains naturally tune in to what's unexpected, unpredictable, or triggers emotion, while tuning out what's ordinary, predictable, and devoid of emotion—or basically, much of what happens in classrooms. As Medina puts it, "If you wanted to create an education environment that was directly opposed to what the brain was good at doing, you probably would design something like a classroom" (p. 5).

When students are off task, it's likely because their brains have decided to tune out of learning because it doesn't register as interesting, novel, or worthwhile. They may have lost interest in it or never found it interesting. Or maybe you've asked them to learn or do something they cannot. It may also be that they lack self-regulation, goal-directedness, or some other issue. We'll address many of these issues on other pathways, but for now, let's start with something that's essential to teaching, and that we know from research is one of the most important things you can do as a teacher: Design every lesson and unit so that it maps onto how students' brains work by capturing their interest, moves at a pace that holds their interest, and engages them in learning activities that challenge them to think about what they're learning.

In a sweeping synthesis of 800 education meta-analyses, John Hattie (2009) found that one of the most effective ways for teachers to support learning is to follow a clearly organized sequence or model of learning. To wit: dozens of studies have found that one such approach, called Explicit Direct Instruction, had a strong, positive effect on learning—among the strongest of any education technique. (Explicit Direct Instruction starts with teachers hooking student interest and setting learning goals at the beginning of a lesson, followed by teaching key concepts directly, then scaffolding deeper learning through guided and independent practice before reviewing learning at the end of a lesson.)

In other words, one of the most important things teachers can do in the classroom—and a foundational practice to designing engaging learning—is to be clear about how everything they do in the classroom fits into a larger scheme or sequence of learning: how A leads to B which leads to C and so on.

Make intentional decisions: Be deliberate in planning

At this phase in your journey, your task is to develop a consistent sequence or model for teaching and learning— an approach for designing and delivering lessons from beginning to end. Your school or district may already have a model in place. If so, that's great, you should use it. It's also possible that your district or school hasn't provided you with a model—or has provided you with more than one. The two tools that follow— "Expand Your Toolkit of Hooks" and "Master the Model"—will help you become skilled in sequencing learning in a consistent way.

Include them in your lesson planning, try them out, and pay attention to how they go.

Become responsive | Build awareness
Assess and analyze your impact | Make intentional decisions

Expand Your Toolkit of Hooks

Why do it: Because novelty is key to engagement, when you expand your repertoire of teaching and learning activities, students are more likely to stay engaged. Once you've developed a solid familiarity with the previous model, begin to enhance your use of it by "plugging in" best practices that engage (and *hook*) students throughout each of its eight steps.

How to do it: There are countless resources online that provide lists of instructional strategies that enhance student engagement. Here, we highlight just a few and encourage you to expand your toolkit and intentionally plug one in to your lesson model to engage students during any part of your lesson.

- **Picture prompt:** Show students an image (related to the content you are planning to teach) with no explanation. Ask them to identify, describe, and/or justify their thinking as they look at the image. What do they know about this picture? What inferences are they making? You may even ask them to write as much as they can about the picture using as much terminology as they can. Do not give any information until they have completely shared their thinking. This works best as a group activity. When finished, continue to introduce your content and allow students to make connections to their thinking as you teach.

- **Pro and con grid:** Throughout the lesson, pause occasionally and ask students to create an ongoing list of the pros and cons for a given subject. Another version of this is to partner students with each other. In these pairs, students take opposite emotional sides of a conversation and engage in discussion. Pause at several points during the lesson and ask students to talk with their partner.

- **Visible thinking:** Give each student three sticky notes. As you make your way through the lesson, pause at several points and give students an opportunity to write down an "aha" (something they've just learned) or a question that they have. After a minute, ask them to stand and share their thinking with a neighbor. The neighbor should answer the question if they are able. When the lesson is nearing the end, collect the sticky notes and use them to identify the learning that has taken place.

- **Rank the information:** Place students in small groups of 3–4. After introducing the concept you are teaching, pause and ask students to determine the three most important things they've learned so far. They must all agree on the same three pieces of information and write them down. Continue with your lesson and then pause again. Ask groups to identify the three most important things they've learned so far. If they need to add a new item to their earlier list, they must cross off another item first. They can only keep three items on their list. Continue with this process until the end of the lesson. At the end of the lesson, ask groups to compare their ranked list of information with other groups and discuss why they placed the items they did on their list.

When to do it: These activities can be used during any lesson at any time. Select one to try at a time.

While doing it: Notice student engagement. What happens when you make learning more interactive?

Master the Model

Why do it: Students are more engaged when lessons are well designed and delivered with a lively pace. You can adopt (or adapt) this tool, based on McREL's six-phase model of learning, as a template for designing lessons and units that align with how students learn, thus helping them stay engaged and on task.

How to do it: Design learning opportunities for students with these phases of learning in mind.

Phase 1: Become interested. To launch learning, help students become interested in learning using strategies such as these:

- Spark curiosity. Use mystery, suspense, surprising truths or facts, or academic controversy to hook student interest.

- Connect learning with positive emotions. Help students connect positive emotions—such as joy, helpfulness, optimism, eagerness, or enthusiasm—to learning.

- Mind the gap. Prepare students for learning by helping them to recall background knowledge and reveal curiosity-provoking gaps in their current knowledge.

Phase 2: Commit to Learning. Next, help students commit to learning with these strategies.

- Provide a big picture. Frame learning as an investigation of big ideas or essential questions.

- Show students what's in it for them. Help students see why something is important to learn.

- Provide learning objectives and success criteria. Show students what they'll learn in achievable steps and how they'll ultimately demonstrate deep learning.

- Encourage personal learning goals. Help students set personal goals for mastery (e.g., become a better writer) rather than performance goals (e.g., get a good grade).

Phase 3: Focus on new learning. As you introduce new content to students, use these strategies to help them actively engage in visualizing, verbalizing, and thinking about their learning.

- Nonlinguistic representations. Use visual aids (photos, diagrams, models, manipulatives) to support learning.

- Alternate worked problems with problems students must solve. Give students examples to follow as they independently work new problems.

- Telling and showing. Use concrete examples to illustrate abstract ideas and make explicit abstract ideas or patterns embedded in concrete examples.

- Note taking. Encourage students to take (handwritten) notes and draw pictures to actively engage in learning and enhance memory.

- Self-questions and close reading. Encourage students to quiz themselves while learning new content to boost comprehension and retention.

Phase 4: Make sense of learning. Use these strategies to help students process learning by clustering, categorizing, and linking it to prior learning.

- **Chunk learning into segments to support processing.** Periodically pause during learning to help students make mental connections.

- **Ask probing questions.** After introducing new concepts, use high-order questions with "wait time" to help students connect dots with new learning.

- **Cooperative learning for processing.** During pauses in instruction, use cooperative learning (e.g., reciprocal teaching, classroom dialogue) to help students process learning.

- **Similarities and differences.** Engage students in classifying and comparing new learning.

- **Summarizing.** Encourage students to rephrase key ideas, principles, and insights from new learning in their own words.

Phase 5: Practice and rehearse. After students have focused on and made sense of new learning, help them embed new learning into long-term memory with these strategies.

- **Guide initial practice.** Observe students as they rehearse new learning to ensure they learn procedures correctly and avoid misconceptions.

- **Interleave and space independent practice.** Have students practice different skills during the same session and repeat practice of the same skill over time to support recall.

- **Provide formative feedback.** Give students descriptive feedback as they learn, helping them to reflect on their learning and identify next steps toward mastery.

- **Support frequent retrieval practice.** Use ungraded quizzes and other techniques that encourage students to recall prior learning to boost retention of new learning.

Phase 6: Extend and apply. As you conclude a learning sequence (i.e., a unit), give students opportunities to transfer learning to new situations and/or think critically about what they've learned to embed new learning.

- **Create challenging learning tasks.** Help students develop deeper knowledge by engaging them in challenging work that ensures they think about their learning or explore essential questions—for example, investigations, analyses, and syntheses.

- **Sharpen student thinking via writing.** Writing about learning (in all subjects) supports deep learning, meaning making, and transfer of learning to new situations.

- **Anchor learning in performance assessments.** Assess learning with projects, writing assignments, and other demonstrations of students' ability to extend and apply learning.

When to do it: The purpose of this task is to develop a consistent approach to designing teaching and learning experiences for students. So, you can use this model as a template for lesson and unit planning.

While doing it: Pay close attention to student engagement as you work your way through each of the six phases of learning. What do you notice?

Adapted from *Student Learning That Works* (Goodwin, 2018). © McREL. Used with permission.

Assess and analyze your impact: Notice learning

At this point, you've likely had a few (or many) "aha" moments along the way and your thinking has begun to shift. Fostering higher levels of student engagement might seem like a large mountain to climb; it's OK, you can start with the foothills! It's also OK if you stay here a while and develop consistency in your practice. First is the initial question that got you started on this pathway: *How do I keep students focused and on task?* And as you strive for consistency in your lesson delivery, including capturing students' engagement early on, there are a couple other questions you might want to ask yourself. How has your teaching changed? How has student learning changed? Use the prompts below to guide your reflections about both.

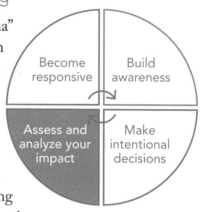

Reflect on Teaching	Reflect on Learning
• Which of the steps in the lesson design template (or whatever model you use) come most naturally to you? Which are harder to remember? • After a lesson, notice which parts of the lesson you were able to teach as planned. Which parts did you skim over or miss completely? • What is your favorite "hook" to use to increase engagement? How often do you plan for it and use it?	• How are your students responding to your consistent lesson-delivery model? • If you ever vary from your lesson plans (which we all do), how do students respond? What does that tell you? • How are you defining student engagement? What behaviors are you looking for? When are you seeing them? When are they absent? • When you use certain "hooks" in your classroom, notice how students respond. File that information away for times you want to engage students in that same manner.

Become responsive: Make changes

Using a trusted, consistent model of instruction while simultaneously incorporating various attention-grabbing strategies can yield significant gains in student engagement rates. As you're growing in your skills in the classroom—and building that reflective muscle—you're probably noticing that these are necessary, though not sufficient, approaches. The more you learn, the more you realize you don't know. That's the beauty of self-reflection and your openness to grow as a professional!

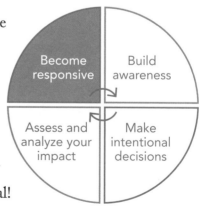

Meanwhile, here are some questions that you might want to bring to a trusted colleague—a "critical friend" or an instructional coach or mentor—to reflect on what's improved and what your next steps might be:

- ❖ How are you incorporating what you know about your students into the lesson-delivery model?

- ❖ When do you first notice the students' focus/engagement waning? How are you responding?

- ❖ What specific steps are you taking throughout the lesson to *keep* students focused and on task?

It's time to heed that ageless advice, "Look back to look ahead." The question you sought to answer at the beginning of this pathway was *How do I keep students focused and on task?* Now think how you'd answer it. Here are three simple ways to return to your problem of practice and deepen your reflective capacity:

- ❖ Jot some notes down in a learning journal or another place where you might be able to archive your thinking and access ideas, musings, questions, and other ponderings later.

- ❖ Find a trusted colleague or two to engage in a dialogue with you. Exchange thoughts, suggestions, critical feedback, and celebrations together.

- ❖ Engage your administrator, instructional coach, department chair, or another member of your support network in a discussion about this question, your journey thus far, and any shifts in perspective you've noticed.

Your newfound focus on lesson structures and engagement tools is likely benefiting your planning process and initial buy-in from your students, though you may find that your new clarity of focus is surfacing other problems and raising different questions. For example, you may wonder if the higher engagement rates are fleeting, and if you may be forced to augment your content and delivery with elaborate tricks that are simply attention-getters, not engagement-builders. If so, you may want to tackle the problem on the next page, *How do I make learning interesting to students?*

Or, if you find yourself with another nagging question, turn to the grid on p. 16, find that question, and turn to the page where we help you address it.

How do I make learning interesting to students?

Be consistent *Teacher-owned, Student-experienced*	**Be connected** *Teacher-directed, Student-connected*	Differentiate *Student-engaged, Teacher-facilitated*	Empower *Student-owned, Teacher-guided*

Welcome to the second phase of the "Designing engaging learning" pathway. In this phase, you'll begin to notice a significant shift in your focus. Yes, you're still very much in charge of building lesson plans, following a structured format, and attempting to hook students in lessons. The difference is that now, your attention is drawn to what (and how) students are learning and how they're responding to your lessons. Your practice is becoming more *connected* as you're beginning to see more clearly the cause-and-effect relationships between your actions and your students' learning. This is an exciting place to be in your journey, as your classroom is becoming more *teacher-directed, student-connected*.

 If you're joining us from another pathway, or if you're skipping ahead to this problem of practice without reading the previous phase in its entirety, we suggest you skim through or review the previous section just to get your bearings.

Build awareness: Note cause-and-effect relationships

How do I make learning interesting to students? Having well-organized and precisely delivered lessons is great, but only gets you so far. In fact, maybe you've found that the better you've become at following a well-defined model or sequence for teaching, the more predictable and, well, *boring* your lessons become. *(Anyone? Anyone? Bueller? Bueller?)* Perhaps you're even tempted to throw out the sequence altogether in favor of something more organic and unexpected. But don't do that! Especially not if you're building your lessons on a logical, brain-based sequence of learning. Instead, let's figure out how to take your teaching

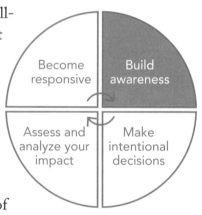

to the next level by tapping into something that helps your students keep moving along at the pace you've set for them: their motivation to learn. Here, you'll learn to weave together two big ideas from research: 1) the power of well-designed lessons that reflect the science of learning and 2) the power of students' intrinsic motivation to learn. As you learned and experienced in the previous phase along this pathway, designing and delivering lessons with a sequence or model in mind provides a foundation for your teaching as it gives an arc to your lessons that engages students in active learning. Now, you're going to work on igniting their interest to learn.

As we grow as reflective practitioners, we increasingly see cause-and-effect relationships between our teaching and students' learning, recognizing that every action we take as teachers, no matter how large or small, has an impact on learning. As you've increasingly and more consistently aligned your lessons to a teaching sequence or model, you've noticed that your students have adapted to the sequence—they're more on task and are able to move readily from one phase or activity to the next. You also have a "feel" for the sequence and experience few, if any, rough transitions, dead space, or a need to scramble to "beat the clock" at the end of a lesson. In short, you've begun to worry less about what you're doing as a teacher and are able to pay more attention to what your students are doing. Thus, you've begun to notice that while your students are more on task, they're not always 100 percent motivated to learn—or at least, not *intrinsically* motivated to learn. So, you're now asking yourself, *How do I make learning interesting to students?*

This is a powerful question to ask. Studies have found that a variety of non-school factors have even more influence on student learning than their schools or teachers; as much as 80 percent of the perceived variance in student achievement, in fact, reflects a handful of external (and internal) influences in students' lives: namely, their home environment, their motivation, and prior knowledge. We share these data not to blame students for poor performance or dismiss some as unteachable, but because they point to powerful drivers of student learning that have long been ignored (as it's "rear-view mirror" data from schooling as it's *been*, not necessarily how it *could be*). In short, if teachers can tap into these drivers—starting with student motivation—they can dramatically accelerate student learning. That's because student motivation predicts student success more than IQ or teacher quality.

Make intentional decisions: Plan, then implement

So, how do we motivate students to learn? Despite what you might have seen in the movies, motivating students is less a matter of delivering moving speeches or adorning classrooms with motivational posters than of designing everyday learning in a way that engages students, fueling their natural desire to learn—namely, their curiosity. The following two tools—"Double Ledger Planning" and "Spark, Flame, and Fire"—will help you build on the foundational work you did in the last phase to adopt a learning model or sequence to create more engaging learning experiences for students. As you implement these strategies, you'll find it important to observe their impact on student learning, which is, after all, the essence of the *connected* phase of this pathway.

Double Ledger Planning

Why do it: Use a "double ledger" plan to identify what you'll do as a teacher and what students will do during each episode of learning. Planning what we want *students* to think about and do at each point in a lesson or unit helps to ensure every learning activity is challenging, meaningful, and engaging.

How to do it: To write double ledger lesson plans, identify both the objective for your lesson and subsequent teaching strategy that you'll use to drive learning. Create a two-column graphic organizer with labels as seen below. As you break down each action step to implement the strategy, consider what that action will lead students to know, understand, or be able to do. Jot down notes similar to the sample chart below and on the next page. Anticipate and make note of any misconceptions or common errors students might have. As you walk through each step, you are identifying a cause-and-effect equation. This provides indicators to follow in your implementation of your strategy, as well as indicators of student thinking and learning to measure the impact of your teaching. Take a look at the example below:

> **Objective:** *Students will know the academic vocabulary of photosynthesis.*
>
> **Strategy Category:** *Advance organizer and nonlinguistic representation (graphic organizer)*
>
> **Teacher Strategy:** *The Frayer Model of graphical organizer (Frayer, Frederick, & Klausmeier, 1969)*

Teacher Action	Resulting Student Action
Identify the essential academic vocabulary ahead of time.	Students have the list of words. Students begin to connect familiar words to current schema and make predictions around meaning.
Develop a Frayer Model form with spaces for the definition, characteristics, example, non-example, and a symbol or picture. Have enough forms for each word for each student.	Students are provided a Frayer Model for each word. They begin to examine the ways to articulate the meaning of academic vocabulary.
Model how to complete the Frayer Model with one of the words. Ask for clarifying questions.	Each student is filling out the Frayer Model as the teacher talks through each part. Students are listening, imitating, repeating, and clarifying for understanding.

Teacher Action	Resulting Student Action
Ask students to work with a partner to complete a Frayer Model for the next word. Model how to have a collaborative conversation before filling out one part of the form.	Students work in pairs to each fill out their own Frayer Model for the same word. They talk and share their ideas about each part of the model, associating, comparing, and determining meaning from text. They are validating thinking through peer discussion and collaboration.
Ask students to complete the other three words independently.	Students work alone using the text to complete the remaining three words. They are interpreting information from text in order to determine meaning.
Walk around the room giving individual feedback, noting thinking, and recognizing effort.	Students generate questions and make their thinking visible when you stop by to observe.
Ask students to get into triads and compare thinking with one another. Walk around and note the feedback you hear students give to each other.	Students compare and adjust their Frayer Models based on collaboration with their peers. They test meaning, argue and defend points of view, and come to consensus.
Encourage students to use their new academic vocabulary in context and to make their own Frayer Model as they encounter new words.	Students use the academic vocabulary during group work and other learning activities. They experiment with and deduce meaning of unknown words using the association strategies learned through the Frayer model.

When to do it: This task can feel tedious at first, but is guaranteed to deepen your thought processes and clarify your focus throughout a lesson. We recommend engaging in this task with at least two lessons a week.

While doing it: Notice the clarity of thought that this activity brings your way, shifting your focus from teaching to learning. What do you notice about student engagement as you teach this lesson?

Spark, Flame, and Fire

Why do it: Curiosity motivates learning in different ways at different points in the learning process. This tool will help you use curiosity to fuel student engagement at all points in the process.

How to do it: Follow these steps when planning each lesson. How will you spark, flame, and fuel the fire of learning?

Spark their interest. How will you grab students' attention?

- Mystery
- Weird fact/contradiction . . . a "why is that?" fact they don't expect
- Riddle
- Puzzle
- Incomplete sequence
- Cliffhanger narrative
- Make a prediction or guess
- Controversy/debate
- Provocation
- Experiential confrontation with problem or obstacle
- Personal connection

Fan the flame of focus. What new wrinkles, surprises, and twists will you add as the lesson unfolds?

- Questions that will drive new discoveries
- Student goal-setting ideas
- Student choices for exploring the topic
- Ways you'll provide feedback

Fuel the unforgettable fire. How will new learning be deliberately practiced and rehearsed by your students?

- Student choices for sharing their work
- Self-reflection tools
- Practice schedule
- Opportunities for student collaboration

When to do it: This simple three-step frame is a great way to keep student engagement at the forefront of our minds when teaching. Use this during your lesson planning process, during a lesson, and to reflect after a lesson.

While doing it: Pause during a lesson and ask yourself: In which of the frame's three steps are you currently operating? How do you know? Are your students responding as you expected?

Assess and analyze your impact: Recognize the results of your actions

As you focus your mental energy on ways to effectively engage students in cooperative groupings, you'll notice your attention turning to the direct impact of your efforts. So when you assess the impact of your actions, reflect on your guiding question for this phase: *How do I make learning interesting to students?*

The more you intentionally implement engagement-building strategies, the more you're probably noticing higher levels of curiosity in your students. Engagement rates may well be on the rise. Perhaps your spark-flame-fire approaches have occasionally yielded a crackling bonfire of learning in selected lessons! What are the metrics you're looking for to gauge student engagement rates? And perhaps even more importantly, how did your actions contribute to these changes? Remember: Cause and effect are your allies in this journey. *When I do X, students respond with Y* or *If I want students to do Y, then I'll do X.* The path to expertise is paved with deep understanding about how our teaching actions directly impact our students' learning outcomes. The questions below are designed to help you to further hone and shape your mental models by engaging in self-reflection and dialogue with your colleagues.

Reflect on Teaching	Reflect on Learning
• In addition to preparing Double Ledger lesson plans, how might you monitor the cause-and-effect relationship between your actions and your students' actions in class?	• When was the last time you asked your students what they are interested in or curious about? What did they tell you? What can you do with that information?
• How might you use what you know about your students to design activities and prompts that further engage them in their learning?	• What happens to engagement rates when you use certain Spark, Flame, and Fire strategies? Pick a different student randomly each day to watch closely when you implement a strategy. What do you notice?
• How can you remain focused on—and consistent with—implementing Spark, Flame, and Fire strategies to keep the fire of engagement alive for your students?	• When do your students tend to be more engaged? When are they less engaged? What might you do with this information?

Become responsive: Respond to the needs you see

As you've begun to use more and different engagement strategies (from implementing consistent lesson structures to interjecting novel prompts that pique students' interest) in your classroom, you're probably noticing a lot of cause-and-effect relationships. One is that responses to your efforts vary from day to day, and from student to student. Maybe that's a result of inconsistent application on your end. Maybe it's the nature of your students. Overall, though, student engagement in your classroom is probably improving. And this was the goal that prompted your original question: *How do I make learning interesting to students?* Upward trends are always encouraging, right? To continue your growth, here are some questions you might ask to help you and your colleagues reflect on what's improved for you and your students and what steps to take next.

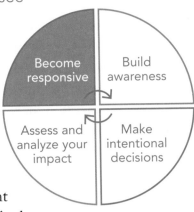

- ❖ Do you ever find yourself slipping into standard lesson designs that yield very little engagement? How might you remind yourself to stay focused on this element?

- ❖ Are some of your lessons or lesson segments more engaging than others? What is the difference? How might you replicate the engaging ones?

- ❖ What are your colleagues' favorite approaches for raising student engagement rates? How might you incorporate some of their ideas in your classroom?

As you grow, you're well aware that you haven't mastered this element yet. A new reality has probably presented itself: Engagement rates are great, but you're interested in engaging each and every one of your students. Individually. At all times. You're not going to settle with vague assessments like "most" students are "generally" engaged. As a result, you may begin to fret about capturing each student's interest and homing in on their innate curiosity and willingness to learn. If so, you may want to tackle the problem on the next page, *How do I get every student to engage in learning activities?*

Or, if you find yourself with another nagging question, turn to the grid on p. 16, find that question, and turn to the page where we help you address it.

How do I get every student to engage in learning activities?

Be consistent *Teacher-owned Student-experienced*	Be connected *Teacher-directed, Student-connected*	**Differentiate** *Student-engaged, Teacher-facilitated*	Empower *Student-owned, Teacher-guided*

Welcome to the third phase of the "Designing engaging learning" pathway. Here, you may notice a significant change as you begin to focus more on motivating and engaging all students—even the hard-to-reach students—which requires you to differentiate learning for your students and to consider what motivates them as individuals. This important shift happens in every pathway as we move into the *differentiate* (or *student-engaged, teacher-facilitated*) phase. Addressing this problem of practice requires increasing depth of knowledge of not only how learning works, but also of the principles of intrinsic motivation—knowledge you've been developing during the first two phases of this pathway.

 If you're joining us from another pathway, welcome! Before diving headlong into this challenge, though, we suggest you review the previous phase of this pathway to get your bearings.

Build Awareness: Zoom in on the details

How do I get every student to engage in learning activities? Researchers have long found a strong, positive link between freedom of choice and intrinsic motivation. A meta-analysis of 41 studies, for example, found that when students have choices in their learning—for example, how to cycle through learning stations, what essay topic to write about, or how to demonstrate their learning—their intrinsic motivation, task performance, and willingness to take on challenging tasks increase (Patall, Cooper, & Robinson, 2008). However, giving students too many choices (e.g., more than five) often decreases their motivation, likely because students spend too much mental energy agonizing over which choice to make, rather than digging into learning. For younger students, even fairly simple and instructionally irrelevant choices (e.g., choosing what color pencil to use or which sequence to follow with learning stations) can have a positive effect on motivation and behavior.

Consider a small study at the University of Northern Colorado (Powell & Nelson, 1997). Researchers observed Evan, a second-grader diagnosed with ADHD. When directed to work on the same assignment as his classmates, he exasperated his teachers by engaging in undesirable behaviors (e.g., wandering away from his desk, staring off into space, and not doing his work) roughly 30–90 percent of class time. However, when Evan could choose from among three (and *only* three) assignments of equal ardor—for example, working on spelling lists, reading silently, or doing grammar and punctuation exercises—the frequency of his undesirable behaviors dwindled to 10–30 percent of class time—far from perfect, but a big improvement. Moreover, when students choose among assignments, they don't opt for the path of least resistance, but instead tend to dial in at a level that challenges them (Kohn, 1999) and also work harder (Wang & Stiles, 1976).

So, the first key to engaging all students in learning is to provide a small array of choices that engage their interests and varying levels of challenge. Here's the second key: being crystal-clear about *why* you're asking them to learn something.

As it turns out, clearly understanding the meaning and purpose of what we're doing is a powerful motivator—more powerful, in fact, than the traditional motivational tools of rewards and punishments. As Daniel H. Pink observes in his book, *Drive: The Surprising Truth About What Motivates Us* (2011), when it comes to engaging in challenging, complex tasks like learning, the best motivators are internal, namely: 1) *autonomy* (providing people with some choices in their actions), 2) *mastery* (helping people continually advance toward higher levels of performance), and 3) *purpose* (giving a rationale of why something is worth doing and/or a deeper purpose for doing it).

Indeed, you may also find yourself reexamining your own deeply held beliefs about how to motivate students. As Harvard professor Alfie Kohn (1999) noted in a sweeping review of research on student motivation, for decades, the *behaviorist* school of thought has held sway over education. Behaviorism says the best way to motivate students is external rewards (e.g., grades, gold stickers, and prizes) and consequences (e.g., demerits, detention, and loss of privileges). Yet using carrots and sticks to motivate learning often backfires, producing diminishing returns over time by convincing students that learning is drudgery and something they must endure while they wait to pursue more fulfilling endeavors.

For example, Kohn writes, when students are off task, teachers often resort to using external rewards or consequences to get them back on task, without asking, "What is the task?" (p. 218). And is it a task worth doing? "Right now," he adds, "a good deal of what students are required to do in school is, to be blunt, not worth doing" (p. 216). Yet if we resort to bribes and rewards to engage students, it "conveniently spares us from asking hard questions about why we are asking people to do things that are devoid of interest in the first place" (p. 89).

Make intentional decisions: Develop a clear vision

Building this *differentiated* classroom requires you to engage and motivate students at different levels (if you'll pardon us using the root to define the word). We will help you connect the dots by tapping into your students' internal motivators to get all students more engaged in their learning. At this phase, our guidance will be a little less prescriptive and a little more cerebral. That's because at this point on the pathway, your professional practice will increasingly reflect your developing mental models of if-then responses (*If I see students doing or needing X, then I do Y*). The following tools—"Choice Boards" and "WIIFM"—will encourage you to ask those hard questions and develop approaches to learning based on a different (and more powerful) set of assumptions about how to motivate students: their internal motivators.

Choice Boards

Why do it: Giving students a handful of choices increases their motivation to engage and persist in learning (Patall, Cooper, & Robinson, 2008). Choice boards allow students to choose how they will learn and offer a series of activities that focus on students' specific learning needs, interests, and abilities. Structured like tic-tac-toe, choice boards allow students to decide which activity they are most comfortable completing first. Once they've mastered that activity, they can move on to more challenging tasks.

How to do it:

1. Identify the instructional focus and learning outcomes of your lesson and/or unit. What do you want students to know, understand, and be able to do by the end of it?

2. Design nine different tasks that meet your students' various interests, needs, and learning styles. Arrange each task so it has its own grid on the tic-tac-toe board.

3. Select one required task for all students. This task should be placed in the center of the board.

4. Ask your students to complete three tasks, one of which must be the one in the middle. They complete three tasks to cross off a row.

When to do it: This powerful tool can be used each week. The tasks on the choice board can be revised to fit the learning outcomes you have as you teach each lesson/unit.

While doing it: Ask yourself, are these tasks worth doing? Would completion lead students closer to mastery of a standard and/or deep learning? Which do students gravitate toward? What does this tell you about their learning needs?

Option 1	Option 2	Option 3
Option 4	**Required Task**	Option 5
Option 6	Option 7	Option 8

WIIFM

Why do it: Students are more motivated to learn when they see how it will benefit them and are more likely to retain learning when they find personal meaning in it (Souza, 2011). This tool will help you to develop for students what advertising executives refer to as WIIFM (or what's in it for me?). When we do not (or cannot) answer this question for students, their engagement suffers.

How to do it: Teachers intentionally employ the self-reference effect throughout the lesson, helping students to connect what they're learning with their own personal experience. These prompts require advance preparation. Here are some examples:

- Think about someone you know who is as generous as the Giving Tree. What kind of *metaphor* might you use to describe them?

- If you had to describe your own home in political terms, would you describe it as a dictatorship, oligarchy, democracy, anarchy, or some other term?

- Most wars are fought for a cause—freedom, religion, justice. What causes, if any, would you find worth fighting and dying for?

- We just learned how to measure the perimeter of a quadrangle. See if you can come up with a way you might use this knowledge in your own life and turn that into a story problem.

When to do it: This tool can be used throughout any lesson and can be built upon for deeper learning.

While doing it: Notice the connections students make between learning and their personal lives. How does this strategy shift ownership from teacher to learner?

Assess and analyze your impact: Transfer the vision

OK, you're in the midst of an important mental shift in your approaches to garner student engagement and their intrinsic motivation. You're probably scrutinizing your lesson plans and learning activities for the elements of autonomy, mastery, and purpose—all important in hooking your students and keeping them all connected. Now, as you assess and analyze the impact of your actions up to this point, we remind you to keep your guiding question in mind: *How do I get every student to engage in learning activities?*

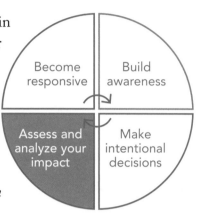

This is expert-level thinking: blending your knowledge of pedagogical practices with your students' unique learning needs and interests. Yes, it is complicated work, and you may find yourself frazzled at times. During those moments, take a deep breath and seek out a thought partner. Experts don't go it alone; they consult with one another to diagnose and solve problems. With a "critical friend," use the following reflective questions (and then create your own to add to the list) to help you to develop your expert mental models and challenge each other's thinking:

Reflect on Teaching	Reflect on Learning
• How (and how often) can you weave elements into your lessons that address students' autonomy, mastery, and purpose?	• How do students' responses to choices vary? Does this surprise you? Validate you? Make you curious about something?
• How do choices impact student engagement? What's the sweet spot for offering choice in various lessons, standards, and activities?	• When students make their own decisions, what do you notice about their effort, engagement, and quality of work?
• What are some ways that you bring the why to life in your classroom?	• How do you respond when students ask, "Why are we doing this?" How do they respond when you ask?
• What challenges have you encountered in trying to make education a differentiated journey for your students? How are you addressing these challenges in your lesson planning and teaching?	• Students mastering standards is one of the key metrics in education. So, what trends are you noticing in your classroom with regard to student mastery of standards? What are you doing to ensure the results are increasing?

Become responsive: Respond in the moment

The third phase in this pathway marks a seismic shift in your thinking, as well as your actions. As you've pursued the question that launched this pathway—*How do I get every student to engage in learning activities?*—you've started to reap the rewards of this newfound focus. Students are more engaged in lessons, they complete their work with a little more ownership, and off-task behaviors are diminishing. As you orient your thinking and your attention to your students as individual learners, you are keen to signs of engagement and disengagement.

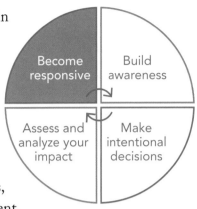

Remember that this is a major shift for your students, too, so remind everyone to be patient with each other. We're all travelers on this journey together, after all, and like the saying goes, a rising tide lifts all boats. Take a moment and reflect on your professional growth from the beginning of this pathway until now, and challenge yourself (and a trusted colleague, instructional coach, or administrator) with a few bonus reflective questions:

❖ How do you truly define and measure *engagement*? How about *motivation*, *commitment*, and *effort*?

❖ When you notice off-task or disengaged students, when and how do you respond? Do the responses vary based on what you know about your students? How so?

❖ What is the difference between a compliant student and a committed student? Can you tell? How?

You've done quite a bit to design engaging lessons. Through the infusion of autonomy, mastery, and purpose, you've seen a stronger connection between your lesson design, instructional methods (as facilitator, rather than deliverer), and your students' motivation to attend and learn. That's a lot of ground to cover, but we can never rest on our laurels, because climbing to a new level may surface a new set of challenges. For example, you may realize that engagement in a lesson is different than truly becoming a "lifelong learner," and that's an aspiration you'd like for each and every one of your students. If so, you may wish to turn to the next page to consider, *How do I help students be curious, persistent, and independent learners?*

Or, if you find yourself with another nagging question, turn to the grid on p. 16, find that question, and turn to the page where we help you address it.

How do I help students be curious, persistent, and independent learners?

Be consistent	Be connected	Differentiate	**Empower**
Teacher-owned, Student-experienced	*Teacher-directed, Student-connected*	*Student-engaged, Teacher-facilitated*	**Student-owned, Teacher-guided**

Welcome to the fourth phase of the "Designing engaging learning" pathway. Here, you'll begin to *empower* students to develop their curiosity in a *student-owned, teacher-guided* environment. This is no subtle shift, either. Building your students' capacity to truly become self-directed learners requires steady, significant development of your own capacity—both as a master of the technical elements of teaching and as a reflective practitioner. Getting to this point requires building on the foundation of everything you've learned, the acute awareness you've built, the many steps you've taken with great intentionality, and your ability to gauge your impact and make midcourse corrections as necessary.

 If you're joining us from another pathway, we encourage you to review the previous three phases in this pathway to ensure you're ready to address this challenge.

Build awareness: Bring all the variables together

How do I help students be curious, persistent, independent learners? As you've become a more reflective practitioner, you've learned to "go meta" with your own practice—employing metacognitive thinking (thinking about thinking) about your own teaching practices. That's the whole purpose of this book, of course. As noted earlier, it also reflects what distinguishes experts from novices. The ability to "go meta" with learning and emotions about learning is also what separates effective learners from struggling ones. Two decades ago, in an academic report titled *A Theory-Based Meta-Analysis of Research on Instruction*, Robert Marzano (1998) examined the effects of instructional strategies in three domains: the *self*-system (which guides whether we see learning as valuable and believe we can be successful in it), the *cognitive* system (the processes we use to develop new knowledge and skills), and the *metacognitive* system (which monitors learning in relation to goals we set for ourselves). In simple terms, our metacognitive system oversees our learning and prompts us to pause, reflect, and redirect when we detect a breakdown in our learning. It's also the part of our mind that sizes up a problem (e.g., calculate the area of a circle) and retrieves stored mental scripts (e.g., $\pi \times r^2$) for solving those problems.

Basically, our metacognitive system serves as a sort of symphony conductor in our minds, monitoring, guiding, and controlling our thought processes. A lazy conductor lets things slide; an active conductor redirects when our thinking and learning go awry. The metacognitive system doesn't set learning goals, mind you (that occurs in the self-system); rather, it monitors our progress and keeps us on track to achieve our learning goals. The self-system decides whether something like paying attention in class is important; the metacognitive system keeps our mind focused on achieving the goal (e.g., taking notes). Together, these two systems serve as powerful gatekeepers of learning for obvious reasons: If we don't care to learn something, our metacognitive system shuts down, and we're unlikely to set goals for learning. By the same token, if the self-system is willing but the metacognitive is weak and unable to keep our mind focused on acquiring new knowledge or self-correcting to learn or apply a new skill with precision, learning is unlikely to occur.

Marzano examined strategies used by teachers and students and found those used by *students* had a greater effect on learning than those used by *teachers*. In particular, helping students clarify their goals for learning and providing them with feedback on the strategies they select for achieving their goals had tremendous effect sizes—equivalent to raising average student achievement by 34 and 26 percentile points, respectively, on standardized achievement tests. Marzano noted that "feedback is particularly useful when the focus of feedback is process-oriented" (pp. 127–8). In other words, feedback is most helpful when it supports students' meta-cognitive systems, helping them to reflect on their own learning strategies (e.g., Did I quiz myself on the chapter after I read it? Did I skip any steps when attempting to solve the problem?).

A few years after *A Theory-Based Meta-Analysis*, Marzano translated the findings from this study into a more widely read publication, *Classroom Instruction That Works* (Marzano, Pickering, & Pollack, 2001) which identified nine categories of effective instructional strategies, such as questions, goal setting, and feedback. Although the original study had found that many of these strategies could trigger and support cognition, metacognition and the self-system, in practice, many teachers have tended to regard them solely as *instructional* strategies, overlooking their effects on *learning*—that is, how these strategies "work" by helping students understand and guide the process of learning in their own minds.

At this point in your journey, though, you've mastered how to sequence lessons and units so they support learning, you've grown adept at sparking student curiosity to support the process, and have helped students find meaning and purpose in their learning (employing their self-system). Now, you're ready to take the next step: helping students "go meta" with their learning, reflecting on what's happening in their own minds so that increasingly, they can guide their own learning, something children at all ages can do; even young children can learn to think about their thinking (e.g., What things can you do when you see a word that's new to you?).

So, how do you bring all of these ideas together in your classroom? The ability to do this—both consistently and consistently *well*—is often referred to as the art of teaching. You're way past the focus on *what* you are going to do to address this challenge; indeed, you're now thinking about *how* all of these strategies and approaches blend together to create an assessment design. *Empowering* students in such a classroom environment does not happen by accident, and it's no coincidence that your growth as a reflective practitioner has accompanied—in fact preceded—this shift in practice.

Because of the complexity and uniqueness of your situation (no one has ever faced exactly what you're facing before, with exactly the students you have), you're in uncharted territory, as it were. How cool is that? But it also means there's no step-by-step guide that we (nor anyone) can offer. Instead, we can offer guiding principles designed to support students' metacognition (thinking about their own learning) and help them become increasingly independent in self-assessing and self-correcting their learning. The following two tools—"Socratic Seminar" and "Reciprocal Teaching"—can help you to continue this journey with confidence.

Socratic Seminar

Why do it: This tool acknowledges the highly social nature of learning and embodies the belief that students build ownership in learning when they are involved in the process of constructing meaning. The Socratic Seminar is a formal discussion, based on a text, in which students help one another understand the ideas, issues, and values reflected in a text through a group discussion format. Within the context of the discussion, students listen closely to the comments of others, thinking critically for themselves, and articulate their own thoughts and their response to the thoughts of others.

How to do it: A Socratic Seminar is best done when students are divided into two groups and sitting in two circles, inner and outer. The inner circle is the speakers: These are the students who discuss the questions. The outer circle is the recorders. These students silently record notes on the discussion. After a set amount of time, both circles switch so that all students have had a chance to be in each circle.

- **Choose a text.** Socratic Seminars work best with authentic texts that invite authentic inquiry.

- **Prepare your students.** Ask them to read and prepare for the discussion in advance. Provide sticky notes for annotation as they prepare.

- **Prepare the questions.** As you introduce this strategy to your students, you'll fill the role of discussion leader until students are ready and able to handle the responsibility. Generate as many open-ended questions as possible, aiming for questions whose value lies in their exploration, not their answer. Start and end the discussion with questions that relate more to students' lives so the conversation is grounded in the context of real experience. Pass these questions out to the students to give them a frame to drive the discussion.

- **Establish student expectations.** Set norms for the conversation; distinguish debate from discussion. Ask students to hold themselves accountable for the norms they agree upon.

- **Establish your role.** The teacher should not be a significant participant in the pursuit of questions. Limit your role to reminders about procedures and let students own the rest of the discussion. Resist the urge to correct or redirect, relying instead on other students to keep the discussion on track.

- **Assess effectiveness.** Engage students in reflective writing after the discussion to assess the effectiveness of the activity.

When to do it: This highly effective tool can be utilized toward the end of a unit or compilation of lessons to summarize content and facilitate student ownership of learning.

While doing it: Each time you utilize this tool, choose three students to observe. Take notes of their contribution to the discussion. What evidence of ownership of learning do you see?

Reciprocal Teaching

Why do it: If our goal is to achieve deeper levels of student engagement and ownership of learning, it makes sense to use strategies that encourage students to critically think, be actively involved, and learn through socialization with peers. In reciprocal teaching, students become the teachers in small groups. Teachers model, then help students learn to guide group discussions around four parts: summarizing, question generating, clarifying, and predicting. In math, the four parts might be predicting, clarifying, solving, and summarizing.

How to do it:

1. The summarizer reads a short passage and summarizes what has been read, heard, or seen. Other students may add to the summary at this time. When students first begin reciprocal teaching, they are generally focused at the sentence and paragraph levels. As they become more proficient with the technique, they are able to integrate information from multiple paragraphs and passages.

2. After the summarizer finishes, the questioner asks questions that are designed to help identify important information. He or she presents information in question form, and the rest of the group answers the questions in order to go deeper into the text. As students learn this process, they are taught to generate questions at deeper levels. For example, teachers might require students to ask questions that require the group to infer or apply new information from a text.

3. The clarifier, as the name suggests, clarifies any vocabulary words, pronunciations, or terms the group may not already know or understand well. This student is taught to look for aspects of a passage that might make it hard for his or her classmates to comprehend the passage and do what is necessary to make the meaning clear (e.g., reread, ask for help).

4. The final role in this process is that of the predictor. Before the group moves forward to the next passage, this student asks for predictions about what will happen next. He or she can record the predictions on chart paper or a computer and return to these predictions for verification after reading. To do this successfully, the predictor must review the relevant information that the group already possesses about the topic. By generating these predictions, students have a purpose for continued reading—to confirm their predictions.

When to do it: This discussion strategy can be used on a regular basis to shift ownership from teacher to student during learning. With practice, students will strengthen their discussion skills and develop their ability to learn from one another and construct meaning.

While doing it: Observe the discussion and take note of student behavior.

Adapted from *Classroom Instruction That Works* (Dean, Hubbell, Pitler, and Stone, 2012). © McREL. Used with permission.

Assess and analyze the impact of your actions: Assess with purpose

At this phase in the pathway, you're using your deep knowledge and skills to help students take ownership of their learning journeys. Some may observe your engagement techniques and consider such *empowerment* in your classroom to be innovative and creative divergence. As a committed, reflective practitioner, you're well aware that you've reached a place in your professional development that is only possible because of your consistent, intentional focus on growing, learning, gauging, and tinkering with your practices to better meet individual students' needs. You know the most important part of any classroom isn't

what you're doing as a teacher, but rather, what's going on in students' minds; thus, you want to design classroom experiences that add real value to student learning—helping them to learn and do things together they couldn't do independently. Your initial question is truly guiding your inquiry: *How do I help students be curious, persistent, and independent learners?* Do the strategies and structures you've designed for students support deep learning? With that in mind, gather some colleagues, administrators, coaches, and your teammates and lead a discussion based on the following questions (and feel free to add your own):

Reflect on Teaching	Reflect on Learning
• What are some other strategies that elicit deep thinking and honest contributions? How can you incorporate them in your lessons and units? • How can you encourage even more students to open up and contribute their thinking to Socratic Seminars and open-ended questions? • How are your colleagues confronting these same challenges? How can you engage them in conversations about ways to address this problem of practice together?	• When you pose open-ended questions, how do students respond? Which students are more eager? Which are more reluctant? • What are your students curious about? Interested in? How do you know? • What do you notice when students take the reins as "teacher" in their reciprocal teaching groups? How does this impact participation? Motivation? Learning?

Become responsive: Trust your intuition

Student engagement, you've no doubt found, is a fickle beast. Like the rising and falling of tides, student engagement rates fluctuate from class to class, moment to moment, and even student to student. The approaches you've investigated, embraced, implemented, and tweaked have probably yielded you some pretty encouraging results. And yet . . . there's still room for improvement. You may find yourself reflecting on ways to further refine your practice. That's because the journey never ends—even though you've made it to the final phase

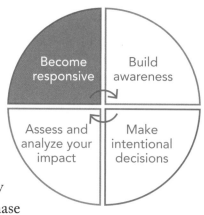

of this pathway. Learning is iterative, cyclical, and ongoing. There is no finish line, simply the continued pursuit of knowledge, understanding, application, and so forth. Trust your inner voice. At this point, your reflective capacity has developed to a point where you're attuned to your students' needs and how to address them, both in the moment and from a grander perspective. And if you'd like to couple your inner voice with those of your trusted colleagues, we invite you to reflect on the following questions together, challenging each other's thinking to continue to refine your practice:

❖ What lingering questions do you still have about student engagement? What haven't you learned yet? How might you go about answering those questions?

❖ How can you truly discern when (and to what extent) an individual student is deeply engaged in his or her learning?

❖ Have you determined what practices and structures tend to increase *all* students' engagement? How do you use them? And when they don't work for *each* student, how do you intervene?

You're probably wishing there were more phases in this pathway, right? Well, we agree, and we want to acknowledge a couple of realities: First, you've really grown as a thinker and a practitioner as you've learned about and implemented strategies designed to truly engage your students. Second, though you've progressed through this chapter, there really is no end to this work. You can always grow, you can always improve, and you can always learn and refine your approaches. Yes, there's a lot to celebrate, and yes, there's still a lot on the horizon.

Final thoughts on designing engaging learning

As you've come to the end of the "Designing engaging learning" pathway, it's important to take stock of your journey, appreciate the phases you've mastered, and note the growth you've made. In short, this is a wonderful time to appraise your professional development.

First, let's look at the pathway from the 10,000-foot level:

| Be consistent
Teacher-owned,
Student-experienced | Be connected
Teacher-directed,
Student-connected | Differentiate
Student-engaged,
Teacher-facilitated | Empower
Student-owned,
Teacher-guided |

You've made significant strides in transforming your classroom from one that's inherently *teacher-owned* (and student-experienced) to one that is becoming more *student-owned* (and teacher-guided). Through a systematic process of identifying key questions that either confound or interest you (or both), you've investigated and addressed four critical problems of practice all related to the "Designing engaging learning" pathway. Along the way, you repeated a very predictable, very deliberate pattern of reflective steps that a) built your self-reflective capacity and b) enhanced your professional acumen. That pattern, the Reflective Cycle, really ought to be second nature to you by now:

❖ Build awareness about the problem of practice by asking key questions and conducting research to learn more.

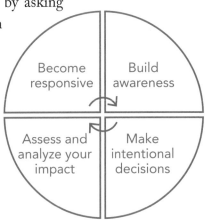

❖ Make intentional decisions about implementing strategies, based on the research and your desired goal.

❖ Assess and analyze the impact of your actions to determine the effectiveness of particular strategies over a period of time.

❖ Become responsive to the changing needs you notice in order to better meet your (and, more specifically, your *students'*) needs

❖ Repeat, repeat, repeat, and repeat again and again and again.

Remember the Theory of Action that drives this combination of approaches:

Theory of Action	IF we start with key problems of practice, use research-based best practices to solve them, and reflect on our practice as teachers, THEN we will become more expert in our practice, better able to meet our students' needs, and engaged in career-long professional growth that will allow us to become amazing, unstoppable teachers in whose classrooms learning will flourish.

Though you've come to the end of this particular pathway, you're far too astute to believe the journey is over. Learning is cyclical—a progression that leads you ever upwards, not unlike a spiral staircase—and you realize there will be times that you need to backtrack, regroup, and revisit some of the foundational elements of this pathway to solidify and enhance your effectiveness. And of course there's more yet to learn, different approaches to implement, and all sorts of new ways of looking at—and solving—your newfound problems of practice. Indeed, the growth you've made is more than just about raising engagement rates in your classroom; in addition, you're becoming masterful at the art of growing as a reflective practitioner and transferring your learning into the classroom.

And as you've certainly noticed, cultivating a comprehensive instructional plan to engage your students in deep learning is just part of a robust, powerful, successful schooling experience for students. Now your task is to weave the other refinement pathways into your work in a seamless expression of excellence, ensuring that all students thrive and flourish. ✳

Or, if you find yourself with another nagging question, turn to the grid on p. 16, find that question, and turn to the page where we help you address it.

Chapter 6
Motivating with feedback

You've likely seen all the catchphrases about feedback—how it's the breakfast of champions, the key to improvement, and fit for mass consumption. Yet in practice, whether it's giving or receiving feedback, we've likely had it fall on deaf ears (including our own); feel like nit-picking ("The little lights are not twinkling"—thanks, Griswolds); vague, redundant, or unhelpful ("This sentence is awkward"); or worse, aggravating if not demotivating ("Your singing voice is too screechy").

In other words, for all its benefits, feedback can fizzle or backfire—something we've probably all witnessed as teachers when our students' eyes glaze over, their backs go up, or they scarcely bother to read our painstakingly written feedback prior to depositing it in the recycle bin on their way out the classroom door. On this pathway, you'll learn how to perfect your ability to deliver feedback that not only guides learning, but also motivates learners, helping them tap into their innate desire to find themselves "in the zone"—welcoming and seeking feedback to grow in their learning.

Take charge of your own professional growth

To help you consider how to use feedback practices that guide and motivate students to deep learning, we'll start with *your own curiosity*—questions you're likely to ask about your classroom. You may have found yourself asking one (or all) of the questions below. To help you meet your pressing needs and address your current problem of practice, we've placed a page number next to each so you can flip ahead and engage in some self-guided exploration:

- ❖ How do I guide students to do better? (p. 116)
- ❖ How do I help students become more receptive to feedback? (p. 123)
- ❖ How do I tailor feedback so it's meaningful for every student? (p. 130)
- ❖ How do I help students give one another effective feedback? (p. 136)

How do I guide students to do better?

Be consistent Teacher-owned, Student-experienced	Be connected Teacher-directed, Student-connected	Differentiate Student-engaged, Teacher-facilitated	Empower Student-owned, Teacher-guided

Welcome to the first phase of the "Motivating with feedback" pathway. Not surprisingly, the focus here is on your actions as a teacher: what you are doing, what is expected of you, and what it will take for you to be successful. This pattern of thinking is typical of the *teacher-owned, student-experienced* phase, and as you proceed through the Reflective Cycle and expand your reflective vision, you'll begin to become more consistent in your approaches, allowing you to better meet your students' needs.

Build awareness: Observe

How do I guide students to do better? As you follow the other pathways in this book—in particular those in which you set high expectations for students, engage them in goal setting, and create challenging learning opportunities for them—you're likely to face a new concern: Helping students meet the bar you've set for them. You want them to understand their progress as learners—what they've mastered, have yet to master, and what they must do to achieve mastery. At the same time, we must help students *want* to improve—to be open to feedback, using it to improve.

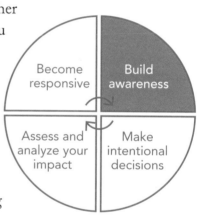

We may sometimes feel frustrated with students who don't "get it," who seem either unable or unwilling to improve their learning. We may find ourselves searching for an elusive key to unlock their understanding or feeling like we've led horses to water that just won't drink. Our frustrations can turn to anxiety that if our students don't improve, we're going to look bad and/or be judged poorly. We may even feel that when our students fail to achieve mastery, we've failed them as teachers. Basically, what you're experiencing here is a dual challenge: figuring out *what* guidance students need to stay on track and *how* to deliver it so that instead of ignoring or resenting it, they'll take it to heart.

The good news is that research can help us unpack these challenges. For starters, we know feedback is one of the most powerful tools we have at our disposal as teachers strive to improve student learning. Multiple studies have shown that providing consistent, specific feedback translates roughly into students scoring 28 percentile points higher on standardized achievement tests than comparison groups who receive no feedback (Beesley & Apthorp, 2010). And in his analysis of 800 meta-analyses of studies of education research, Hattie (2009) found that the effects of feedback dwarfed those of most other common teaching and schooling practices, prompting him to declare that a key to raising student achievement is giving them "dollops of feedback" (p. 238).

However, like many practices, not all feedback is effective feedback. In fact, while most studies have found positive effects for feedback, as many as a third of all studies on feedback have actually found negative effects (Shute, 2008). Why should that be? For starters, the quality of feedback can vary. When it remains too broad or vague for students to grasp, it results in uncertainty, confusion, decreased motivation, and diminished learning. Case in point: a study of sixth graders in Israel found that providing students with feedback in the form of written comments (e.g., "You thought of quite a few interesting ideas; maybe you could think of more ideas?") resulted in significantly higher achievement than providing students with numeric score or no feedback at all (Wiliam, 2011).

The first key principle here is that feedback must be specific. Students should be able to do something with the feedback you provide; it should point them toward specific behaviors they can develop, actions they can take, or learning they can pursue to meet their learning goals. A second key principle from research is that feedback should be timely—that is, coming at the right moment for the learning at hand. In most cases, immediate feedback is preferable, which isn't surprising given that students do not learn much from a corrected test or paper returned weeks after the class has moved on to a different topic. When learning procedures (e.g., long division), students often need real-time guidance to avoid learning the process incorrectly (Bangert-Drowns, Kulik, Kulik, & Morgan, 1991). Yet in some circumstances feedback can be too immediate; students may come to rely on teachers for answers (or peek ahead to see them) rather than persevere and figure problems out on their own (Bangert-Drowns et al., 1991). When you're asking students to think critically—creating, synthesizing, analyzing, or applying knowledge—they need some "space" to wrestle with ideas and engage in productive struggle.

Make intentional decisions: Be deliberate in planning

What all of this means is that it's helpful to "pre-plan" our feedback, considering in advance what kinds of feedback students may need—anticipating misconceptions and mistakes, and then structuring units and lessons to ensure plenty of opportunities to provide students with feedback while they can still use it—for example, while students are still drafting an essay, planning a science fair project, or learning how to calculate how much concrete is needed to build a staircase. The two tools that follow— "Plan Your Checkpoints" and "The Feedback Four"—will

help you become skilled in pre-planning your feedback so that it's both specific and timely.

Plan Your Checkpoints

Why do it: To ensure that our feedback is specific, timely, and ultimately, effective.

How to do it: As you plan your lesson for the upcoming week, identify when your students will be engaged in each of the following tasks and determine what type of feedback you'll provide, and when. We encourage you to write out several examples of feedback that you might be likely to give. Keep them readily available to use when teaching your lesson.

CHECKPOINTS When students are:	When to provide feedback:	Example of feedback that encourages reflection and offers guidance for next steps:
Learning a new process or skill (e.g., guided practice)	Immediate, often in real time to ensure students don't learn a process incorrectly or develop bad habits.	*Remember what to do if the numbers in a column add up to more than 10? That's right, "carry" the one.*
Practicing a learned process or skill (e.g., independent practice)	Timely, yet delayed long enough to let students complete and reflect on the process.	*Your descriptions of the setting, with words like "balmy" and "the buzzing of mosquitoes," really helped me to picture your setting. Keep using vivid language while focusing on writing even more complex sentences like those we've been working on.*
Learning declarative knowledge (facts)	Timely to avoid misconceptions, while encouraging students to wrestle with new ideas.	*So, what do the rest of you think? Does the earth "lean into" the sun in summer and "away from" it in winter like some of you have said? If we imagine the sun being in the middle of our classroom, can you walk this globe around the room to describe why we have seasons?*
Taking quizzes	Ideally, within a day of the quiz to help students recognize and correct gaps in their knowledge or refine skills they have yet to master.	*I noticed several of you got area and perimeter mixed up on yesterday's quiz. Perhaps that's because it's been too abstract for you. So, today we're going to figure out the area and perimeter of our classroom.* *I noticed that you did a great job with the multiplication problems that were multiples of 4 and 5. The 4 problems you missed were all multiples of 6 and 7. That's a good place to focus your efforts this week.*

CHECKPOINTS When students are:	When to provide feedback:	Example of feedback that encourages reflection and offers guidance for next steps:
Applying new knowledge and skills on an independent learning task	During periodic checks-ins to provide students with opportunities to think independently, self-evaluate, and correct their work, while still receiving some guidance from you or their peers with guiding protocols (e.g., Two Stars and a Wish, Praise and Polish).	*The revision you made to your introduction yesterday really draws readers into your essay and makes your thesis statement clear. Now, where do you want to focus on rewriting today to make you really show (not tell) your readers what you're trying to say?* *Using more scientific words in your revised study design sounds a lot more like a scientist! We can't really test if bean sprouts "need" or "like" sunlight because we don't know their feelings. What might be something related to sunlight that you could observe in bean sprouts in your experiment? Answering that question is a good next step in setting up your experiment.*
Completing an end-of-unit assessment or assignment	No more than a few days after the test/ assignment so that students can reflect on their learning. Bear in mind that letter grades or numeric scores often cause students to ignore feedback, so letting students correct assessments or assignments for improved grades can increase their learning.	*I see you highlighted and corrected important parts of the test. Your new answers are more detailed with specific examples, too! Did you see how that really makes your thinking visible? As you prepare for the next test, I think you'll find it really helpful to see you can provide those kinds of more elaborate answers as you quiz yourself.*

When to do it: As you plan each week, reference this chart and plan intentionally for feedback to be timely and specific.

While doing it: Look for evidence that your feedback is working. Are your students learning as a result of your increased focus on timeliness and specificity? Do you see an improvement in their work? Is there evidence of increased student motivation?

The Feedback Four

Why do it: Feedback should cause thinking. Resist the urge to evaluate and judge student performance. Studies of effective teaching and learning (Dinham, 2005, 2007a, 2007b) have shown that learners want to know where they stand in relation to their learning goals. Providing answers to the following four questions will help provide quality feedback that is specific, motivating, and leads students to think more deeply about their learning.

How to do it:

Before offering feedback, whether in written or oral form, ask yourself these four questions. We call them the Feedback Four:

1. What has the student *shown* that s/he can do?
2. How does this evidence of knowledge or skill *compare* to the desired outcomes or goals of learning?
3. What is *missing*?
4. What is the *next step* in this student's learning?

With these answers in mind, craft careful feedback statements that propel students to articulate their thinking.

Instead of:	Try this:	
You give lots of evidence in your essay, but no supporting citations.	*You gave several examples of how plastics are harming aquatic life, which, as a reader, I found powerful.*	What the student has *shown* s/he can do.
	A level 3 on our rubric, though, says "all evidence is cited" and a 4 says "from trustworthy sources." I know your goal is to persuade your readers to stop using products with plastic beads in them.	Show how it *compares* to desired outcomes/goals.
	Yet, I only see citations for a couple statistics, and a lot without citations, so, as a reader, I might be skeptical if it's all true.	Show what's *missing*.
	So, on your next draft, if you'll cite all your evidence and ensure it comes from reputable sources (no Wikipedia, right?) you'll make your argument even more persuasive.	Provide the *next* step.

When to do it: Before offering feedback, reference the Feedback Four and use the questions to guide your thinking as you provide comments about learning.

While doing it: Keep in mind the purpose of feedback: Feedback should prompt thinking about learning.

Assess and analyze your impact: Notice learning

At this point, you've likely had a few (or many) "aha" moments along the way and your thinking has begun to shift. As your thinking changes, so do your actions. Your feedback practices are probably a little different, and you're considering feedback through a slightly different lens. These are healthy changes, and they'll lead to long-term benefits in your classroom, especially if you keep your initial question on your mind: *How do I guide students to do better?* Meanwhile, there are considerable other questions to ask yourself. How has your teaching changed?

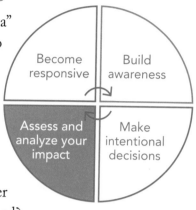

How has student learning changed? Use the prompts below to guide your reflections about both:

Reflect on Teaching	Reflect on Learning
• When do you typically give feedback to your students?	• What do you notice about how students respond to your feedback?
• How intentionally do you plan for opportunities to give feedback during a lesson or unit? What do those moments look like in your lesson plans?	• Do students' responses to your feedback change if the feedback is written? Oral? Digital?
• Which parts of the Feedback Four do you find easiest to keep in mind? Which give you the most trouble?	• Consider conferring with one student and going through some written feedback together. What does the student do with this information afterwards?
• Pay attention to the way you praise students. Are you praising simply to praise them, or was that supposed to be a "dollop" of feedback? How do you know what the purpose of that interaction is?	• How do your students respond to praise?

Become responsive: Make changes

You've probably become aware by now that for your students to do better as a result of your feedback, *you've* got to do better at delivering specific, timely feedback in the first place! So as you're noticing your own feedback habits, and you're thinking carefully about how your students respond to that feedback, consider mixing things up a bit. Understand that not everything's going to go as planned; there's messiness inherent in learning, and that's OK. Your willingness to learn, adapt, and grow will see you through the messes! Here are some questions that you might want to bring to a trusted colleague—a "critical friend" or an instructional coach or mentor—to reflect on what's improved and what your next steps might be:

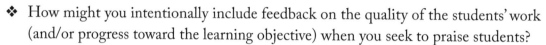

- ❖ If you change the mode (from written to oral, for instance) or the timeliness (at the end of class today instead of waiting until tomorrow, perhaps) of your feedback, how do you predict students might respond? Try it and find out.

- ❖ Does your instruction style facilitate or inhibit feedback? Is feedback a natural part of your lesson delivery, or are there times you have to be conscious about including it?

- ❖ How might you intentionally include feedback on the quality of the students' work (and/or progress toward the learning objective) when you seek to praise students?

- ❖ What can you do to intentionally keep the Feedback Four in the front of your mind when opportunities to give students feedback present themselves?

It's time to heed that ageless advice, "Look back to look ahead." The question you sought to answer at the beginning of this pathway was *How do I guide students to do better?* Now think how you'd answer it. Here are three simple ways to return to your problem of practice and deepen your reflective capacity:

- ❖ Jot some notes down in a learning journal or another place where you might be able to archive your thinking and access ideas, musings, questions, and other ponderings later.

- ❖ Find a trusted colleague or two to engage in a dialogue with you. Exchange thoughts, suggestions, critical feedback, and celebrations together.

- ❖ Engage your administrator, instructional coach, department chair, or another member of your support network in a discussion about this question, your journey thus far, and any shifts in perspective you've noticed.

As you continue to learn, implement, and revise your feedback processes, you may well find that you're feeling confident about how good your feedback is getting . . . and this could be uncovering a new wrinkle. You may have new, unforeseen questions invading your mental space. For example, you may become frustrated that your students aren't always willing to accept this feedback and do something with it, even though it's so *good*. If so, you may want to tackle the problem on the next page, *How do I help students become more receptive to feedback?*

Or, if you find yourself with another nagging question, turn to the grid on p. 16, find that question, and turn to the page where we help you address it.

How do I help students become more receptive to feedback?

Be consistent *Teacher-owned, Student-experienced*	**Be connected** ***Teacher-directed, Student-connected***	Differentiate *Student-engaged, Teacher-facilitated*	Empower *Student-owned, Teacher-guided*

Welcome to the second phase of the "Motivating with feedback" pathway. In this phase, you're still very much in charge of providing feedback to your students—using a variety of strategies at different intervals in the lessons—and now your attention is shifting to how students are responding to the feedback you provide. In other words, your teaching is becoming more *connected* as you're beginning to observe cause-and-effect relationships between your actions and student learning. As your feedback has become more specific and timely, you've likely noticed that some students receive it better than others. That's typical, and it's a great reminder that your classroom is becoming *teacher-directed, student-connected.*

 If you're joining us from another pathway, or if you're skipping ahead to this problem of practice without reading the previous phase in its entirety, we suggest you skim through or review the previous section just to get your bearings.

Build awareness: Note cause-and-effect relationships

How do I help students become more receptive to feedback? Does this sound familiar? You're aware of the elements of effective feedback, and you're trying like crazy to implement specific, timely feedback into your classroom. One day this goes swimmingly, and students respond by rewriting their essays with enthusiasm and clear direction. The next day it backfires, as your students toss their papers and throw up their arms in exasperation. Up go your arms as well, right? This is a common experience at this phase of the journey, as you're encountering the promise and peril of feedback. Take heart: There's a well-worn path through this jungle.

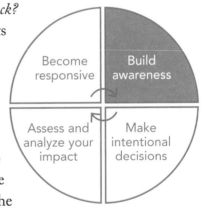

This challenge leads us into psychological research on motivation, starting with the simple fact that when it comes down to it, no one likes to be told what to do. Research shows, for example, that even positive feedback undermines student motivation if it comes across as attempting to coerce students to comply with the teacher's wishes (Deci, Koestner, & Ryan, 1999)—for example, telling kids "Yes! That's what I want to see from you." However, if we deliver praise simply as information about how students are performing against a predefined standard (e.g., "This reflects all of the criteria we discussed for a strong thesis statement"), teachers can boost performance with little or no negative effect on motivation.

In addition, a meta-analysis of studies of the effects (positive and negative) of student-teacher interactions (Cornelius-White, 2007) found that one of the most effective teacher behaviors was something called "non-directivity"—that is, delivering feedback in a purely informational way, not as value-laden judgments or attempts to coerce or cajole students into changing their behavior.

What all of this comes down to is that we cannot force students to learn anything. Sure, sometimes browbeating ("No recess for you") and guilt-tripping ("Please, do it for me") work, but at best, both are just short-term solutions. And over the long haul, they're apt to further diminish student motivation because they quickly see it for what it is: an attempt to control their behavior. That's why it's best to remove controlling language from our teacher talk and student feedback, and focus instead on encouraging, motivating, and guiding their learning.

A second big idea for motivating with feedback comes from studies that have found praising students can backfire when we focus our praise on their talents or abilities (e.g., "You're so smart!"). The implication of the Carol Dweck study, discussed on p. 44, for teachers is profound; it means as teachers, we may inadvertently diminish student motivation and achievement by praising them for ability instead of effort.

Make intentional decisions: Plan, then implement

You're at a crossroads in this pathway, which is an exciting development. You've learned several handy tidbits about how feedback must be organized (specific and timely) and what contributes to it being motivational (focused on effort and/or information, as opposed to praising talents). The time has come to implement feedback with these characteristics in a way that *connects* students to their learning progression. Planning it is one thing; putting it into place consistently and reliably is another. So, how do we deliver feedback that motivates students? Try using these two tools— "Shifting Control" and "Growth-Mindset Feedback"—to bring your feedback to life for your students. As you implement these tools, you'll find it is important to observe their impact on student learning, which is, after all, the essence of the *connected* phase of this pathway.

Shifting Control

Why do it: It's no secret that a sense of control is the root of human motivation. In the classroom, a student's sense of control will influence both their efforts and subsequent mindset. The goal of all educators is to teach students to adopt a narrative that gives them a learning mindset in which successes and failures are temporary and can be changed. We do this, in part, by offering feedback that shifts control over learning to the student.

How to do it: Before your next lesson, identify three students that you will target for this strategy. Consider the type of feedback you might typically provide, script a sample on paper, and then rewrite the script to emphasize student control of learning. Use the samples below to guide you as you begin to revise your statements.

Emphasis on Teacher Control of Learning	Emphasis on Student Control of Learning
I'm disappointed in your performance. You should've done what I recommended.	*Your work on this particular assignment didn't reflect advanced performance. I believe you can do better.*
Your essay was good. That's the level of work you should be doing if you're serious about college.	*I see that you worked hard and put a lot of thought into that essay. It was college caliber. How do you feel about your effort toward this assignment?*
You had a lot of careless mistakes in your homework. You need to check it more carefully before turning it in to me.	*I noticed a lot of careless mistakes in your homework. I think you would've caught all of these on your own if you'd just spent a few minutes double-checking your work before you turned it in.*
You'd better buckle down and study hard for this test.	*I think there's a great student inside you just waiting to come out. But I can't make him/her come out. That's up to you.*
I'm so pleased with your report! Keep up the great work.	*You paid special attention, in your report and presentation, to include facts that many people might not know. You also did a nice job of anticipating common misconceptions about this topic.*

When to do it: Crafting feedback that emphasizes student control of learning is not easy. To successfully tackle this, it is important that time is spent before each lesson to identify what shifts in feedback will look like/sound like for specific students.

While doing it: Notice and record student reactions. How does this shift in feedback impact the student? Make a mental note of any differences you notice.

Growth-Mindset Feedback

Why do it: As students engage in learning activities, it can be easy to become distracted and caught up in the learning tasks and assignments themselves. Growth-minded language guides, encourages, and reminds students to remain focused on the process of learning rather than completion of the task. It emphasizes recognition of the struggle, the meaning-making, the personal strategies, and the thinking that leads to deep learning.

How to do it: Use these language frames when interacting with your student in the following situations.

When students struggle despite strong effort:

- *When you think you can't do it, remind yourself that you just haven't done it yet.*

- *Mistakes are welcome here! They are a huge part to all learning.*

- *Let's identify how much progress you've made so far. Do you remember how much more challenging this was (yesterday/last week/last year)? Sometimes we need to stop and remember past successes.*

- *Of course it's tough! Learning is hard work. What do you need to be ready to tackle this again?*

- *Let's stop here and return tomorrow with a fresh brain.*

When students struggle and need help with strategies:

- *I know you're frustrated. Everyone learns differently. We'll keep at it and find your best way to master this.*

- *Describe your process for completing this task.*

- *Let's do one together—walk me through your thinking.*

- *What parts are difficult right now? Let's look at them together. I know you can do this.*

- *Let's ask _____ for advice. S/he may be able to explain/suggest some ideas and/or recommend some strategies.*

- *What parts are confusing for you? Talk me through what is happening in your brain.*

When students are making progress:

- *That's a complex program/task/concept that you've been working on for a while. What strategies are you using?*
- *Your hard work is clearly evident in your process/project/essay/assignment.*
- *What kind of conversation goes on in your brain as you work to keep you so focused on your task?*
- *Your amazing persistence and resilience will pay off.*
- *I know there are a lot of big words in this book, but as long as you're not bumping into more than five words per page that you don't know, keep with it. It's making your brain stronger.*

When they succeed with strong effort:

- *The effort that you put into this assignment/task was extremely evident.*
- *You did not give up and look what you have to show for all of that work!*
- *Congratulations! You really used great strategies for studying and managing your time/behavior.*
- *All of your hard work and effort paid off!*
- *The next time you have a challenge like this, what will you do?*
- *What advice can you give to others when they face challenging tasks for learning?*
- *Drawing in 3-D perspective is very difficult. I can tell you had to work hard at this.*

When they succeed easily without effort:

- *It looks like your knowledge and skills weren't really challenged by this assignment. Let's talk about ways we can apply this learning in a deeper way.*
- *It's important that you advocate for your own learning. We don't want you to be bored because you're not challenging yourself. Next time, come speak with me and we'll identify ways to take this learning to a more challenging level.*
- *You're ready for something more difficult. Let's talk about what that might look like.*

When to do it: Use these frames when interacting with your students during lessons.

While doing it: Notice what students tell themselves when they encounter a setback. Sometimes, simply being aware of mindset can make a difference as we tackle a new challenge or receive helpful feedback.

Adapted from Mindset Works, Inc. (www.mindsetworks.com). Used with permission.

Assess and analyze your impact: Recognize the results of your actions

As you've focused your mental energy on ways to effectively engage students in cooperative groupings, you'll notice your attention turning to the direct impact of your efforts. So when you assess the impact of your actions, reflect on your guiding question for this phase: *How do I help students become more receptive to feedback?*

Are students becoming more receptive to feedback? Do they *ask* for feedback? Do they appear to be developing a growth mindset? To what extent can you draw cause-and-effect conclusions between your feedback-delivery actions and your students' feedback-utilization responses? In order to continually grow as an expert, you'll want to continue to ask these questions, as they'll guide your future actions, too. Remember: *When I do X, then students do Y . . . ergo, if I want students to do Y, I should do X.* The questions below are designed to help you to further hone and shape your mental models by engaging in self-reflection and dialogue with your colleagues.

Reflect on Teaching	Reflect on Learning
• Is your feedback aligned to desired outcomes or goals of the learning task? How do you know? • How often does your feedback foster student control (as opposed to sink into teacher control)? • How can you encourage student participation and ownership of the feedback process?	• When you offer feedback intended to enhance growth mindset, how do students respond? • When you catch yourself providing feedback that enhances fixed mindset, how do students respond? What can you do to reorient your feedback? • When you notice students asking for feedback, what is going on? What sorts of tasks are they engaged in? What is the learning objective? Why is it captivating their motivation? And how can you use this information in the future?

Become responsive: Respond to the needs you see

You've got a lot going on in your head right now, don't you? For feedback to be effective, it's got to be specific, timely, and focused on information, cultivating a growth mindset, and empowering students to own it. Holy smokes, are you noticing that sometimes you're so concerned with getting the words right that your students aren't buying it? That's the essence of the question you asked to begin this phase: *How do I help students become more receptive to feedback?* Well, there are a lot of reasons for that, of course, and you can scratch your head trying to figure it out. In fact, we encourage that approach . . . along with some targeted reflections, of course.

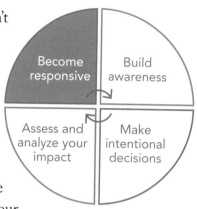

So if the results aren't exactly what you're going for (*Students didn't do Y, or they did only a vague resemblance of Y*) despite your very focused efforts (*I'm pretty sure I did X, and I think it was spot-on, for heaven's sake*), try scratching your head with the following questions, either by yourself or with your colleagues:

- ❖ When your feedback doesn't result in student agency, renewed focus, or a "lightbulb" moment, peel back the layers to try to figure out why. What happened? What preceded the feedback interaction? What history do you have with feedback and this particular student? This activity? This learning objective?

- ❖ Bring your concerns to a colleague and ask your colleague to bring you a professional concern. Engage in a "critical friends" protocol to see if you can come up with a plan of attack.

- ❖ Continue to tinker with your focus, your specific language, and your nonverbal communication when you provide feedback. Do those impact your students' responsiveness? How so?

When you provide feedback to students, they always respond somehow. It may not always be how you *want* them to respond, but it still provides data for you to analyze. The key is for you to then respond in a way that gets you all back on track, and that helps to move the students closer to owning their learning journeys. Take heart: The path is long. If you're finding that there's still variation in students' responses to your feedback, you may wonder how to refine your feedback practices to truly connect each individual student to deep learning. If so, you may want to tackle the problem on the next page, *How do I tailor feedback so it's meaningful for every student?*

Or, if you find yourself with another nagging question, turn to the grid on p. 16, find that question, and turn to the page where we help you address it.

How do I tailor feedback so it's meaningful for every student?

Be consistent	Be connected	**Differentiate**	Empower
Teacher-owned Student-experienced	*Teacher-directed, Student-connected*	*Student-engaged, Teacher-facilitated*	*Student-owned, Teacher-guided*

Welcome to the third phase of the "Motivating with feedback" pathway. Here, you'll begin to focus on taking what you've learned in the first two phases of the pathway and applying it with greater precision in your interactions with students—focusing on how to provide every student with the right feedback at the right moment. It's becoming a little less about you and a little more about how your students are responding. This important shift happens in every pathway as we move into the *differentiated* (or *student-engaged, teacher-facilitated*) phase. Addressing this problem of practice requires deeper knowledge of not only how feedback works, but also the principles of intrinsic motivation—knowledge you've begun to develop during the first two phases of this pathway.

 If you're joining us from another pathway, welcome! Before diving headlong into this challenge, though, we suggest you review the previous phase of this pathway to get your bearings.

Build awareness: Zoom in on the details

How do I tailor feedback so it's meaningful for every student? You've probably seen firsthand that even the most thoughtful feedback doesn't have much impact if students aren't receptive to it. Research tells us as much: Students are more receptive to feedback when they have a so-called "learning orientation"—that is, when they view improving their own abilities as the goal of learning, as opposed to a "performance orientation"—when they view being evaluated well by others (i.e., getting a good grade) as the goal of learning (Shute, 2008). For teachers, 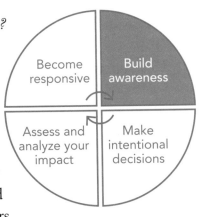 this means we can avoid feedback falling on deaf ears by helping students develop a learning orientation and buy into their learning objectives (not performance goals). In short, when students commit to their learning objectives, they're more apt to welcome feedback because they see it as helping them to accomplish something meaningful. This means that as teachers, we must have not only deep knowledge of what we're teaching students—the common misconceptions, mistakes, and barriers to understanding in the content students are learning—but also the knowledge and acumen needed to size up how individual students are doing so we can provide them with real-time feedback targeted to their needs.

Make intentional decisions: Develop a clear vision

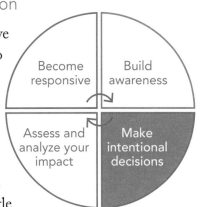

As you're growing more knowledgeable about effective feedback practices, you're likely becoming quite attuned to what your students need to be able to receive and engage with your feedback as they strive to master their learning goals. Now it's time to truly take this to the *differentiated* student level, where your feedback is geared specifically towards each student: where they are in relation to their goal, what their next steps are, and how to motivate them to push further. At this phase, our guidance will be a little less prescriptive and a little more cerebral. That's because from this point on, the refinements to your practice will increasingly reflect branching decision trees of if-then responses (*If I see students doing or needing X, then I do Y*). You're probably starting to size up your students, viewing them as active learners rather than passive recipients, and gauging how best to convey their progress (or lack thereof) to them in a way that inspires them to roll up their sleeves and get after it.

The two tools we provide on the following pages—"Differentiated Feedback That Targets Learning vs. Performing" and "Creating a Student-Led Culture for Feedback"—will help you ask the right questions and develop approaches to feedback that are based on different and more powerful assumptions about how to motivate students: their internal motivators.

Differentiated Feedback That Targets Learning vs. Performing

Why do it: For differentiated feedback to be effective, we must begin to link it to students' individual learning goals, rather than performance goals. When our feedback is directly connected to an individual's learning journey rather than performance, we tap into internal motivators.

How to do it: During lesson planning, identify three students who seem more focused on performance than learning. Jot down their individual learning goals associated with the lesson you're planning. Be careful to disassociate learning goals from performance goals. Studies show that performance-oriented goals foster avoidance of challenging tasks due to anxiety about failure (Dweck & Leggett, 1988). Once their learning goals are clear to you, provide differentiated feedback which is linked to those goals using the three characteristics below.

Differentiated feedback reminds/clarifies the learning goal:

One of the goals you set for yourself with this speech is to construct an attention-grabbing opening that taps into the emotions of your peers. The prevalence of autism is a startling statistic, but I noticed your classmates were really interested when you shared with them how well your cousin who has autism plays the piano. How might you use that observation to guide your thinking as you spend time next week revising this message?

Differentiated feedback facilitates the development of self-assessment in learning:

I know that learning your three- and four-times tables is your goal for this week. You've learned your threes really well, but the fours seem a bit trickier for you. What is your brain telling you right now? Do you agree? What were some of the strategies you used in learning your threes that you could use with the fours? How will you know if those strategies are helpful to your learning?

Good feedback gives students high-quality information about their learning:

I recall your setting a goal earlier this year to take more organized and complete notes and to be able to use them for studying. You mentioned that one of your biggest frustrations has been capturing the important information fast enough while I'm teaching. So far, you have experimented with handwritten informal outlines, webbing, and Cornell notes. I've noticed that you seem more confident as a learner when you use Cornell notes. How do you feel about each of these strategies? What have you learned about yourself through this process?

When to do it: This type of feedback is best provided in written form and given to students to drive personal reflection and self-evaluation. It works well when students are given time to process and then asked to write (or orally share) a response to your questions. Start by targeting students who struggle to engage or are focused on performance over learning.

While doing it: Observe and take notes of student thinking during this process. Notice the shift in perspective about learning: Do students view growth in their abilities as the goal of learning? Or do they still believe getting good grades is the target?

Creating a Student-Led Culture for Feedback

Why do it: Students' difficulties with understanding and using feedback have been well researched. Evidence shows that in many classrooms the purpose of feedback is unclear. Students struggle to make sense of something that hasn't been explicitly taught. When we value feedback as an integral part of learning and shift ownership to students, they become more involved and feedback becomes more meaningful.

How to do it: Set aside time to create the following chart with your students. Ask for their input and ideas as you fill in each section. Collate their answers, unpack concepts, and assess their understanding through the discussion. Throughout the year, refer to the chart and repeatedly model and provide students with opportunities to practice. Sample answers have been provided to drive your thinking.

Feedback is an important part of the learning process. What is feedback? When is feedback given? Who gives the feedback? How is feedback given? What is the purpose? Why is feedback given?	
Here's what it sounds like to . . .	
Request feedback:	*I'm wondering if my thinking is on the right track.* *Can you please give me feedback on _____?* *Would you be willing to listen to my thinking about this problem and give me feedback?*
Clarify feedback you've received:	*I have a question about _____.* *Can you explain _____.* *This part doesn't make sense _____.* *I'm confused about something you said.* *Can you please clarify _____?*
Discuss feedback you've received:	*Your comment here leads me to think _____.* *I am interested in hearing more about this part of your feedback: _____.* *Well, that's not what I meant. I meant _____.*
Challenge feedback you've received:	*I disagree with _____ because _____.* *I understood your point that _____; however, _____.* *I don't think that will work because _____.*
Take action using feedback you've received:	*The feedback I received made me think differently about _____. As a result, I am going to _____.* *I used to think _____, but now I know _____.*

When to do it: This powerful tool can be used in all grades. It should be introduced at the beginning of the year and referenced repeatedly throughout. It is not uncommon for students to want to add to the chart as they take more ownership of the feedback process.

While doing it: Assess student understanding and thinking. Be cognizant of the overall purpose of the activity: to transfer ownership of the feedback process to students.

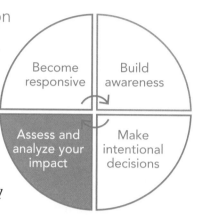

Applying multiple strategies is likely affording you a new way to look at feedback and its relationship to motivation. Most likely you're really taking your time and concentrating your efforts to build a culture of learning, one in which feedback plays a vital role. And now, as you assess and analyze the impact of your actions up to this point, we remind you to keep your guiding question in mind: *How do I tailor feedback so it's meaningful for every student?*

You're probably also noticing that the more you give students feedback, you're viewing their responses as feedback about your feedback . . . which may create a healthy feedback loop in which you and each of your students are active partners. How are you using this information? How is this feedback process impacting student learning? Motivation? Effort? Self-talk? Perseverance? Grit? As you collect data (formal and/or informal), you're applying your reflective muscle like experts do: learning, trying, and tinkering with an eye on the goal. You're using feedback *from* your students to improve the feedback you're *giving* your students! As you well know, experts don't go it alone; indeed, they consult with one another to diagnose and solve problems. With a "critical friend," use the following reflective questions (and then create your own to add to the list) to help you to develop your expert mental models and challenge each other's thinking:

Reflect on Teaching	Reflect on Learning
• How aware are you of whether your feedback has a learning orientation or a performance orientation? How automatically do you provide learning-focused feedback?	• As you shift your feedback practices, what changes do you notice in student performance and learning? How does this frame your next steps?
• How do you know when to put a score on student work?	• When you do put a score on a student's work, what happens next?
• How might you use anchor charts to support students giving feedback in your classroom? How might you encourage students to refer to them frequently?	• What are some of the pros and cons of creating a culture of feedback? What's working? What still needs to be addressed? What information (feedback) are your students giving you about this culture you're trying to create?

Become responsive: Respond in the moment

The third phase in this pathway marks a seismic shift in your thinking, as well as your actions. As you've pursued the question that launched this pathway—*How do I tailor feedback so it's meaningful for every student?*— you're realizing the changing nature of feedback in your class. Rather than something static you *give* them, it's become a fluid process that greases the wheels of learning. Have you noticed this? As you're growing as a reflective practitioner, you're more keen to catching yourself if your feedback practices are unhelpful (read: vague,

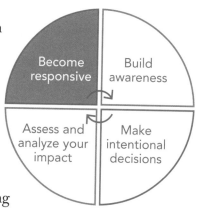

mistimed, performance-oriented, or simply a score or letter grade). The ability to catch yourself repeating a less-than-ideal practice is another landmark in your growth: You're becoming adept at reflecting *in* action, as opposed to waiting until later and reflecting *on* action. Do whatever you can to keep your metacognitive system online! Take a moment and reflect on your professional growth from the beginning of this pathway until now, and challenge yourself (and a trusted colleague, instructional coach, or administrator) with a few bonus reflective questions:

❖ What signals do you look for that indicate the feedback isn't helpful?

❖ How quickly do you respond with a new feedback prompt/strategy/approach when you notice a gap between your intention and the results?

❖ To what extent is your classroom becoming a culture of feedback? How can you tell? What are your next steps to strengthen that overarching idea?

Your reflections, and your metacognitive thinking about your thinking, are propelling you along this pathway. If you were to pause and look back at all that you've learned, implemented, and revised about your feedback practices, motivating students, and emphasizing a growth mindset, what would you notice? What sort of feedback would you give yourself? How might that propel you even further on this journey? What new obstacle might your self-reflections surface? If you're like most, and you're interested in continuing to strengthen the culture of feedback in your classroom, you're probably starting to wonder how you can share the workload with your students. For example, you may want your students to support each other's learning and truly embrace the notion of community. When they own their learning together, they don't need to wait for you! If so, you may wish to turn to the next page to consider, *How do I help students give one another effective feedback?*

Or, if you find yourself with another nagging question, turn to the grid on p. 16, find that question, and turn to the page where we help you address it.

How do I help students give one another effective feedback?

Be consistent *Teacher-owned, Student-experienced*	Be connected *Teacher-directed, Student-connected*	Differentiate *Student-engaged, Teacher-facilitated*	**Empower** *Student-owned, Teacher-guided*

Welcome to the fourth phase of the "Motivating with feedback" pathway. Here, you'll begin to *empower* students to pursue deep learning in a *student-owned, teacher-guided* environment. This is no subtle shift, either. Building your students' capacity to guide their own learning journeys requires steady, significant development of your own capacity—both as a master of the technical elements of teaching and as a reflective practitioner. Getting to this point requires building on the foundation of everything you've learned, the acute awareness you've built, the many steps you've taken with great intentionality, and your ability to gauge your impact and make midcourse corrections as necessary.

 If you're joining us from another pathway, we encourage you to review the previous three phases in this pathway to ensure you're ready to address this challenge.

Build awareness: Bring all the variables together

How do I help students give one another effective feedback? When considering the feedback process, there are a lot of elements to juggle. It's not as easy as slapping a "+14/15" and a "Great job!" sticker on a student's paper and calling it good. In fact, now that you've developed your thinking in this area to this point, a practice like that almost seems laughable. "For heaven's sake," you might say. "That does nothing to foster a growth mindset, offer specific connections to lesson objectives, or build upon a learning orientation!"

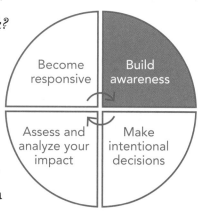

We first discussed the research on metacognition in chapter 5, "Designing engaging learning," and if you have progressed through that pathway already, you are likely making some pretty powerful connections right now. If you haven't read our summary of Bob Marzano's meta-analysis on the matter, we invite you to flip back to p. 106 and you'll see exactly what we're talking about: Your growth in metacognitive practices about your teaching is the whole point of this book; your students' growth in their metacognitive practices about learning is the key to unlocking motivation, engagement, curiosity, and deep learning.

Several years ago, researcher Alison King (1991) demonstrated that it's possible—and quite powerful—to teach metacognitive strategies to students. She set out to see if teaching self-questioning to students, which was effective in reading comprehension, could have equally positive effects on student comprehension of oral lectures. For her study, she taught a class of 9th-grade students to ask themselves higher-order comparison-contrast questions (e.g., "How are Shintoism and Buddhism alike?"), causal-relationship questions ("How did the rise of power of the Shogun affect the development of Japanese culture?"), and analysis questions (e.g., "Which king was best for England?") while listening to history lectures (p. 338). She also gave them "question starters" to model the sort of questions they could ask themselves during lectures and taught them about metacognition, including how to ask themselves questions like, "What do I still not understand about this?" (p. 337). The results were striking. Even though the initial training session on self-questioning had been brief, students taught to use self-questioning techniques scored roughly 16 points higher (out 100) on a test of comprehension and retention compared with students who simply reviewed the lecture material. Even more striking, perhaps, the technique itself seemed to stick with students. When King conducted a second round of her experiment with no prompts about self-questioning, students who had been previously taught the self-questioning technique demonstrated higher levels of comprehension on a test of the new material. Other studies of similar interventions found positive effects persisting months later, which suggests once students become more metacognitive about their learning, they simply appear to become better learners.

Make intentional decisions: Move beyond strategy to design

So, how do you bring all of these ideas together in your classroom? The ability to do this—and to do it consistently and consistently *well*—is often referred to as the art of teaching. You're way past the focus on *what* you are going to do to address this challenge; indeed, you're now thinking about *how* all of these strategies and approaches blend together to create an assessment design. *Empowering* students in such a classroom environment does not happen by accident, and it's no coincidence that your growth as a reflective practitioner has accompanied—in fact, preceded—this shift in practice. Because of the complexity and uniqueness of your situation (no one has ever faced exactly what you're facing before, with exactly the students you have), you're in uncharted territory, as it were. How cool is that? But it also means there's no step-by-step guide that we (nor anyone) can offer. Accordingly, the advice we offer here are really guiding principles designed to support students' metacognition (thinking about their own learning) and to help them become increasingly independent in self-assessing and self-correcting their learning. The following two tools—"Self-Questioning" and "Praise, Question, Suggest"—can help you to continue this journey with confidence.

Self-Questioning

Why do it: Self-questioning is the ongoing process of asking questions before, during, and after learning with the purpose of deepening understanding. This tool requires learners to look for clues that make them wonder, think about possible meanings, surface questions, make predictions, evaluate conclusions, and reconcile differences in their thinking. It supports student metacognition and can teach students to engage in feedback practices that move beyond superficial to deeper meaning.

How to do it: Follow these steps.

After engaging in a new learning task, tell students that they will develop post-learning questions to frame their thinking and make sense of the new learning.

Step 1: Partner students and ask them to discuss and work through the following questions:

- Looking back, I now know _____.
  (Based on what I just learned, how has my knowledge changed?)
- Looking back, I now think _____.
  (Based on what I just learned, do I agree?)
- Looking back, I now question _____.
  (Based on what I just learned, what additional questions do I have?)
- Looking back, I now feel _____.
  (Based on what I just learned, what emotions do I feel?)
- Looking back, I now predict _____.
  (Based on what I just learned, what will future learning include?)

Step 2: Develop an essential question.

- Based on your answers in Step 1, create an essential question that captures the main idea of your learning. This is an open-ended question that is not answerable in a brief sentence. It should stimulate thought, provoke further inquiry, and spark more questions. There should be no "one right answer" to this open-ended question.

Step 3: Craft an answer.

- Develop an answer to your essential question. This answer should be thoughtful and supported with evidence from your learning. It will be lengthy.

Step 4: Debrief the process with your students.

- In what ways do questions support our learning? How does self-questioning help us understand ourselves better as learners? What other questions might we ask to recheck and reflect on learning? How might we use these questions to provide better feedback for our peers?

When to do it: This tool can be used before, during, or after a learning experience. Modify the questions as needed. The questions can also be adapted, revised, and changed at any time. The purpose is to teach students to ask themselves higher-order questions throughout the learning process and build awareness of their thinking. This tool can also be used to guide the peer feedback process.

While doing it: Observe and record students' metacognition. What "ahas" do you have?

Praise, Question, Suggest

Why do it: Peer feedback can be a powerful classroom strategy. This protocol will help students learn the art of listening and providing feedback that supports peer learning. It is important that participants understand that the focus should be on offering feedback that is beneficial to the speaker and leads to deeper learning. Sample feedback stems may need to be crafted first.

How to do it: Provide product descriptors and/or a rubric as a clear guideline of the expectations and criteria for the product. If the product is written, copies for the feedback group are helpful.

Procedure:

- As a whole group, create a list of possible feedback questions based on the rubric for the product.
- Model the procedures with the whole group several times before allowing small independent feedback groups.
- Participants work in groups of 2–5. They sit in a circle during the activity.
- One participant of the group is the first presenter. The presenter shares/reads the draft product s/he is submitting for feedback. The presenter asks peers to focus feedback around a particular question or dilemma that s/he is struggling with.
- This feedback is best written on sticky notes and given to the speaker. Peers focus first on what is praiseworthy or working well based upon the rubric. Praise needs to be specific, such as, *"I noticed that you used descriptive picture captions"* or *"You have a catchy title that makes me want to read your piece."* As peers write their notes, they also share aloud and hand the notes to the presenter.
- Next, the presenter reiterates the question or dilemma that s/he is struggling with. Peers will ask clarifying questions directed at the presenter's thinking. The presenter answers each question. This part of the protocol is a verbal discussion only.
- After clarifying the thinking of the presenter, members of the group now offer feedback in the form of helpful suggestions. The feedback should be centered around the presenter's dilemma or question: *"This part is unclear. I wonder if it would be better to change the order." "Maybe you could add some details that would show the reader where it is taking place."* The presenter takes notes as the group shares.
- After each member of the group has offered feedback, the presenter discusses which suggestions s/he wants to implement and thanks the group.
- Others take turns sharing their work and cycling through the feedback process.
- Debrief with the whole class. Discuss examples of feedback that were beneficial and supported learning, as well as kinds of feedback that were too general or negative to be helpful.

When to do it: This tool can be used in any subject with any product or project. It works best during learning, particularly in the independent practice portion of lesson plans.

While doing it: Pay close attention to the conversation. Keep a clipboard or notepad in hand as you monitor these discussions. Write examples of feedback that you want to share with the group. Also take notes on particular students and the thinking that is exhibited. How do these observations guide your learning as a teacher?

At this phase in the pathway, you're using your deep knowledge and skills to help students take ownership of their learning journeys. Some may observe your collaborative feedback approaches and consider such empowerment in your classroom to be innovative and creative divergence. As a committed, reflective practitioner, you're well aware that you've reached a place in your professional development that is only possible because of your consistent, intentional focus on growing, learning, gauging, and tinkering with your practices to better

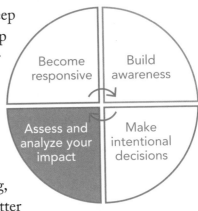

meet individual students' needs. You know the most important part of any classroom isn't what you're doing as a teacher, but rather, what's going on in students' minds; thus, you want to design dynamic feedback experiences that add real value to student learning—helping them to learn and do things together they couldn't do independently. Your initial question is truly guiding your inquiry: *How do I help students give one another effective feedback?* Do the feedback protocols you've designed for students support *deep* learning? With that in mind, gather some colleagues, administrators, coaches, and your teammates and lead a discussion based on the following questions (and feel free to add your own):

Reflect on Teaching	Reflect on Learning
• How are you able to infuse peer-feedback structures into your lesson plans and units? • What are you noticing about your own feedback practices as you attempt to build a culture in which students give each other feedback often? • Where (and how) does feedback fit into the larger scheme of things in your classroom? How can you and your students make it a living, breathing element of learning?	• How are learning outcomes impacted by peer feedback? • You likely have some students who struggle more with peer feedback than others. How might you help them give/ receive such feedback more openly and specifically? • How have your students' learning and motivation been improved as a result of your learning about various feedback processes? What's the next step you're considering? Why?

Become responsive: Trust your intuition

After your conversations with colleagues, open discussions with your students, and some honest self-reflection, you may find yourself wondering how to continue to refine your feedback practices. Of course you are—that's the goal, right? You keep learning, trying things out, seeing how they work, adapting and adjusting . . . and repeat. As you do this, believe in yourself, your learning, and your development. Highly reflective practitioners like you realize there is no finish line, no ending point. Learning is a process that extends beyond any limit you could imagine. And

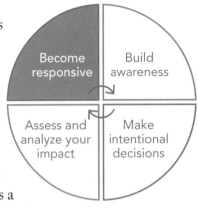

that's the exciting part: No matter how well things are going, there will always be room for improvement. Trust your inner voice. At this point, your reflective capacity has developed to a point where you're attuned to your students' needs and how to address them, both in the moment and from a grander perspective. And if you'd like to couple your inner voice with those of your trusted colleagues, we invite you to reflect on the following questions together, challenging each other's thinking to continue to refine your practice:

- ❖ What's next for you in your learning about feedback practices?
- ❖ How can you share your journey with colleagues, and have them share theirs with you?
- ❖ What steps are you taking to cultivate the little metacognitive voice in your head that reminds you, inspires you, encourages you, and prompts you to keep your eyes and mind open to continued opportunities to learn and refine your practices?

You're probably wishing there were more phases in this pathway, right? Well, we agree, and we want to acknowledge a couple of realities. First, you've really grown as a practitioner as you've restructured the way you think about and use feedback practices in your classroom. Second, though you've progressed through this chapter, there really is no end to this work. You can always grow, you can always improve, and you can always learn and refine your approaches. Yes, there's a lot to celebrate, and yes, there's still a lot on the horizon.

Final thoughts on motivating with feedback

As you've come to the end of the "Motivating with feedback" pathway, it's important to take stock of your journey, appreciate the phases you've mastered, and note the growth you've made. In short, this is a wonderful time to appraise your professional development.

First, let's look at the pathway from the 10,000-foot level:

Be consistent	Be connected	Differentiate	Empower
Teacher-owned, Student-experienced	*Teacher-directed, Student-connected*	*Student-engaged, Teacher-facilitated*	*Student-owned, Teacher-guided*

You've made significant strides in transforming your classroom from one that's inherently *teacher-owned* (and student-experienced) to one that is becoming more *student-owned* (and teacher-guided). Through a systematic process of identifying key questions that either confound or interest you (or both), you've investigated and addressed four critical problems of practice all related to the "Motivating with feedback" pathway. Along the way, you repeated a very predictable, very deliberate pattern of reflective steps that a) built your self-reflective capacity and b) enhanced your professional acumen. That pattern, the Reflective Cycle, really ought to be second nature to you by now:

❖ Build awareness about the problem of practice by asking key questions and conducting research to learn more.

❖ Make intentional decisions about implementing strategies, based on the research and your desired goal.

❖ Assess and analyze the impact of your actions to determine the effectiveness of particular strategies over a period of time.

❖ Become responsive to the changing needs you notice in order to better meet your (and, more specifically, your *students'*) needs.

❖ Repeat, repeat, repeat, and repeat again and again and again.

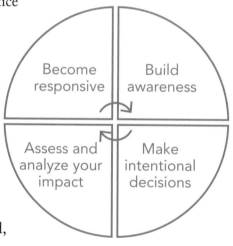

Remember the Theory of Action that drives this combination of approaches:

Theory of Action	IF we start with key problems of practice, use research-based best practices to solve them, and reflect on our practice as teachers, THEN we will become more expert in our practice, better able to meet our students' needs, and engaged in career-long professional growth that will allow us to become amazing, unstoppable teachers in whose classrooms learning will flourish.

Though you've come to the end of this particular pathway, you're far too astute to believe the journey is over. Learning is cyclical—a progression that leads you ever upwards, not unlike a spiral staircase—and you realize there will be times that you need to backtrack, regroup, and revisit some of the foundational elements of this pathway to solidify and enhance your effectiveness. And of course there's more yet to learn, different approaches to implement, and all sorts of new ways of looking at—and solving—your newfound problems of practice. Indeed, the growth you've made is more than just about learning the ins and outs of effective feedback; in addition, you're becoming masterful at the *art* of growing as a reflective practitioner and transferring your learning into the classroom.

And as you've certainly noticed, using various feedback approaches to motivate your students is just part of a robust, powerful, successful schooling experience for students. Now your task is to weave the other refinement pathways into your work in a seamless expression of excellence, ensuring that all students thrive and flourish. ✳

Or, if you find yourself with another nagging question, turn to the grid on p. 16, find that question, and turn to the page where we help you address it.

Chapter 7
Assessing for learning

As we dive into a chapter on assessment, it may be worth acknowledging an uncomfortable truth: For many of us, assessment probably isn't something we want to dive into. You may have saved this chapter for last or felt tempted to skip it altogether.

That's OK. Let's face it, assessments are seldom enjoyable for anyone (teachers or students).

The very word *assessment* may conjure up unpleasant memories of late-night cramming, penciling in bubble sheets, or scrawling in blue books until our eyes went blurry and hands cramped. As teachers, the prospect of grading a stack of tests likely doesn't make us want to jump up and click our heels in joyous anticipation. For many of us, assessment may feel at best like a necessary evil of learning—something done to cajole reluctant kids into learning (and prove to parents and administrators we're doing our jobs)—and at worst, like something that sucks the joy, deeper purpose, and curiosity out of learning.

Such misgivings are normal; yet assessments need not feel like drudgery. As you sharpen your skills in assessing for learning, your view of assessment is apt to change, too. As you move along this pathway, developing your skills in assessing student learning accurately and effectively, you'll also discover whole new applications of assessment that will help you see it as central to learning—a process that can actually unleash student curiosity and joyful learning in your classroom.

Seriously.

Done right, assessments can actually be enjoyable. But don't take our word for it; on this pathway, you'll discover for yourself how that can be possible in your classroom. So, don't be afraid to jump on in. You'll find it feels great.

Take charge of your own professional growth

To help you consider how to incorporate assessments in a way that informs and leads to deep learning, we'll start with *your own curiosity*—questions you're likely to ask about your classroom. You may have found yourself asking one (or all) of the questions below. To help you meet your pressing needs and address your current problem of practice, we've placed a page number next to each so you can flip ahead and engage in some self-guided exploration:

- ❖ How do I know whether students are learning? (p. 147)
- ❖ How do I use assessments to adjust teaching and learning if students don't get it? (p. 154)
- ❖ How do I use assessments to make thinking visible and encourage critical thinking? (p. 164)
- ❖ How do I help students self-assess and guide their own learning? (p. 171)

How do I know whether students are learning?

| **Be consistent** *Teacher-owned, Student-experienced* | Be connected *Teacher-directed, Student-connected* | Differentiate *Student-engaged, Teacher-facilitated* | Empower *Student-owned, Teacher-guided* |

Welcome to the first phase of the "Assessing for learning" pathway. Not surprisingly, the focus here is on your actions as a teacher: what you are doing, what is expected of you, and what it will take for you to be successful. This pattern of thinking is typical of the *teacher-owned, student-experienced* phase, and as you proceed through the Reflective Cycle and expand your reflective vision, you'll begin to become more consistent in your approaches, allowing you to better meet your students' needs.

Build awareness: Observe

How do I know whether students are learning? This is one of the age-old questions teachers ask themselves—and rightly so. It appears here in chapter 7 for a reason: As you've progressed along the other pathways in this book—in particular those in which you challenge students to master high expectations—you're likely to have faced a new challenge. How do you know whether your students have actually mastered the content you've so carefully introduced to them? And, perhaps more pressing, to what extent are students in the *process* of mastering that content?

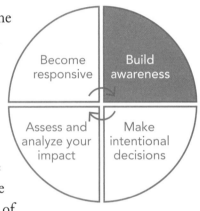

As we dive into this challenge, we'll explore two forms of assessment: *summative* and *formative*. Summative assessments are infrequent, end-of-course assessments that we score or grade. Because there's a finality to summative assessments, they typically (though not necessarily) do little to guide future instruction or relearning. Formative assessments, on the other hand, are much more frequent (and often ungraded) measures that we deliver to guide instruction and relearning. They may include quizzes, homework assignments, classroom discussions, and in-class checks for understanding.

With so much emphasis on high-stakes testing, it's easy to have a rather narrow (if not dim) view of assessments solely as final or summative measures of learning and to fear that we already test students too much, so why test them more? We know from research, however, that students are actually more motivated to learn when we assess them throughout the learning process, giving them multiple opportunities to see what they've learned and have yet to learn. Bear in mind, though, that we're talking about more formative assessments here, not summative.

A good deal of research points to the power of formative assessments to accelerate student learning. In his analysis of more than 4,000 studies over four decades, Dylan Wiliam (2007) found that when teachers use formative assessment and checks for understanding to guide instruction, they can double the rate of student learning. And here's the key: When used most effectively, formative assessments help you understand where your students are in the learning journey by exposing their knowledge (correct and incorrect answers) and illuminating their thinking. It's that second part—our awareness of how our students are thinking, processing, incorporating, and implementing their learning—that is most informative for you as a teacher.

The point here, though, isn't that formative assessments are good and summative assessments are bad. Rather, when integrated, these two forms of assessment can challenge and support students, especially when we design and use them thoughtfully.

Make intentional decisions: Be deliberate in planning

When considering the role assessment plays in your classroom, keep this in mind: Assessment isn't testing. The purpose isn't to determine how many correct answers the student knows, or to grab a quick grade. A comprehensive assessment approach at the classroom level balances both formative and summative tools. This balance of information creates a clear picture of where a student is relative to learning targets and standards. At the same time, the picture includes minute details about individual students as they engage in the learning process and points

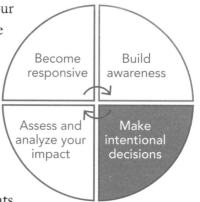

you in the direction that you need to go to adjust instruction to ensure successful learning. Try the following two tools—"One-Minute Papers" and "LODA"—in this midst of lessons and/or as Exit Tickets at the end of lessons to help you gauge student learning. Both are cornerstone formative assessment strategies that can be used in any subject.

One-Minute Papers

Why do it: Without formative assessments, the first indication that a student doesn't grasp the material is when they fail a quiz or test. Effective and engaging formative assessment strategies like this can take failure out of the classroom. This assessment technique provides quick feedback on whether the teacher's main idea about learning, and what the students perceived as the main idea, are the same.

How to do it: One-minute papers are usually done at the end of a lesson, sometimes at the end of a class period or even a day. Students, in groups or individually, are asked to answer 1–2 questions in writing. They write as much as they can in one minute. The papers are collected and analyzed by the teacher to gain awareness of the students' understanding. One-minute papers have been found to be most effective when done on a frequent basis. Questions can be modified, making this a very adaptable tool.

Sample Form: The One-Minute Paper

In concise, well-planned sentences, please answer the question(s) below.
Sample questions to use:

- *What was the main point of learning today?* _____
  _____

- *Which area(s) of the lesson did you struggle to grasp?* _____
  _____

- *Which parts of the lesson are still not clear enough in your mind?* _____
  _____

- *Describe the most surprising concept.* _____
  _____

- *What are the two [three, four, five] most significant [central, useful, meaningful, surprising, disturbing] things you have learned today?* _____
  _____

- *What questions do you need answered now?* _____
  _____

- *What connection did you make between our learning today and yesterday's learning?* _____
  _____

When to do it: This formative assessment tool can be used each day with different questions. Done frequently, it can provide both teachers and students with invaluable information about learning.

While doing it: The purpose of this tool is to illuminate the thinking that is leading to learning. Look beyond correct answers. This is NOT about getting something "right." Identify what the answer exposes about student thinking and learning. Ask yourself: What concepts might a student be misunderstanding? How might that direct my instructional decisions tomorrow?

LODA (Learning Outcomes Drive Assessment)

Why do it: All formative assessment strategies are not created equal. While there are countless to choose from, it is important that we select an assessment that will provide us the information we are looking for—information that connects directly to our learning outcomes and subsequently guides our instructional decisions.

How to do it: Before your next lesson, match the learning outcomes from your lesson to one of the assessments we've listed below and plan to use it. Keep in mind that most formative assessment strategies (what we're calling assessment for learning) happen while learning is still underway. When selecting from the list, ask yourself these questions:

"What information will this assessment provide me?"
"How will it support my instructional decision making?"

Index Card Summaries/ Questions	Distribute index cards and ask students to write on both sides with these instructions: Side 1: Based on our study of _____, list a big idea that you understand and word it as a summary statement. Side 2: Identify something about _____ that you do not yet fully understand and word it as a statement or a question.
Hand Signals	Ask students to display a designated hand signal to indicate their understanding of a specific concept or process: Thumbs Up: *"I understand _____ and can explain it."* Thumbs Down: *"I do not yet understand _____."* Wave Hand: *"I'm confused about _____."*
Misconception Check	Present students with a common or predictable misconception about a designated concept. Ask them whether they agree or disagree and explain why. Using chart paper or sticky notes, ask them to write their thoughts down. Put them in small groups and ask them to discuss their thinking with one another, supporting their claims with evidence. Ask the groups to create a list of questions they have. Use their questions to drive your instruction as you address the misconception.

Analogy Prompt	Present students with an analogy prompt: _____ (concept you're teaching) is like _____ because _____. Students should work in pairs or triads to create an analogy that best illuminates their thinking on the subject.
Brain Dump	The three-minute pause provides a chance for students to stop, reflect on the concept and ideas that have just been introduced, make connections to prior knowledge or experience, and seek clarification. Using the sentence starters below, provide students with an opportunity to talk with peers and share thinking aloud. I changed my attitude about _____. I became more aware of _____. I was surprised about _____. I related to _____. This reminds me of _____. I'm wondering about _____. I was confused by _____.
5 Words	What five words would you use to describe _____? Explain and justify your choices. Be prepared to tell why you chose the words you did.
Twitter Post	Define _____ in under 280 characters.

When to do it: Formative assessment practices should be woven into every lesson as you begin to look for evidence of student learning exhibited through student thinking.

While doing it: Refrain from looking for "correct" answers and push yourself to notice student thinking. What does their thinking tell you about their learning?

Assess and analyze your impact: Notice learning

At this point, you've likely had a few (or many) "aha" moments along the way and your thinking has begun to shift. So, let's pause a moment to notice a few important things that have happened in your classroom as you've begun to hone how you use formative assessments to gauge student learning and the thinking that accompanies it. This self-reflection time is a critical piece of your own professional growth, helping you to make that all-important connection between your actions and student responses. Keep that initial question in mind, too: *How do I know whether students are learning?* Also, ask yourself these big questions: How has your teaching changed? How has student learning changed? Use the prompts below to guide your reflections about both:

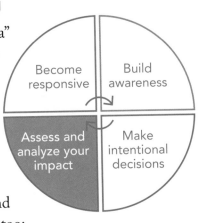

Reflect on Teaching	Reflect on Learning
• When do you typically assess student learning? • What is the purpose of these assessments? • How have you incorporated formative assessment tools (such as One-Minute Papers and LODA) into your lesson planning? • How has your thinking about assessment strategies changed since you began down this pathway?	• What information do you gather from assessment tools? • What does this information tell you about how students are progressing toward their learning goals? Where are they (as a whole, and individually) compared with the standard? • How are students responding to formative assessment tools? • What part of the *formative assessment* process are students struggling with? Which parts are they embracing as part of the journey?

Become responsive: Make changes

There's a temporal element of student-learning assessment strategies that you may have recognized: It's not a static measurement (they either got it or they didn't) because learning is fluid, and you're acknowledging that you can log into your students' brains to catch a glimpse of their thinking at any given moment. And because learning is a process, what you've learned is going to inform your next steps. This is what professional growth and strengthening your reflective muscle is all about, right?

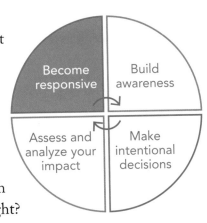

Here are some questions that you might want to bring to a trusted colleague—a "critical friend" or an instructional coach or mentor—to reflect on what's improved and what your next steps might be:

- ❖ What challenges are you experiencing as you shift your focus from "learned" to "learning"? How are you adapting to this cognitive workload?

- ❖ As you pore over the results of formative assessment tools, what do they tell you about student learning? How is this helpful for your future lesson planning?

- ❖ What changes will you make to your lessons tomorrow as a result of collecting these data today?

- ❖ What changes will you make to your archived lessons for next year (or next semester) as a result of the data you have now?

It's time to heed that ageless advice, "Look back to look ahead." The question you sought to answer at the beginning of this pathway was *How do I know whether students are learning?* Now think how you'd answer it. Here are three simple ways to return to your problem of practice and deepen your reflective capacity:

- ❖ Jot some notes down in a learning journal or another place where you might be able to archive your thinking and access ideas, musings, questions, and other ponderings later.

- ❖ Find a trusted colleague or two to engage in a dialogue with you. Exchange thoughts, suggestions, critical feedback, and celebrations together.

- ❖ Engage your administrator, instructional coach, department chair, or another member of your support network in a discussion about this question, your journey thus far, and any shifts in perspective you've noticed.

At this point, you may also find that your new clarity of focus has begun to surface other problems and raise new questions. For example, more frequent checks for understanding or increased use of constructed-response items may have begun to reveal student misconceptions or limited understanding of important concepts. So, now you're wondering what you can do to help them be successful. If so, you may want to tackle the problem on the next page, *How do I use assessments to adjust teaching and learning if students don't get it?*

 Or, if you find yourself with another nagging question, turn to the grid on p. 16, find that question, and turn to the page where we help you address it.

How do I use assessments to adjust teaching and learning if students don't get it?

Be consistent	**Be connected**	Differentiate	Empower
Teacher-owned, Student-experienced	***Teacher-directed, Student-connected***	*Student-engaged, Teacher-facilitated*	*Student-owned, Teacher-guided*

Welcome to the second phase of the "Assessing for learning" pathway. As you've begun to design and deliver more frequent formative assessments, your attention has likely begun to shift from what you are doing to how your students are responding to your teaching. As your assessments become more precise and aligned with high expectations, you've become increasingly aware of gaps in student learning. Observing the cause-and-effect relationships between your assessment strategies, your teaching approaches, and your students' responses is an indicator that your classroom is becoming more *teacher-directed, student-connected.* Indeed, you are *connecting* the dots that lead to increased student learning outcomes.

 If you're joining us from another pathway, or if you're skipping ahead to this problem of practice without reading the previous phase in its entirety, we suggest you skim through or review the previous section just to get your bearings.

Build awareness: Note cause-and-effect relationships

How do I use assessments to adjust teaching and learning if students don't get it? As your assessment practices have improved, you've likely unearthed times when your students simply aren't picking up what you're laying down. Sure, you could shrug it off and figure *that's their problem.* You probably know teachers who cop that attitude—who are what we might call "chicken feed" teachers, scattering knowledge with little regard for who picks it up. That's not who you are, though. By virtue of asking the question, you clearly want your students to succeed, yet may be unsure what to do differently.

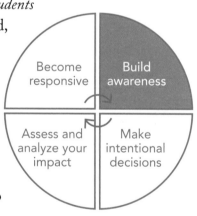

Let's take a moment to consider what may be going on here. In simple terms, the learning process is breaking down for your students. You're introducing them to new knowledge and skills, but for whatever reason, they've not been able to engage with, comprehend, or retain the knowledge and skills they need to master—at least not yet. The learning has become for students like a leaky pipe, leaving nothing coming out the end. With this in mind, let's take a moment to connect your teaching practices to what's happening (or should be happening) inside students' minds.

We're simplifying tremendously here, but what we know from cognitive science is that for learning to occur—for new information to find a home in our long-term memory—it takes a long and perilous journey, passing through three types of memory (short-term, working, and long-term) reflecting these phases:

- ❖ **Becoming interested and committed to learning.** Our senses are constantly bombarded with stimuli, so our brains tend to filter out most of what's around us. Stimuli that trigger fight-or-flight responses get our attention first, followed by those with emotional valence, and finally, opportunities for new learning (Souza, 2011). That suggests we must first feel safe and emotionally engaged before we're ready to learn. After that, new information must capture our interest (e.g., make us curious) and ultimately, because learning rarely happens by accident, we must decide if new information is worth learning—and commit to learning it.

- ❖ **Focusing on new learning and making sense of it.** Once we decide to pay attention to new information, we must hold it in our working memory, which consists of three mental systems: one for processing auditory signals, one for processing visual signals, and one for coordinating these two systems (Souza, 2011). Because these systems work closely together, we're more apt to absorb and retain new information (6.5 times more likely, in fact) when it's presented to us both orally and visually (Medina, 2008). Our working memories also have some serious limitations: Generally, they can only hold 5–9 bits of information at a time (even fewer, for younger people). So, if we're exposed to too much information at once, our working memories get fatigued—and we feel frustrated. We can work around this limitation if we're able to mentally cluster information into larger concepts or into a bigger idea rather than a list of smaller concepts (Bailey & Pransky, 2014). In addition, our working memories tend to time out after 10–20 minutes (less for younger people) (Souza, 2011), so we learn better when it's "chunked" into shorter segments with opportunities to process new learning after each segment.

- ❖ **Practicing and applying new learning.** Ultimately, whether knowledge finds a home in our long-term memory depends on a variety of factors, including what may be the most important key to long-term memory—repeating and rehearsing our new learning and practicing new skills. Doing so reinforces the neural pathways in our brains, increasing automaticity and making it easier to retrieve what we've learned later—especially when we spread out our practice sessions over time (Rawson & Kintsch, 2005) or engage in elaborative rehearsal—paraphrasing, summarizing, teaching others, making predictions, and generating questions about what we've learned (Benjamin & Bjork, 2000). On top of that, one of the most important things we can do to strengthen our learning is to apply it in new settings—especially real-world problem solving, which makes learning more meaningful and creates additional mental pathways for retrieving new learning from memory (Souza, 2011).

So, what does this have to do with adjusting teaching and learning? Well, perhaps everything. When we consider that learning is a process, when students fail to learn, some part of the process is breaking down. So, to use the metaphor of a leaky pipe, we can look for the leak to see where the repair is needed:

- ❖ The "leak" may be occurring early in the process of learning—students may simply not be interested in their learning. When this happens, we may need different "hooks" to draw them into their learning. Or if their interest wanes, they may need more clarity about, or ownership of, their success criteria to commit to their learning.

- ❖ Sometimes, students may be interested and committed to learning, yet still struggle to master new knowledge or skills. If so, they may need to focus on new knowledge in different ways, perhaps with visualizations, manipulatives, or opportunities to see a new skill modeled. Or they may need additional opportunities to make sense of their learning by, for example, engaging in cooperative learning activities that help them connect new knowledge to prior knowledge or cluster it into more manageable big ideas.

- ❖ If you find, however, that students are forgetting what they've learned or their new skills are fading quickly (e.g., they demonstrate learning on mid-point quizzes but not end-of-unit exams), they may need more opportunities to practice and rehearse their learning, which doesn't necessarily mean more homework, but rather, distributed practice opportunities that help them rehearse new knowledge and skills over time. Or if they are struggling to retrieve new knowledge, they may need additional opportunities to extend and apply their learning—using new skills to solve real-world problems or integrate knowledge through creative application of what they're learning.

Make intentional decisions: Plan, then implement

So, how do you make meaningful adjustments to instruction in response to student learning needs? Let us answer bluntly: You plan for it. Some student struggles will arise unexpectedly, though most fall into the categories we just explained—which makes them predictable. So, too, can be your responses to addressing a leaky pipe in your classroom. Intentionally preparing learning activities that cover the learning progression in the first place will solve many of your students' learning needs; this is a function of reliable, consistent, intentional core instructional practice.

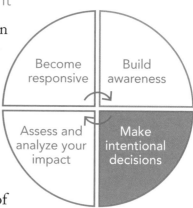

Having an array of assessment strategies that helps you to identify where students' learning breaks down, then, leads you to needing a tool belt full of intervention approaches, alt-teaching strategies (*teaching in a slightly different—alternative—manner; if they didn't get it the first time, why try it again the same way?*), and touch-up tactics. The tools on the following pages—"Direct Links" and "Break it Down"—will help you reflect more deeply on what might be happening when students appear to be struggling to master new knowledge and skills. As you implement these tools, you'll find it important to observe their impact on student learning, which is, after all, the essence of the *connected* phase of this pathway.

Direct Links

Why do it: When we make student thinking visible through formative assessments, we get a window into what students understand, as well as how they are understanding it. What follows is our instructional decision-making based upon the information we've gleaned. This response is what catapults us from *learning to teach to learning to teach well*.

How to do it: Choose three students who showed evidence of struggle on recent formative assessments. With their assessments in front of you, use the frame below to guide your thinking. Ask yourself these questions and connect what you know about the students' thinking and learning to your instructional decisions. The big question here is: *How might I shift my practice to address the learning needs I see through this assessment?*

Focus on Student Learning	Focus on Teacher Practice
Based on the evidence of thinking in front of me, what does this student know?	What instructional decisions did I make that led to this learning?
Where is his/her thinking breaking down?	How was this concept addressed in previous lessons? Can I identify any reason why there was this breakdown in student thinking?
What misconceptions might be operating?	Did I address these misconceptions in the previous lesson? How might I (re)address the misconception tomorrow to bring clarity? Is this something that needs to be clarified/retaught to the whole class, small group, or individually?

Focus on Student Learning	Focus on Teacher Practice
What is this student's next step in both thinking and learning? What needs to be addressed next?	What type of specific feedback does this student need to develop their thinking? (See chapter 6, "Motivating with feedback.")
Does this student need intensive instruction in a small group or one-on-one setting to address the learning needs I see?	How will I adjust my lesson plans or utilize other resources to provide this student with the intensive instruction they need?
In what type of environment/setting does this student do their best thinking? Whole class, small group, paired, individually? Are there any behavioral issues that impede learning?	How will tomorrow's lesson be different based upon the information I've gathered here? How will I adjust my instruction with this student in mind?

When to do it: This thinking guide is a powerful tool to help us begin to make connections between student learning and teacher practice. Use it after collecting formative assessment information to guide your next decisions.

While doing it: Notice what happens when you make changes in your practice based upon a specific student learning need. Document the changes in student thinking and learning that you begin to observe.

Break it Down (When Learning Breaks Down)

Why do it: Let's be real. There are times when our best intentions fall short and the learning process breaks down. In these moments, it's important to remain in "assessment mode" and continue to seek to understand and make sense of individual student needs to make the best instructional decisions possible.

How to do it: Use this chart to identify the six phases of learning (also reflected in *Master the Model* on p. 88), and common pitfalls. The ideas depicted below are intended to provide a frame to guide our thinking in moments when it seems there is no hope for learning. This is not a comprehensive list, but a place to start.

Phase of learning	How learning can break down	Pathway of adjustment
Become interested	Students aren't emotionally ready to learn, so they fail to focus. Students remain disinterested in the topic at hand.	Provide emotional/ curiosity hooks into learning. Help students connect learning to their own lives.
Commit to learning	Students are unclear about what they're supposed to learn. Students don't see the purpose for their learning.	Provide students with success criteria. Encourage students to develop their own success criteria.
Focus on new knowledge	New learning remains vague or unclear. Students fail to actively engage (i.e., think about) their learning.	Provide more visualization of learning. Model the new practice. Use questions and allow students to work with partners to encourage active engagement.

Phase of learning	How learning can break down	Pathway of adjustment
Make sense of learning	Students become overwhelmed with/are unable to absorb new learning. Students fail to connect new knowledge to prior learning. Students are unable to see a big picture for their learning.	Chunk direct instruction into shorter segments. Provide more opportunities for processing. Encourage students to summarize what they've learned.
Practice and rehearse	Students fail to develop automaticity with new skills. Students develop misconceptions. Students develop only superficial understanding of new learning.	Give students massed practice, followed by distributed practice. Provide more frequent feedback on student practice opportunities. Provide students with more elaborative rehearsal opportunities.
Extend and apply	Students are unable to develop deep understanding of new learning. Students appear to master new skills or knowledge, but then it quickly fades.	Engage students in cognitively demanding learning tasks that require them to apply learning to new problems/creative tasks.

When to do it: There are times when formative assessment practices reveal a need for a whole new approach to learning.

While doing it: Ask yourself, "Is this working? Is this not working? How do I know?" This chart offers a pathway that will lead to new strategies and propel us from *learning to teach*, to learning to teach *well*.

Adapted from *Student Learning That Works* (Goodwin, 2018). © McREL.
Used with permission.

Assess and analyze your impact: Recognize the results of your actions

As you've focused your mental energy on ways to effectively engage students in cooperative groupings, you'll notice your attention turning to the direct impact of your efforts. So when you assess the impact of your actions, reflect on your guiding question for this phase: *How do I use assessments to adjust teaching and learning if students don't get it?*

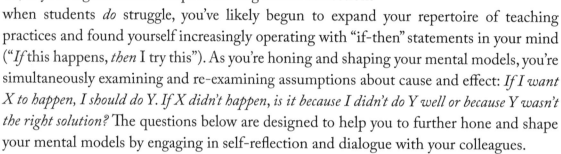

Students will struggle with their learning—that's predictable, and it's a healthy part of the learning process. So, as you've grown more adept at making course corrections when students *do* struggle, you've likely begun to expand your repertoire of teaching practices and found yourself increasingly operating with "if-then" statements in your mind ("*If* this happens, *then* I try this"). As you're honing and shaping your mental models, you're simultaneously examining and re-examining assumptions about cause and effect: *If I want X to happen, I should do Y. If X didn't happen, is it because I didn't do Y well or because Y wasn't the right solution?* The questions below are designed to help you to further hone and shape your mental models by engaging in self-reflection and dialogue with your colleagues.

Reflect on Teaching	Reflect on Learning
• What adjustments in your teaching have you made in the last week? Why did you make those changes?	• When you first notice a student struggling, when and how do you make the connection to how you taught the concept?
• What formative assessment data did you use to make a recent instructional adaptation?	• When you alt-teach a concept, procedure, or lesson, how do your students respond?
• How do you plan to assess your students to identify their pressing learning needs?	• How do you use what you know about your students as learners to build interventions and address learning gaps?
• How do you weave the six phases of learning (from the "Break it Down" strategy) into your lesson plans? What about your intervention plans? Your 1:1 conferences with students?	• When you use the six phases of learning to address students' learning needs, are there strategies that tend to yield better results than others? Are students more responsive to some approaches than others? Why is that?

Become responsive: Respond to the needs you see

OK, let's catch our breath for a minute. But only for a minute. So far we've unpacked the concept of formative assessment being a helpful element for learning. And we've seen the power of formative assessment in the classroom (Wiliam, 2007)—so you're right in your new thinking, *I should be assessing my students' learning often*. Picking up a couple of formative assessment tools helped to clarify that assessment and testing aren't the same thing, and you needn't wait for a test to gauge how your students are doing; in fact, you've learned that clever,

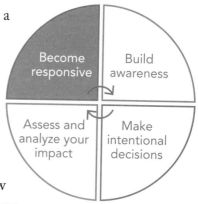

intentional assessments are an intricate and essential part of the learning process. And you're gaining so much knowledge about your students as learners! A mistake or a confused look used to make you wring your hands, and now you see them as goldmines of information! That was the question that prompted this investigation, right? *How do I use assessments to adjust teaching and learning if students don't get it?* Here are some questions you might ask yourself—and your colleagues—to reflect on what's improved for you and your students and what steps to take next.

- ❖ Even after you've taught a lesson brilliantly, you should expect that some students will struggle. How do you predict what the struggles will be? What might you do to change the outcomes?

- ❖ What is your process for continuing to unpack students' struggles to find the root cause? How do you know if its origins are teaching-related, learning-related, or somehow a blend of both?

- ❖ When students struggle and you provide an alt-teaching opportunity or a redo, and students continue to struggle, what is your next step? How many rounds of interventions are you prepared to attempt?

Even with these refinements, you're likely to find that everything's far from perfect in your classroom, though. No worries, that's the case for all of us. And even as you're beginning to understand and implement savvy assessment strategies, some new problems may emerge. For example, you may wonder why some students respond to various interventions and others don't. Or why some students respond well to interventions one time but not every time. If so, you may want to turn to the next page, where we explore the question, *How do I use assessments to make thinking visible and encourage critical thinking?*

Or, if you find yourself with another nagging question, turn to the grid on p. 16, find that question, and turn to the page where we help you address it.

How do I use assessments to make thinking visible and encourage critical thinking?

Be consistent *Teacher-owned Student-experienced*	Be connected *Teacher-directed, Student-connected*	**Differentiate** *Student-engaged, Teacher-facilitated*	Empower *Student-owned, Teacher-guided*

Welcome to the third phase of the "Assessing for learning" pathway. Here, you'll take what you've learned in the first two phases and apply it with greater precision in your interactions with students to help them develop critical thinking skills—their own individual, original thinking. This approach reflects an important mental shift that happens as you move into the *differentiate* phase of your teaching—on this and every other pathway—as you seek to make your classroom *student-engaged* and *teacher-facilitated*. You'll be considering individual students and their learning needs, building assessments that capture and build students' critical thinking skills. Basically, you're ready to explore assessing not just learning, but thinking.

If you're joining us from another pathway, welcome! Before diving headlong into this challenge, though, we suggest you review the previous phase of this pathway to get your bearings.

Build Awareness: Zoom in on the details

How do I use assessments to make thinking visible and encourage critical thinking? As you've become more precise with your ability to assess learning and have begun to adjust your teaching practices to help students "get it," two new challenges have emerged.

First, you've found yourself increasingly able to pinpoint *what* students know and don't know, but not always *why* they don't know it—or what's gone missing from or gotten tangled up in their learning. In short, you find yourself wishing you could "listen in" to their thinking to hear what might be happening.

Second, as you've developed better assessments that go beyond simply measuring students' ability to recall knowledge and apply rote skills, you're increasingly wondering how to encourage their deeper thinking, especially as you've noticed students often view assessments as the be-all-end-all of learning. For many students, if it's not on the test, they don't much care to learn it. So, how can you provide assessments that both facilitate and measure critical thinking skills?

As we've already noted (and you've likely observed), selected-response tests (such as multiple choice) often reveal little about students' thought processes or misconceptions.

You've likely already begun to use assessments, both formative and summative, that make student thinking visible, revealing what your students have learned and have yet to learn. As you move through this phase, you'll further refine your skills in these areas, developing new and improved ways to make individual students' thinking even more visible. Let's start with the fundamental challenge: Student thinking happens where we cannot see it—inside their brains. So, as teachers we must devise ways to help students express their thinking—which itself is often a frightening prospect for students.

Here are a few big ideas we can draw from research about what it takes to make student thinking visible in the classroom (Ritchhart, Church, & Morrison, 2011). For starters, if we want to see what students are thinking, we must provide them with opportunities to *think* in the classroom—not to simply *do* something (like an activity).

So, what exactly do we mean by thinking? One helpful list comes from observations of thousands of students (Ritchhart, Palmer, Church, & Tishman, 2006) that identified eight key types of student thinking in the classroom:

1. Observing closely and describing what's there.
2. Building explanations and interpretations.
3. Reasoning with evidence.
4. Making connections.
5. Considering different viewpoints and perspectives.
6. Capturing the heart and forming conclusions.
7. Wondering and asking questions.
8. Uncovering complexity and going below the surface of things.

The researchers observed that students of all ages could apply and demonstrate these thinking skills and recommend that teachers provide direct instruction and show students how to engage in all of them. Moreover, teachers can design checks for understanding around them and also use them as the basis for providing students with a deeper, more robust form of assessment that encourages them to think deeply about new learning and make their thinking visible. In other words, a performance assessment.

For some, encouraging students to engage in thinking tasks and encouraging them to share their thinking may sound like common sense; yet common sense isn't always that common. Often, students engage in tasks that require very little reflection, puzzling through, mulling over, or wondering about what they're learning. It's not uncommon, for example, during a task such as "make a collage about spiders" to see students thinking more about finding, cutting, and pasting pictures of spiders than conjuring thoughts about spiders themselves! So, for every task we assign, we should think about what we want students to think about—which in turn ought to reflect the kind of critical thinking that occurs in the respective content area (for example, what type of thinking do scientists employ?).

Consider what kind of thinking these various subject areas require:

- ❖ Science: Making and testing hypotheses, conducting close observations, and supporting reasoning with evidence.

- ❖ Mathematics: Looking for patterns and engaging in logical reasoning.

- ❖ Social studies: Considering different perspectives, supporting reasoning with evidence, uncovering complexity, and going beyond surface explanations.

- ❖ Writing: Considering different viewpoints and perspectives, capturing the heart, and drawing conclusions.

Shifting the focus of our assessments—particularly formative assessments—toward student thinking tends to have profound implications for the learning environment you create for your class. Increasingly, you'll be encouraging individual thinking and helping students find their own meaning in what they're learning. As you make this shift, you'll likely find students becoming more actively engaged in their learning.

Make intentional decisions: Develop a clear vision

Yes, we understand what we've asked you to do: Make the invisible *visible*. Clearly, there is no end to the roles teachers play: educator, mentor, coach, nurse, therapist, chauffeur, chef, cheerleader, and even magician. However, there's no sleight of hand at play here. Instead, you're going to wrestle with ideas, ruminate over options, strategize with colleagues, and reflect on the utility of a couple of approaches to accomplish that complex—yet very reachable—goal. As with the other pathways, at this phase our guidance will be a little less prescriptive and a little more 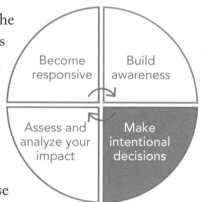 cerebral. That's because at this phase on the pathway, your professional practice is increasingly reflecting your development of expert mental models of if-then responses (*If I see students doing or needing X, then I do Y*). And you're connecting it all back to the goals you're trying to accomplish for yourself and your students: to provide just-right interventions that provide course corrections for students based on their thinking at the *differentiated* level. The two tools that follow, "Claim-Support-Question" and "3-2-1 Bridge" (adapted from Ritchhart, Church, & Morrison, 2011) should demystify this process for you.

Claim-Support-Question

Why do it: Teachers and students come across declarations of fact (claims) all the time. This tool leads students to develop a valuable pattern of thinking aloud and provides a structure for the examination of their ideas by the teacher. It can be used in multiple ways: as a tool to generate new understanding and teach critical thinking skills, as a tool to make student thinking visible, and as a tool to formatively assess learning.

How to do it:

Step 1: Set up.

- The idea of a claim is introduced to the class. It encompasses conjecture, speculation, generalization, assertion, statement of fact, theory, etc. Present a situation and tell the class the goal is to figure out "What's going on here?"

Step 2: Identify claims.

- Ask your students, "What claims, explanations, or interpretations might you have already on this topic?" Or, "Now that we've been studying this topic for some time, what claims can you come up with that offer us an explanation of our topic?" However they are generated, write the claims on chart paper for the class to see.

Step 3: Identify support.

- Ask students, "Now that we have these claims to consider, what can we see, notice, know, or find that might give support to them?" Students might be encouraged to draw on previous knowledge. Have students articulate supporting evidence for each claim. This should be written on chart paper as well. This step is really about asking students to consider the reasons why anyone might stand behind a given claim.

Step 4: Raise questions.

- In this step, a teacher asks students to be skeptics of the claims. Invite students to think beyond the support already articulated and consider what might make one hesitant about the accuracy or truth of it. "Now that we've given some support for these claims, is there opposing evidence? What questions do we need to raise about these claims to closely examine their credibility?" Write questions on chart paper and post to the opposite side of the claims as the support statements.

Step 5: Share the thinking.

- Documenting the routine as it evolves makes student thinking visible throughout the process and allows students to build on one another's thinking. Ask students to rank the claims from "still questioning" to "definitely believe."

When to do it: This tool provides a structure for examining and analyzing ideas. It is not meant to get students to all agree or disagree about a topic. It is not a tool to teach "one right way" of thinking. If students suspect this is about right and wrong answers, they will find the routine pointless. Use this strategy often to make thinking visible.

While doing it: Notice how often and in what contexts students are spotting and making claims. Do they recognize when claims lack support? Do they look for generalizations? These are indicators that they are processing information analytically.

Adapted from *Making Thinking Visible* (Ritchhart, Church, and Morrison, 2011). © Wiley. Used with permission.

3-2-1 Bridge

Why do it: The purpose of this tool is to help learners recognize and name their own learning and development. This strategy develops students' ability to step back and examine their thinking and learning. It focuses on the associations one has around a topic, linking prior knowledge, questions, and thoughts to help students understand themselves as learners. It provides a way for teachers to understand student thinking.

How to do it:

1. **Set it up.** Decide how you will have students record their response. Students will need to come back to their initial 3-2-1 after an extended period of time. You'll want to make sure they don't lose their responses.

2. **Ask for three words.** Ask students to generate three words that quickly come to mind when they think of the topic. This isn't a test. You are interested in their associations with this topic.

3. **Ask for two questions.** Ask students to generate two questions that quickly come to mind when they think of the topic. You are interested in uncovering their initial, surface ideas at this point.

4. **Ask for one metaphor or simile.** Ask the students to create a metaphor or simile for this topic.

5. **Provide an instructional period.** This may be a video, text, image, story, or experiment that conveys new information. There is no time limit. You may spend the next week on this.

6. **Perform the second 3-2-1.** Repeat steps 2–4 above. This time, ask students to select words, questions, and metaphors prompted or used in the instruction.

7. **Bridge the thinking.** Invite learners to share with partners both the initial and new responses. In sharing, partners should discuss what they noticed about their thinking on the topic. They should identify where their thinking shifted or where changes have taken place. Capture these shifts and elaborate on them through class discussion.

When to do it: This activity is a great frame for making thinking visible throughout a lesson. Use it as often as you see fit. The more frequently it is used, the more changes in critical thinking you will see with your students.

While doing it: Refrain from using this tool as a test or otherwise graded assessment. Notice the emphasis on making thinking visible and guiding students to understand themselves as learners.

Adapted from *Making Thinking Visible* (Ritchhart, Church, and Morrison, 2011). © Wiley. Used with permission.

Assess and analyze your impact: Transfer the vision

At this point in your journey, you're really thinking like an expert, relying on your knowledge of effective assessment strategies to help students understand their place in the learning journey. As this becomes clearer, you're beginning to pair feedback with your goal of encouraging deep learning and transferable academic skills within each of your students. And now, as you assess and analyze the impact of your actions up to this point, we remind you to keep your guiding question in mind: *How do I use assessments to make thinking visible and encourage critical thinking?*

You're also weaving together many big ideas and complex techniques, so it's likely to be messy, especially at first. Time to practice what you preach and link your own assessments to your own critical-thinking goals! As you well know, experts don't go it alone; indeed, they consult with one another to diagnose and solve problems. With a "critical friend," use the following reflective questions (and then create your own to add to the list) to help you to develop your expert mental models and challenge each other's thinking:

Reflect on Teaching	Reflect on Learning
• What's the difference between assessment of learning and assessment of thinking? • How do you know what questions to ask students that will elicit their best, deepest thinking? • How do your students respond to prompts that are designed to inspire divergent thinking and defensible arguments, rather than fishing for correct answers?	• When you ask for it, how confidently are students making the transition from correct-answer to visible-thinking displays? How does this confidence vary from student to student? • What parts of this process do students struggle with the most? Why do you think so? What can you do to help them move forward? • As you increase the open-endedness of your questions and offer more cognitively demanding tasks, what are you noticing about levels of student engagement, mastery of standards, and other measures of student learning? • What misconceptions (about your topic, the learning goals, standards, etc.) are you noticing that students display, and how might you address them?

Become responsive: Respond in the moment

The third phase in this pathway marks a seismic shift in your thinking, as well as your actions. As you've pursued the question that launched this pathway—*How do I use assessments to make thinking visible and encourage critical thinking?*—you're likely transitioning from a) simply measuring students' mastery of standards, to b) assessing to gauge where they currently sit on the learning trajectory, and then to c) providing interventions to attempt to corral students back into learning, and now to d) using powerful cognitive strategies that engage your students and encourage them to share their thinking. This allows you to take steps to further support their learning at the individual student level. Hopefully, you've begun to see new student behaviors taking root, like their delightfully surprising ability to articulate their own ideas and perspectives and engage in reflective learning. You may have observed some new behaviors and thinking taking hold in yourself, including new insights into what students are thinking, which is particularly helpful in designing learning interventions. Still, you likely have room to grow—ways to make your developed practices even more powerful and engaging. Take a moment and reflect on your professional growth from the beginning of this pathway until now, and challenge yourself (and a trusted colleague, instructional coach, or administrator) with a few bonus reflective questions:

❖ Are your students becoming more capable of (and willing to) engage in exercises that open their thinking up to observation, scrutiny, and challenge? How can you continue to encourage them to do so?

❖ To what extent are you using your awareness of individual students' thinking to intervene to support their learning? How are you leveraging your students' visible learning into deeper learning outcomes?

❖ How often do you respond immediately—in the moment—when you hear student thinking that illustrates a misconception or an error in processing? How do you respond? How can you increase your response time (when timeliness matters)?

Individualizing your attention to detail has now led you to help students to reveal their thinking in an exquisitely magical (think Disney, not Copperfield) way. And yet . . . new challenges keep finding their way into your master plan. Remember: This is a journey with no real finish line—simply the pursuit of improvement: your own teaching and your students' learning. As you strengthen that reflective muscle and improve your assessment practices, you may find yourself scurrying about the classroom attempting to intervene with every misconception at a deeply differentiated level. By now, your students should be able to engage in some of this rigorous metacognitive reflection on their own, right? If that's what's on your mind, you may wish to turn to the next page to consider, *How do I help students self-assess and guide their own learning?*

 Or, if you find yourself with another nagging question, turn to the grid on p. 16, find that question, and turn to the page where we help you address it.

How do I help students self-assess and guide their own learning?

| Be consistent
*Teacher-owned,
Student-experienced* | Be connected
*Teacher-directed,
Student-connected* | Differentiate
*Student-engaged,
Teacher-facilitated* | **Empower**
*Student-owned,
Teacher-guided* |

Welcome to the fourth phase of the "Assessing for learning" pathway. Here, you'll begin to *empower* students to utilize self-assessments in a *student-owned, teacher-guided* environment. This is no subtle shift, either. Building your students' capacity to guide their own learning journeys requires steady, significant development of your own capacity—both as a master of the technical elements of teaching and as a reflective practitioner. Getting to this point requires building on the foundation of everything you've learned, the acute awareness you've built, the many steps you've taken with great intentionality, and your ability to gauge your impact and make midcourse corrections as necessary.

> If you're joining us from another pathway, we encourage you to review the previous three phases in this pathway to ensure you're ready to address this challenge.

Build awareness: Bring the variables together

How do I help students self-assess and guide their own learning? As your practices have become more sophisticated and you've begun to encourage students to engage in more critical thinking, you've seen them become increasingly engaged in their own learning, asking good questions in the classroom, and becoming more comfortable with making their thinking visible. At this point, you may find yourself wondering what it would take for them to go one step further, discovering what may feel like the holy grail of schooling: becoming self-directed learners. After all, studies of college students reveal that grades and college entrance exams predict less than one-third of their success; what appears to matter more is their ability to set goals, keep themselves focused on learning, and actively engage in their classes (Goodwin & Hein, 2016). So, if we send students out into the world without the ability to self-assess and direct their own learning, they're apt to struggle; it's perhaps no surprise that 40 percent of students who enroll in college fail to graduate.

So, what can we do as teachers to help students learn how to become *learners*—self-assessing their progress and adjusting their learning to ensure mastery?

Here are a few key ideas from research:

- ❖ **Give students rubrics and show them how to use them.** Contrary to what you might think, rubrics do not necessarily make teachers better or more consistent graders (Jonsson & Svingby, 2007). However, they've been shown to dramatically raise student performance—by as much as a full letter grade (Howell, 2011). How? By making teachers' expectations for learning explicit, rubrics help students assess themselves, become more receptive to feedback, and feel more motivated to learn, which has led researchers to conclude that the most important reason for using rubrics in the classroom may simply be to let students "know why they are doing what they are doing" (Jonsson & Svingby, 2007, p. 139).

- ❖ **Encourage self-questioning.** Research shows that teaching learners to tame and focus the voice in their heads can make the difference between their success and failure. Guiding students to ask themselves questions that address comparison-contrast, causal-relationship, analysis, and meta-cognitive processing often leads to increased comprehension and retention (King, 1991; Wanzek, Wexler, Vaughn, & Ciullo, 2010). In fact, in its review of hundreds of studies on reading comprehension, the National Reading Panel (U.S. Department of Health and Human Services, 2000) called out student self-questioning (teaching students "to be aware of their understanding of the material" and "ask themselves questions about the various aspects of the story") to be among the seven most effective strategies to emerge from decades of research on reading comprehension strategies (p. 15). Not only can self-questioning strategies be taught fairly quickly (in about 90 minutes), students appear to internalize them, creating a virtuous circle in which they begin to see themselves as better learners, creating a little voice in their head that says, *I can do this.*

- ❖ **Support a mastery orientation.** Students often view grades (i.e., getting an A or passing a class) as the goal of learning, rather than, well, learning itself. Such a mindset, notes Stanford University psychologist Carol Dweck, reflects a performance orientation—a common affliction among students which can prevent them from seeing assessments as part of the learning process. Often, they tend to fixate on performance goals, which are all about, in Dweck's words, wanting "to look smart (to themselves or others) and avoid looking dumb" (Dweck, 2000, p. 15). Such an orientation makes it difficult for students to self-assess their progress accurately or engage in productive self-talk when they fall short of their goals. If we want students to see assessments as part of the learning process, we need to help them develop a mastery orientation, which, Dweck notes, reflects "a desire to learn new skills, master new tasks, or understand new things—a desire to get smarter" (Dweck, 2000, p. 15). While a performance orientation says, *I want to get an A on my persuasive essay*, a mastery orientation says, *I want to write more persuasively*. In a 1988 study,

Dweck and a colleague found, in fact, that students with a performance orientation are more apt to feel helpless, condemn their own abilities, and give up in the face of challenge (Elliott & Dweck, 1988). On the other hand, those with a mastery orientation worry less about looking dumb, take initial frustrations or setbacks in stride, and are more apt to learn from feedback. In short, they're more apt to self-assess their learning.

❖ **Provide opportunities for relearning.** Finally, if we want to empower students to self-assess and self-correct their learning, we need to give them opportunities to relearn—to for example, redo an assignment based upon teacher feedback or to restudy and retake a test. Nonetheless, teachers (and parents) may be reluctant to embrace such measures because they fear students won't apply themselves the first time around if they know they'll get a second chance. They may argue that the real world doesn't provide second chances, so why should schools? Here are a few things to consider. For starters, outside of school, students often can retake assessments—including drivers' license tests and college entrance exams. In the business world, product designers often create so-called "minimally viable products" to test and improve. Moreover, research going back decades shows by forcing us to recall information, testing actually enhances knowledge retention (Roediger & Pyc, 2012). So, if we really want students to learn something, why not test them on it—many times—on low-stakes tests that help them identify gaps in their knowledge? We might call such tests quizzes. Some teachers balance concerns about promoting student laziness or lack of preparation by asking them to complete a request to retake a test, which identifies what they'll do differently to better prepare themselves. The point here, though, is really to help students see assessment as a means, not the end, of the learning process.

Make intentional decisions: Move beyond strategy to design

So, how do you bring all of these ideas together in your classroom? The ability to do this—both consistently and consistently *well*—is often referred to as the art of teaching. You're way past the focus on *what* you are going to do to address this challenge; indeed, you're now thinking about *how* all of these strategies and approaches blend together to create an assessment design. *Empowering* students in such a classroom environment does not happen by accident, and it's no coincidence that your growth as a reflective practitioner has accompanied—in fact preceded—this shift in practice.

Because of the complexity and uniqueness of your situation (no one has ever faced exactly what you're facing before, with exactly the students you have), you're in uncharted territory, as it were. How cool is that? But it also means there's no step-by-step guide that we (nor anyone) can offer. Instead, we can offer guiding principles designed to support students' metacognition (thinking about their own learning) and help them become increasingly independent in self-assessing and self-correcting their learning. The following two tools—"Student-Centered Rubrics" and "Redos & Retakes"—can help you to continue this journey with confidence.

Student-Centered Rubrics

Why do it: Rubrics have many possible uses, from making students aware of success criteria and supporting peer feedback to helping assess or grade a project. Most conversations surrounding rubrics revolve around types and creation. Yet design is not nearly as important as the way a rubric is utilized. Ask yourself, *Are the rubrics I use simply serving as a vehicle for me to assess student work, or are they a way to put students in control of their own learning and strengthen their critical thinking skills?*

How to do it: Select a rubric you currently use in your classroom. In addition to asking yourself the question above, also ask, *What purpose do you have in mind when you use your tool? How might you utilize it differently?* Read through the possible alternate uses below and identify ways you might shift to a more student-centered purpose.

Track learning growth through self-evaluation	Rubrics should lead students to understand and track their thinking and learning growth. Ask students to play an active role in their learning process by recording ongoing progress on rubrics. Note: We highly recommend the use of critical thinking rubrics for this purpose.
Develop criteria for self-evaluation	Asking students to create their own critical thinking rubric is a powerful way to reinforce those skills and teach students to evaluate their own thinking. These rubrics don't necessarily need to be content- or skill-centered. They should focus on the critical thinking skills that lead to learning. They are most successfully created in small groups where discussion and negotiations can take place as students dissect concepts and ideas for each dimension.
Creation of models	Knowing criteria on a rubric is important, but it is nowhere near as helpful as having a clear model. When students are asked to create a model for each dimension or column on the rubric, it not only provides support for all students, but it cements understanding of the type of learning the rubric describes.
Self-questioning	Self-questioning is one of the most effect strategies to teach critical thinking skills. Using your rubric, ask students to create questions that they might ask themselves to drive their thinking to the highest level on each part of the rubric.

When to do it: Our goal at this point in our learning is to shift from teacher-directed to student-centered instruction. Use this approach to support this shift.

While doing it: Notice student thinking. Where might it be breaking down? How can you support it with careful questioning and feedback?

Redos & Retakes—Let's Make Them Meaningful

Why do it: One of the simplest ways for students to respond to assessment feedback is to let them redo assignments, retake tests, or rewrite papers. Teachers may worry that if they provide opportunities for do-overs, students will stop working hard on their first attempt as they know they can improve the work later. As it turns out, though, research shows that students tend to learn more from correcting their own mistakes, and redoing their work actually tends to *increase* their motivation to do well.

How to do it: This is a strategy to use with assessment tools. Before diving in, consider the following steps from Wormeli (2011):

1. Ask students who redo assignments to submit the original attempt with the new one and to write a brief letter comparing the two. What is different and what did they learn as a result of redoing the work?

2. If the same student repeatedly asks for redos, something's wrong. The content is not developmentally appropriate, there are unseen issues at home, or perhaps there's an undiagnosed learning disability. Investigate. Ask the student questions about their struggles and seek to know more about their thinking.

3. Choose your battles. Push hard for students to redo anything associated with the most important curriculum standards and less so with work associated with less important standards.

4. Unless an assessment is complex and interwoven, allow students to redo just the portions on which they performed poorly, not the entire assessment.

5. Often, redos can be a brief interview at the teacher's desk while the rest of the class is engaged in an activity. Consider alternate ways for students to show that they've learned the material and/or mastered the standard: Think products, performances, and portfolios.

When to do it: Our goal with this tool is to help students self-assess and guide their own learning. Use this approach any time a student struggles to demonstrate learning through your primary assessment strategy.

While doing it: Notice the new learning that takes place during this process. What increases in learning do you see?

Assess and analyze the impact of your actions: Assess with purpose

At this phase in the pathway, you're using your deep knowledge and skills to help students take ownership of their learning journeys. Some may observe your assessment practices and consider such *empowerment* in your classroom to be innovative and creative divergence. As a committed, reflective practitioner, you're well aware that you've reached a place in your professional development that is only possible because of your consistent, intentional focus on growing, learning, gauging, and tinkering with your practices to better meet individual students' needs. You know the most important part of any classroom isn't what you're doing as a teacher, but rather, what's going on in students' minds; thus, you want to design assessment experiences that add real value to student learning—helping them to learn and do things together they couldn't do independently. Your initial question is truly guiding your inquiry: *How do I help students self-assess and guide their own learning?* Do the assessment techniques you've designed for students support deep learning? With that in mind, gather some colleagues, administrators, coaches, and your teammates and lead a discussion based on the following questions (and feel free to add your own):

Reflect on Teaching	Reflect on Learning
• How do you use rubrics? Are there times where you incorporate them for different reasons? Why? • What is your philosophy on redos and retakes? When might they be appropriate? When might they not? How might you explore this big idea with colleagues to generate some sort of consensus for your systemic practice? • How do you remind yourself to consistently encourage students to show their thinking and self-assess their work, rather than look to you to grade or evaluate it?	• How do students' demonstrations of learning change when they have access to clear rubrics that describe levels of performance? • When students opt for a redo, what do you notice? How does their learning change? What new learning occurs during this process? • How often do students' self-assessments match your assessments of their performance? When they don't match, why not?

Become responsive: Trust your intuition

Did you ever think that a chapter on assessments would end up including information about students analyzing their own performance against clear rubrics, monitoring their own metacognitive processes, and self-correcting as needed, using various redo and retake options? It's not all about teaching to the test, Scantron forms, and writing *distractors* in multiple-choice exams. Yet here we are, and here *you* are, guiding your students along the path of self-discovery, curiosity, and innovation. And since this path has no ending point, you're probably already considering ways to continue to expand, deepen, and refine your impact on your students, your colleagues, and your profession. That's just what highly reflective practitioners do. Trust your inner voice. At this point, your reflective capacity has developed to a point where you're attuned to your students' needs and how to address them, both in the moment and from a grander perspective. And if you'd like to couple your inner voice with that of your trusted colleagues, we invite you to reflect on the following questions together, challenging each other's thinking to continue to refine your practice:

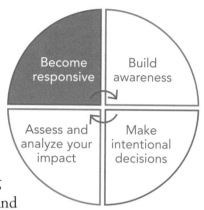

- ❖ What is assessment for, anyway? How can you ensure that the form (the tool, quiz, performance, etc.) matches the function (purpose, outcome, etc.)?

- ❖ How will you know if your students have truly internalized their learning journeys? What will you look for? Listen for? Ask?

- ❖ When the assessment results do not match your expectations, how do you determine which course-correction approach to take? How can you possibly plan for all the misconceptions, errors, and unidentified learning needs that students might display?

You're probably wishing there were more phases in this pathway, right? Well, we agree, and we want to acknowledge a couple of realities: First, you've really grown as a thinker and a practitioner as you've built assessment approaches that directly relate to student motivation and achievement. Second, though you've progressed through this chapter, there really is no end to this work. You can always grow, you can always improve, and you can always learn and refine your approaches. Yes, there's a lot to celebrate, and yes, there's still a lot on the horizon.

Final thoughts on assessing for learning

As you've come to the end of the "Assessing for learning" pathway, it's important to take stock of your journey, appreciate the phases you've mastered, and note the growth you've made. In short, this is a wonderful time to appraise your professional development.

First, let's look at the pathway from the 10,000-foot level:

Be consistent *Teacher-owned, Student-experienced*	Be connected *Teacher-directed, Student-connected*	Differentiate *Student-engaged, Teacher-facilitated*	Empower *Student-owned, Teacher-guided*

You've made significant strides in transforming your classroom from one that's inherently *teacher-owned* (and student-experienced) to one that is becoming more *student-owned* (and teacher-guided). Through a systematic process of identifying key questions that either confound or interest you (or both), you've investigated and addressed four critical problems of practice all related to the "Assessing for learning" pathway. Along the way, you repeated a very predictable, very deliberate pattern of reflective steps that a) built your self-reflective capacity and b) enhanced your professional acumen. That pattern, the Reflective Cycle, really ought to be second nature to you by now:

- ❖ Build awareness about the problem of practice by asking key questions and conducting research to learn more.

- ❖ Make intentional decisions about implementing strategies, based on the research and your desired goal.

- ❖ Assess and analyze the impact of your actions to determine the effectiveness of particular strategies over a period of time.

- ❖ Become responsive to the changing needs you notice in order to better meet your (and, more specifically, your *students'*) needs.

- ❖ Repeat, repeat, repeat, and repeat again and again and again.

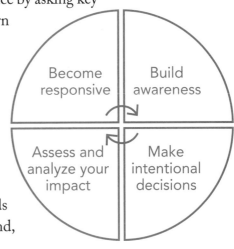

Remember the Theory of Action that drives this combination of approaches:

Theory of Action	IF we start with key problems of practice, use research-based best practices to solve them, and reflect on our practice as teachers, THEN we will become more expert in our practice, better able to meet our students' needs, and engaged in career-long professional growth that will allow us to become amazing, unstoppable teachers in whose classrooms learning will flourish.

Though you've come to the end of this particular pathway, you're far too astute to believe the journey is over. Learning is cyclical—a progression that leads you ever upwards, not unlike a spiral staircase—and you realize there will be times that you need to backtrack, regroup, and revisit some of the foundational elements of this pathway to solidify and enhance your effectiveness. And of course there's more yet to learn, different approaches to implement, and all sorts of new ways of looking at—and solving—your newfound problems of practice. Indeed, the growth you've made is more than just about building a sturdy assessment plan; in addition, you're becoming masterful at the art of growing as a reflective practitioner and transferring your learning into the classroom.

And as you've certainly noticed, utilizing assessments as a tactical learning strategy is just part of a robust, powerful, successful schooling experience for students. Now your task is to weave the other refinement pathways into your work in a seamless expression of excellence, ensuring that all students thrive and flourish.

Or, if you find yourself with another nagging question, turn to the grid on p. 16, find that question, and turn to the page where we help you address it.

Chapter 8
Creating dynamic group learning

We've all been there: at our wit's end with a class of unruly students. Even experienced teachers can find themselves watching in dismay as a classroom slips away from them. Sometimes it might just be a student or two, or for a lesson, or a day or two. But at other times, it may feel more chronic with disruptive behavior begetting more bad behavior, spreading around a classroom, and turning what had been a group of focused, cooperative students into something verging on anarchy.

So, we begin this pathway with something that can leave teachers feeling they've reached the end of their rope: off-task, distractible, unfocused, or even oppositional student behavior. If you've flipped to these pages in desperate need of a lifeline, take heart. You're not alone, and you've come to the right place. As you follow this pathway, you'll learn tried-and-true strategies for redirecting students away from off-task behavior and into productive learning.

Once you've mastered that, we'll help you go a step further: creating classrooms where students work together productively. Yes, we know that for many teachers, the very thought of group work may turn your stomach. Perhaps it brings back memories of your own school days when so-called cooperative learning often devolved into one or two kids doing all the work while the others slacked off and freeloaded from more conscientious students. And you were probably that kid doing all the work. So, we understand if you have misgivings about group work. Not to worry. On this pathway, you'll also learn how to ensure group work in your classroom is actually productive, collaborative, and cooperative—and not one kid doing everyone else's work for them.

Ultimately, this pathway will lead you to an exciting place: a classroom where your students are not only attentive and working well together, but also learning with and from one another, unleashing their creativity and curiosity. We know that depending on your perspective, such talk may sound hopelessly far-fetched or even utopian. Yet believe it or not, there are classrooms where that happens. We know, because we've been in them and seen them—in all kinds of schools. So, trust us. After you've worked through all four phases of this pathway, the notion of a classroom where students stay focused on helping one another learn won't seem hopelessly idealistic, but rather, entirely realistic—as it will be happening in your classroom.

Take charge of your own professional growth

To help you consider how to support students working together effectively and in a way that fuels their curiosity and leads to deep learning, we'll start with *your own curiosity*—questions you're likely to ask about your classroom. You may have found yourself asking one (or all) of the questions below. To help you meet your pressing needs and address your current problem of practice, we've placed a page number next to each so you can flip ahead and engage in some self-guided exploration:

- ❖ How do I manage unwanted behavior so students can learn? (p. 183)
- ❖ How do I get students to participate actively in group work? (p. 190)
- ❖ How do I match cooperative groups to individual needs? (p. 197)
- ❖ How do I create opportunities for students to support one another in deep learning? (p. 205)

How do I manage unwanted behavior so students can learn?

Be consistent *Teacher-owned, Student-experienced*	Be connected *Teacher-directed, Student-connected*	Differentiate *Student-engaged, Teacher-facilitated*	Empower *Student-owned, Teacher-guided*

Welcome to the first phase of the "Creating dynamic group learning" pathway. Not surprisingly, the focus here is on your actions as a teacher: what you are doing, what is expected of you, and what it will take for you to be successful. This pattern of thinking is typical of the *teacher-owned, student-experienced* phase, and as you proceed through the Reflective Cycle and expand your reflective vision, you'll begin to become more *consistent* in your approaches, allowing you to better meet your students' needs.

Build awareness: Observe

Often, one of the most pressing problems for teachers is *How do I manage unwanted behavior so students can learn?* More bluntly, you may wonder: Why won't these kids pay attention/listen/stay focused? We know that teachers often suffer with this concern in private, beating themselves up because they feel that managing a classroom is something they ought to be able to do. It's embarrassing to admit we're struggling to rein in our students. We may feel that if we were to admit such a thing in the faculty lounge the room would suddenly fall into stunned silence with our colleagues staring at us in wide-eyed dismay. *S/he is losing control of her/his classroom! Oh, the horror!*

The reality, though, is that nearly every teacher struggles at some point with classroom management—especially newer teachers, who are more willing to admit it in anonymous surveys (Melnick & Meister, 2008). Despite their best efforts, many preservice programs do little to prepare us for the realities of classrooms, including how to deal with unruly students. As one first-year teacher confessed on a survey, "a bigger bag of classroom management tricks would have been helpful" (Fry, 2007, p. 225). You may even have heard that the key to managing behavior in your classroom is to create engaging, well-paced lessons—and student behavior will take care of itself. That's partly true: As you progress along the other pathways, you're likely to find students *are* more engaged and some previously observed behavior issues have begun to wane. Yet it's only partly true . . . and cold comfort if such advice makes us feel even more professionally inadequate.

So, let's acknowledge that sometimes students get off task. Sometimes they misbehave. Sometimes they're disrespectful. As it turns out, sometimes adults (including teachers) demonstrate the same behavior. So, why should we expect anything different of students?

Here's another news flash: Some students are just plain challenging. They may be easily distracted, oppositional, and try to draw others into off-task behavior. There's no formula. We're talking about humans here, ones that aren't fully matured yet—and by definition, they're going to be unpredictable and challenging to coordinate, to say the least.

So, now that we've called out the "elephant in the room"—that classroom management is a challenge—let's discuss what you can do about it.

Understand the cause of unwanted behaviors. One of the best things we can do when students demonstrate unwanted behaviors is to take a step back and ensure we do not take their misbehavior personally. Rather, as the adults in the room, we can consider what's triggering their behavior. Are they unclear or confused about what's expected? Could they be feeling frustrated or bored? Is the work too challenging or not challenging enough? Do they have unmet needs (physical, relational, control, emotional) that are affecting their ability to be learning-ready (Souers & Hall, 2018)? Considering what's happening when student behavior falls short of expectations can help us to not only keep our cool, but also figure out what actions to take to redirect the behavior (and avoid escalating it).

Plan every minute. Doing so ensures a lively pace, minimizing idle moments that can tempt students to get off-track. Also, as you may recall from the "Designing engaging learning" pathway, students' brains need little breaks to process new learning. So, if you find a classroom becoming unruly, you may need to build in some more of those little breaks for processing—with a variety of clearly defined opportunities for helping students make sense of their learning.

See student behavior infractions as learning opportunities. Years ago, while observing highly effective teachers in urban environments, Martin Haberman (1991) concluded that these "star" teachers tended to see student misbehavior not as distractions, but as teachable moments—opportunities to help students develop social-emotional skills like self-control, empathy, and goal-directedness by redirecting them to becoming better versions of themselves. One of the best ways to do that is by having clear expectations to point to—and pre-scripted responses for correcting and redirecting unwanted behavior.

Engage students in setting classroom rules. Why? Because when students "own" the rules, breaking them isn't defying the teacher, it's violating class norms. The more classroom rules are seen as group norms such as respecting each other, not wasting one another's time, and treating each other with kindness, the likelier students are to create positive peer pressure to stay on task and avoid distracting one another. Also, you'll be tapping into intrinsic motivation, which is more powerful than extrinsic rewards for shaping behavior. If your school has identified values or traits of positive behavior, you might start the conversation by asking students: What would these values look like in our classroom? You can also engage students in identifying the consequences of violating the norms. Finally, be sure to give students a way to return to the group (with an apology, for example) after they've violated the norms.

Focus on behavior, not personality. When students make a mistake, don't make it personal—for you or them. Pointing out the behavior—as distinct from a student's personality—gives students a way to leave it behind. For example, instead of hanging a negative trait on a student—"I wish you weren't so talkative/easily distracted/hyperactive/disrespectful/[fill in the blank]"—you can say something like, "You were disrespectful to your classmates today, which isn't like you." Because students are apt to live up (or down) to our expectations, it's important to let them know you expect—and anticipate—positive behavior. For example, you might let them know you see good things inside them, waiting to come out, by asking them, "What do you need to do to show us the best version of you?"

Catch students in the act of doing things right. Positive rewards are more powerful than negative ones. So, delivering quick praise and positive reinforcement for students who are on task ("I see five people ready to get to work!") can help to reinforce group norms. If you're going to provide rewards for positive behavior, you're apt to find this is best done at the group level. For younger students, you might, for example, fill a jar with marbles for good behavior and provide a reward (a Friday dance party) when the jar is full. For older students, you might simply, at the end of a lesson, reflect upon positive behaviors more anonymously ("I really appreciate how many times today I observed people engaged in active listening").

Be "with it." This means "filling" a classroom with your presence, by getting out from behind your desk and walking around the room and paying attention to what's going on. For example, if students are whispering or passing notes, stand near them. Also, hand gestures can be incredibly effective signaling for students to wait their turn, quiet down, or that you'll call on them next. They say teachers have eyes in the backs of their heads; even if you don't possess that particular physical trait, you can be so keen to your classroom's many goings-on that it may appear you do.

Make intentional decisions: Be deliberate in planning

We know that students will sometimes behave in a way contrary to our expectations, our norms, and/or our directions. In that light, we might say that unwanted behaviors are predictable. The best way to mitigate their effects is to plan for them. The Boy Scouts aren't the only ones who live by the mantra, "Be Prepared," after all. Use the two tools on the following pages: "Create Shared Classroom Agreements" and "5:1 Ratio." They will help you manage unwanted behavior in positive ways so that you can get students quickly back on task.

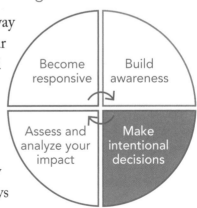

Create Shared Classroom Agreements

Why do it: Establishing a set of shared expectations and rules is an essential step in creating a positive classroom environment. It builds community and creates a culture of mutual respect and collaboration. This tool includes and relies on all students to participate in developing norms, and to maintain these agreements through peer accountability all year long. It reduces disruptive behavior.

How to do it: Start by posting a prompt such as, *What do we need as learners to grow and thrive together?* Next, create an agreement chart using the template below. We've provided a couple of examples. Note how the agreements are phrased in positive language: what we *want* to see rather than what we *don't* want to see.

Agreement	Meaning	Celebration (for students to praise peer behavior)	Prompts (for students to redirect peer behavior)
I am responsible for my own learning and for supporting the learning of others.	I am the boss of myself. I am expected to make wise choices and work and learn in a way that does not detract from the learning of others. I am expected to use my time wisely.	*"Thank you for sitting patiently at your seat while your group was putting away supplies."* *"Thank you for working next to me quietly so that I can concentrate on my learning."*	*"What is your responsibility as a learner right now?"* *"Would you please support our learning by staying on task during this assignment?"* *"What can we do to help you stay on task right now?"*
We are finished as soon as everyone understands and can explain their thinking.	We are collaborators. This means that we attend to the learning of everyone in our group. If I finish early, it is my responsibility to see how I can support the learning of my peers, not just help them finish their work.	*"Thank you for helping me process my thinking out loud. It helped me understand _____."* *"It was great to see _____ today working closely with _____ and supporting her understanding. She didn't just give her answers, she asked good questions to help her thinking."*	*"Would you be willing to come help me explain my thinking?"* *"We're not finished yet. Please support our learning."*

When to do it: Shared agreements should be created at the beginning of each year and revisited throughout. They should encourage students to celebrate and/or prompt one another during learning. Once this process and these skills have been taught, gradually release the students to carry it out with minimal teacher guidance/prompting.

While doing it: Notice the atmosphere of trust that develops when ownership is placed on students to create the norms of learning and accountability. The teacher only steps in when the prompts from peers aren't working.

5:1 Ratio

Why do it: Research supports the idea that there is a "critical ratio" of positive to negative interactions between students and teachers that best supports productive relationships. This tool builds teacher awareness of the type of interactions occurring with individual students and decreases classroom disruption as a result of a more positive classroom environment.

How to do it: The 5:1 Ratio is a practice in which teachers increase the number of positive interactions with a student as compared to negative interactions. Identify three students who exhibit unwanted behavior in your class.

For this tool to be most effective, you'll need to carefully and objectively track your interactions with these students. Our goal is to provide five positive interactions (praise, nonverbal acknowledgment, friendly conversation, etc.) to every negative interaction (criticism, negative comments, negative nonverbal acknowledgment, etc.) for each student. We're not just encouraging you to compliment students more, but to form positive relationships through various positive interactions. So grab a clipboard and a blank sheet of paper. During today's class, let's notice and tally each interaction with these targeted students.

Examples of positive interactions:

- Call students by name. And pronounce the names correctly!
- Express gratitude for understanding the human element. *Thank you for giving me a minute to check my lesson plans to make sure we get this right.*
- Take a moment to check in personally. *What did you do this weekend? How's your dog?*
- Inquire about an interest or hobby. *I saw the start of the Red Sox game last night. Who won?*
- Identify work habits. *You worked really hard on that one. That must feel good!*
- Appreciation togetherness. *I'm so grateful to have such wonderful, smiling students in my classroom!*
- Greet students positively. *Good morning! It's great to see you. Welcome back!*
- Smile, high-five, fist-bump, salute, or offer another friendly gesture.

When to do it: You'll want to pay special attention to students who are exhibiting disruptive behavior first. Then focus on those who are not disruptive to your classroom learning environment. We can learn from paying attention to our interactions with all students.

While doing it: Notice ongoing behavior as you implement the 5:1 Ratio tool. What shifts do you see? What do you notice about yourself as you engage students in this manner?

Assess and analyze your impact: Notice learning

At this point, you've likely had a few (or many) "aha" moments along the way and your thinking has begun to shift. So, let's pause a moment to notice a few important things that may have begun happening in your classroom. And remember the question you set out to answer at the beginning of this path: *How do I manage unwanted behavior so students can learn?* You may see some changes—if you look for them—as you've begun to apply tried-and-true strategies for managing your classroom

and redirecting student behavior in your classroom—both in terms of your actions as a teacher and your students' behavior in response. How has your teaching changed? How has student learning changed? Use the prompts below to guide your reflections about both.

Reflect on Teaching	Reflect on Learning
• What sorts of behaviors do you find most distracting and bothersome? Lead your class in a discussion to create a Shared Agreement about a positive alternative to that behavior.	• Once students cocreate the norms for the class, what do you notice about their behavior?
• When do students' unwanted behaviors occur? Collect some data about time of day, type of activity, subject matter, lesson design, and other factors. This information might help you address the behaviors as a class.	• When students' unwanted behaviors occur, how do their classmates respond? If you need to review the norms and possible ways to respond to peers, feel free to do so. Over time, reduce the frequency of your reviews. What do you notice now?
• Attempting five (or more) positives for each negative interaction with a student might be challenging. What do you notice about your students' behaviors when you go looking for the positives?	• How do your students respond to your positive interactions? Are you keeping up with the five (or more) positives for each negative?

Become responsive: Make changes

Analyzing the impact of the strategies you've just implemented likely yields robust data about your students' behaviors—both on task and off. As a reflective practitioner, you're becoming more aware of what's happening in your classroom, what you can do to alter the outcomes, and how this affects student learning. It's time to hone your focus even more, because let's face it: Having clear norms and emphasizing the

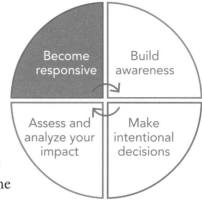

positives probably hasn't solved all your classroom management woes. So you've got to be prepared to adapt your approaches even more. But where?

Here are some questions that you might want to bring to a trusted colleague—a "critical friend" or an instructional coach or mentor—to reflect on what's improved and what your next steps might be:

- ❖ How consistently are you explicitly referring students back to their Shared Agreements?
- ❖ How consistently are you reinforcing students' positive, pro-social behaviors at a 5:1 ratio to negative, disruptive behaviors?
- ❖ What are some ways that you can remind yourself to stay the course, even when it seems like a lost cause?
- ❖ What are some ways that you can predict the behaviors that serve as emotional buttons for you, so you can have an intentional plan to respond professionally . . . and coolly let them slide off your back?

It's time to heed that ageless advice, "Look back to look ahead." The question you sought to answer at the beginning of this pathway was *How do I manage unwanted behavior so students can learn?* Now think how you'd answer it. Here are three simple ways to return to your problem of practice and deepen your reflective capacity:

- ❖ Jot some notes down in a learning journal or another place where you might be able to archive your thinking and access ideas, musings, questions, and other ponderings later.
- ❖ Find a trusted colleague or two to engage in a dialogue with you. Exchange thoughts, suggestions, critical feedback, and celebrations together.
- ❖ Engage your administrator, instructional coach, department chair, or another member of your support network in a discussion about this question, your journey thus far, and any shifts in perspective you've noticed.

At this point, you may also find that your new clarity of focus has begun to surface new issues—after all, you get more of what you focus on, and if you're focused on the disruptive behaviors, guess what you'll be noticing? New questions are probably popping into your head, too. For example, as you've begun to feel more competent with managing student behavior and your students are beginning to jell around some shared agreements for interacting with one another and regulating their behavior, you may be wondering what you can do to foster even more positive interactions among students while working in groups. If so, you may be ready to tackle the problem on the next page, *How do I get students to participate actively in group work?*

 Or, if you find yourself with another nagging question, turn to the grid on p. 16, find that question, and turn to the page where we help you address it.

How do I get students to participate actively in group work?

Be consistent	**Be connected**	Differentiate	Empower
Teacher-owned, Student-experienced	*Teacher-directed, Student-connected*	*Student-engaged, Teacher-facilitated*	*Student-owned, Teacher-guided*

Welcome to the second phase of the "Creating dynamic group learning" pathway. As you've begun to rein in off-task behavior, you're now able to see your classroom more clearly and contemplate what else you might do to create an even more productive learning environment. With unwanted behaviors more under control, you may feel a little more comfortable letting students work together. Great! Learning is a social event, after all. At this point, your teaching is becoming increasingly *connected* to students as you begin to observe cause-and-effect relationships between your actions and student learning, and your classroom is becoming increasingly *teacher-directed* and *student-connected*.

 If you're joining us from another pathway, or if you're skipping ahead to this problem of practice without reading the previous phase in its entirety, we suggest you skim through or review the previous section just to get your bearings.

Build awareness: Note cause-and-effect relationships

How do I get students to participate actively in group work? Even as your classroom management has improved, you may nonetheless fret about turning students loose to do group work. Perhaps you've noticed that students are going off task or struggling to carry the load evenly while working in groups. Let's consider what's going on.

Are students clear about what's supposed to happen during group learning? Student groups are apt to come off the rails if students aren't clear what they're supposed to accomplish together. So, be sure to provide clear directions and role expectations. You may even want to model the process of group work beforehand—for example, inviting a group to the front of the class to model the process and outcomes of reciprocal teaching. It's also helpful to give students a time frame at the start of the group work to help them stay focused on the task at hand and maintain a lively lesson pace. For example, you might say, "In the next five minutes we are going to . . ." Having a timer visible can further help keep students focused on the task at hand.

Are *you* clear about the purpose of group work? This idea reflects something you may have already explored in the "Designing engaging learning" pathway: making intentional choices when designing learning opportunities. As a teacher, it's important to regularly ask

The circular diagram shows four quadrants: Become responsive, Build awareness (shaded), Assess and analyze your impact, and Make intentional decisions.

yourself questions like: Why am I asking students to work in groups? What do I want them to be thinking about when they're working in groups? What will they be learning or doing that they could not do independently or in a whole class setting? Research shows that a key benefit of cooperative learning is providing students with an opportunity to "talk through" material with their peers and thus, learn it in a deeper way than through individual reading or listening (Johnson, Maruyama, Johnson, Nelson, & Skon, 1981). Talking through ideas or solutions for problems helps students become more conscious of the strategies they use to get to an answer, as well as better able to retain new knowledge and skills later. In other words, peer conversations are a great way to help students process or make sense of learning, yet an ineffective way to encounter new learning (Stevens, Slavin, & Farnish, 1991).

In our own observations of classrooms, we often see students doing group work that has, at best, a vaguely defined purpose—sitting in groups of three or four, reading a book chapter to one another, or working through mathematics problems together. What's the purpose of such an exercise? If students are off task while doing such work, we might ask: What was the task? Was it worth doing? Did students see how working with peers would help them to accomplish the task? Or did they view it as "busy" work?

Are you creating positive interdependence for students working in groups? Students tend to be more motivated to learn when they're able to develop a "sink-or-swim together" relationship—something researchers call "positive interdependence" (Johnson & Johnson, 1999). In fact, this quality—group members seeing how every individual must contribute in order for the group to succeed—may well be the defining characteristic of positive groups (Frey, Fisher, & Everlove, 2009). When groups work well, they deliver positive emotional experiences and the "feel good" neurochemical oxytocin to students' brains. When groups don't work well, they create threat conditions, leaving students feeling unsafe and more focused on group dynamics than learning. You can create positive interdependence among student groups by ensuring each student has a well-defined task that supports the overall success of the group.

Do group projects retain some form of individual responsibility? Groups stay more focused when students understand not only what's expected of the group, but also what's expected of them as individuals. Ensuring individual accountability means that group and individual goals are both linked to clear success criteria, so every student knows exactly how they will demonstrate their learning. For example, after completing a group task, you might ask students to write a summary paragraph of what they have learned, and based on their group's work, what they are still curious about. On the following pages, we'll provide some strategies for incorporating positive interdependence and individual responsibility into group work.

Make intentional decisions: Plan, then implement

Sometimes, teachers get stuck on just one or two ways of "doing" group work (e.g., think-pair-share). Filling your toolkit with various approaches will certainly help you build your confidence in tackling this challenge. The key for you here is to plan to use the tools in your toolkit with intentionality—and then follow through by actually putting them into place in your classroom! An unused tool does you very little good. Here are a couple options for expanding your cooperative learning repertoire: "Numbered Heads Together" and "Jigsaw" are both proven strategies that can dramatically improve student learning and academic success. As you implement them, you'll find it important to observe their impact on student learning, which is, after all, the essence of the *connected* phase of this pathway.

Numbered Heads Together

Why do it: This instructional technique builds upon peer collaboration and provides the supports and structure necessary to promote dynamic group learning.

How to do it: Students are seated in small groups of 4–6.

1. **Students number themselves.** In each group, students count off by the number of students in the group. A group of six students will each have a number. If there is one group in the room with five students, one student will have two numbers.

2. **Pose a question or a problem.** The teacher poses a question or problem, either closed- or open-ended, to the class. The teacher provides a specified amount of time to come to consensus on a solution or possible solution.

3. **Students put their heads together.** The students in each group put their heads together to make sure that everyone in the group understands the question or problem. They then have a specified amount of time to come to consensus on a solution or possible solution. When finished, it is their responsibility to confirm that all members of the group understand how they came to consensus on their solution.

4. **Teacher calls a number.** The teacher calls a number from 1–6. The students with that number in each of the groups stand up. One of the standing students is called upon to explain their group's solution. Standing students from other groups can then chime in with their agreement/disagreement. Make sure they explain their groups' rationale for thinking as they speak.

When to do it: When you notice your students struggling to engage in group work, this tool offers a structure that is highly motivational. Even the most disruptive students tend to engage in this format of learning.

While doing it: Observe group interaction during the discussion. Listen in on their thinking. Take notes on each group and their dynamics. What feedback might you give to each group based upon your observations?

Adapted from "The Structural Approach to Cooperative Learning" (Kagan, 1989).

Jigsaw

Why do it: Positive interdependence doesn't just happen. Teachers must model and implement routines to promote relationships that encourage, rather than inhibit, learning. In this activity, a complex learning task is split among group members, creating an opportunity for interdependence.

How to do it: Each student is simultaneously a member of two groups: a home group and an expert group. The home group's goal is to learn the content and complete tasks. The expert group consists of one representative member from each home group. Students meet in their home group to discuss overall goals, and then in their expert group to discuss a specific aspect of content. After mastering the content, members return to teach it to the rest of their home group. Note: The teacher may find it valuable to appoint one student in each group as the "Leader" who can manage time, encourage students to contribute their part, and ensure the group is accomplishing the goals.

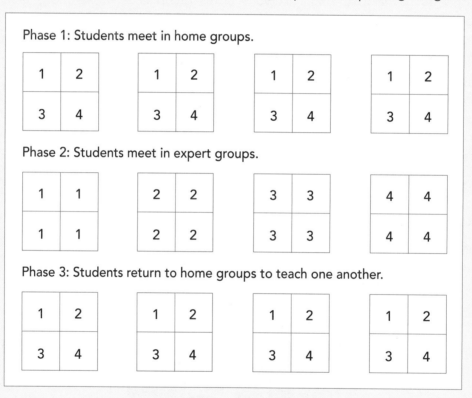

When to do it: Use this tool to introduce large portions of content in a short amount of time. It creates an active learning environment where each student is essential to supporting and enhancing the learning of others.

While doing it: Pay attention and notice student engagement and interaction in the groups. It might be necessary to switch some students around, to ask a disengaged student to be the group leader, or to join a group and model what the sharing of content sounds like. Observe and respond.

Assess and analyze your impact: Recognize the results of your actions

As you've focused your mental energy on ways to effectively engage students in cooperative groupings, you'll notice your attention turning to the direct impact of your efforts. So when you assess the impact of your actions, reflect on your guiding question for this phase: *How do I get students to participate actively in group work?*

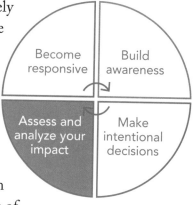

And since student engagement is likely on the rise, you've likely begun to see improvements in student learning too. You're noticing, for example, that certain group arrangements and activities support different forms of student learning. Your students are likely becoming more comfortable with group work, too—spending less time transitioning into group projects, learning the ground rules for different group configurations, and engaging in deeper learning. In short, you're beginning to develop, as experts do, new mental models and theories of action about learning: *When I create X conditions, students respond with Y behaviors* or *If I want students to do Y, then I'll do X.* The questions below are designed to help you to further hone and shape your mental models by engaging in self-reflection and dialogue with your colleagues.

Reflect on Teaching	Reflect on Learning
• Are you clear about the purpose of group work? Do your grouping configurations and projects support the learning goals of your lessons?	• Are students clear about what's supposed to happen during group learning? How do you know?
• How are you creating positive interdependence for students working in groups? How do students respond to these structures?	• When students are set up to rely on each other to complete a task or project, what happens to their engagement, work ethic, and learning outcomes?
• How do you ensure that individuals are still held accountable for their portion of group work?	• How are you gauging individual effort, contributions, and learning in group projects? What resources can you access to help you?

Become responsive: Respond to the needs you see

Even with your expanded teaching repertoire and refinements to your professional practices, you're still likely to find opportunities for improvement. Take heart: This journey, like all the other journeys that precede and follow it, really has no finish line. The benefits you'll reap are ongoing. And as you travel, remember the question that launched you in this phase: *How do I get students to participate actively in group work?* Indeed, the more precise and intentional you become in engaging students in cooperative learning, the more new questions you may find yourself asking.

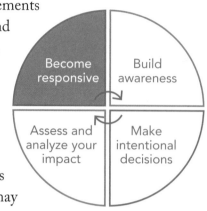

Here are some questions you might ask yourself and your colleagues to reflect on what's improved for you and your students and what steps to take next:

❖ Are there times that students still struggle with learning in a group setting? How might you determine what's the best way to partner students with classmates to maximize learning?

❖ Are you noticing that different students learn better in different settings and contexts? How might you assign students to groups intentionally? Does it change learning outcomes?

❖ What conditions might cause you to change your groupings from one project to the next? How might that affect learning, motivation, behaviors, and learning outcomes?

Perhaps you've heard that homogeneous student groups are a bad idea as they can cause students to have a fixed mindset about their own abilities. However, you know teachers who use ability grouping to differentiate instruction—creating small groups based on student learning needs that allow them to provide targeted teaching and learning opportunities. You also may have heard or read that groups shouldn't be permanent, but rather dynamic, so students don't feel stuck. However, you've seen that as students become familiar with one another, they become better learning partners, and that certain pairs or groups work really well together. So now, you're wondering how you ought to think about student grouping itself, especially because each student seems to have unique learning needs. If so, you may want to tackle the problem on the next page, *How do I match cooperative groups to individual needs?*

 Or, if you find yourself with another nagging question, turn to the grid on p. 16, find that question, and turn to the page where we help you address it.

How do I match cooperative groups to individual needs?

Be consistent *Teacher-owned Student-experienced*	Be connected *Teacher-directed, Student-connected*	**Differentiate** **Student-engaged,** **Teacher-facilitated**	Empower *Student-owned, Teacher-guided*

Welcome to the third phase of the "Creating dynamic group learning" pathway. As you've grown more adept at engaging students in cooperative learning, you've likely started to wonder if you ought to group them more according to their own learning needs—or just the opposite, avoid grouping them by ability to ensure they don't develop a fixed mindset about their own abilities (e.g., "I'm always in the slow group"). These sorts of questions reflect an important mental shift that happens as you move into the *differentiate* phase of your teaching—on this and every other pathway—as you consider individual students and their learning needs and seek to develop expertise to make your classroom *student-engaged, teacher-facilitated*.

> ✓ If you're joining us from another pathway, welcome! Before diving headlong into this challenge, though, we suggest you review the previous phase of this pathway to get your bearings.

Build Awareness: Zoom in on the details

How do I match cooperative groups to individual needs? As it turns out, researchers have asked the same question, and many others just like it, about how to group students to meet their needs yet ensure they don't feel labeled or pigeonholed. They've also arrived at some conclusions that, at least at first, may seem conflicting.

Like-ability groups can support intensive, additional instruction for struggling learners. Guidance from the federally funded What Works Clearinghouse concluded there's *strong* evidence to supporting placing struggling readers in small like-ability groups for 1–3 hours per week of intensive, additional instruction (U.S. Department of Education, 2009).

Like-ability groups appear to widen, not close, achievement gaps. A study of 12,000 students (Sparks, 2018), however, found that students in low-ability reading groups actually progressed more slowly than their peers and were less apt to develop varied interests, an ability to focus, or persist in the face of challenges. Meanwhile, students in high-ability groups tended to stay there despite, in many cases, demonstrating lower reading scores on subsequent exams. International comparisons have also found that countries where ability grouping is more common (such as the U.S., where 9 in 10 students attend schools that practice ability grouping) also have wider achievement gaps and lower overall achievement (OECD, 2012).

Confused even more? You're not alone. Such conflicting conclusions often make educators grumble about (or at least disregard) research, yet there's an explanation.

Like-ability groups tend to become static. Often, students get stuck in the same group (high or low) regardless of changes in their learning or effort. If that happens, they may develop a fixed mindset about their abilities as learners. Also, for anyone, it's easy for our personal, racial, or psychological biases to creep into how we assign students to groups. Moreover, we may feel compelled to provide "equal time" to every group, even though some groups could benefit more from attention or additional instruction than others.

Ability groups should be fluid, not static. Perhaps the first key takeaway from this research is that groups should be fluid—that is, revisited regularly (i.e., every few weeks) to ensure students aren't permanently defined by a particular ability level.

Objective measures should guide the formation of like-ability groups. To avoid bias in grouping students, it's important to use objective measures (e.g., diagnostic assessments) to create like-ability groupings.

Group work itself should be targeted to specific skills (e.g., decoding). For example, you might put students who are at different reading levels together into a small group to focus on, say, fluency, if that's an area where they all have opportunities for growth.

Ability should inform the creation of only specific kinds of groups. Roger and David Johnson (1999), leading researchers in the field of cooperative learning, identified these three types of cooperative learning groups:

❖ *Base groups* are longer duration groups (e.g., a semester or school year) that provide students with peer support for learning; examples include pairing older students as lab partners or forming groups of 3–4 students to help one another with daily tasks or questions they might feel uncomfortable asking in front of the larger group.

❖ *Formal groups* are more structured and may last for days or weeks; they tend to engage students in a variety of different learning activities that support positive interdependence as well as individual responsibility.

❖ *Informal groups* are brief duration groups (e.g., a few minutes to a class period) formed for specific or immediate needs (e.g., checking understanding, reviewing homework, processing new learning); examples include think-pair-share or turn-to-your-neighbor quick conversations.

With this terminology in mind, what all of this research really appears to suggest is that base groups should not reflect ability. At times, though, it may be appropriate for formal groups to reflect ability levels—so long as they're based on objective measures of discrete skills and target the development of those skills. Finally, informal groups should remain randomly assigned and reflect mixed ability.

Make intentional decisions: Develop a clear vision

So, how do you apply all of these ideas to your classroom? That's precisely the challenge we're issuing to you as you attempt to answer the charge of simultaneously using various grouping formations and addressing individual learning needs. You may notice that just like in the other pathways, at this phase, our guidance will be a little less prescriptive and a little more cerebral. That's because your growth as a reflective practitioner demands it. You're beginning to develop expert mental models (*If I see students doing or needing X, then I do Y*) and you're equipped to strategize and problem-solve your way through such dilemmas. As you assess your students' skills, needs, and readiness, and position that information in the greater context of your *differentiated* classroom, your vision for accomplishing your goals will become clearer. The two tools we present on the following pages— "Learning Support Group" and "Learning Cycle Groups"—may help you in your journey.

Learning Support Group

Why do it: Our goal with this type of heterogeneous grouping is to create a small team of interdependent students who can support one another's learning throughout the course of a school year. The purpose of this type of grouping is to improve social competencies, improve self-esteem, build positive relationships between students, foster leadership skills, prepare students for the workplace, and increase student achievement.

How to do it: A *learning support group* is a heterogeneous grouping of three students who meet each week (length of time will vary) to check on and support one another's learning. The teacher does not participate unless needed, but rather, facilitates from afar. The sole purpose is to create interdependent relationships between students for the purpose of learning support. Students will ask one another questions about weekly learning and offer support through guided conversations. Students may bring work to the group and ask for help. They also share successes and applaud effort. Social-emotional learning activities can also be used to develop group dynamics. Use the thinking guide below to plan for a successful learning support group.

1. How might I form groups of three students with mixed ability (academic, social, and behavioral), mixed gender, and mixed ethnic makeup, based on personality types?

2. It is important for students to clearly understand the purpose for meeting. Remember, it will be necessary to remind groups of this purpose each time they meet. What "norms" will need to be established for conversations to be successful? What will conversations sound like when meeting? With student input, consider creating an agreement chart like the one below.

Group Agreements	What will sharing successes and applauding effort sound like?	What will checking for understanding, asking for help, encouragement to achieve, and discussion about concepts being learned sound like?
We will engage in respectful conversations centered on our roles as learners. We will keep our discussion on track and avoid talking about things other than learning. We will be solution-oriented, positive, and always encouraging.	*"This week I worked hard to _____. My efforts paid off."* *"Great job!"* *"That's awesome!"* *"I had an 'aha!' this week. It was _____."* *"I'm still working to _____, but it's getting easier."*	*"What has been your most difficult challenge as a learner this week?"* *"I'm struggling to understand a concept in math and brought a sample problem. Could you help me work through it?"* *"You mentioned last week you were struggling with that science project. How's it going this week?"* *"Did my suggestions help?"* *"You got this! We believe in you."*

3. What will my facilitation look like? Will the groups need me to lead discussions with questions? Will I walk around and listen in while they discuss? What types of discussion questions will I use?

4. What type of targeted feedback will students need from me as they engage with their peers in this manner? (For additional support, see chapter 6, "Motivating with feedback." How might I reinforce the agreements through my ongoing feedback?

5. How often/long will groups meet? (Share this with your students when you pull them together. It is important that they understand the duration of the group.)

When to do it: *Learning support groups* will last throughout the year. While occasionally you will see a need to move students around or restructure, the point is to build long-term relationships within teams.

While doing it: Notice the types of conversations students are having. What information does this give you? What type of feedback do they need to refine and deepen their conversations? Is modeling needed? How might you use one student group to model for others?

Learning Cycle Groups

Why do it: The purpose of this grouping strategy is to bring together students with similar needs for a short amount of time. Students selected for this specific type of group need additional help, time, and practice to master specific content or skill that the teacher has already taught to the class. Caution: Failure to change the group's composition promptly after a skill has been learned can be a detriment to students' self-perception, self-efficacy, and learning itself. Long-term assignment to any type of group works against the positive outcomes of instructional grouping.

How to do it: The creation of a learning cycle group is temporary, lasting one hour, a week, or even a month. It is not permanent. We repeat: It's a *temporary* way for students to work together toward learning with intensive guidance from the teacher. This can happen successfully when we focus our planning around the group learning outcome. Use the thinking guide below to plan for a successful learning cycle group.

> What this group is **NOT**: A seating configuration that allows a teacher to pull six students to a back table and easily work with them as individuals. A "grouping" where students work on individual and independent tasks while the teacher is in close proximity for support. An avenue for the teacher to reteach the same material all over again or keep students on task with an assignment.

1. Based on formative assessment and student needs information, what key skills, big understandings, and misconceptions do I see students still struggling with? How might I create a clear learning outcome for the group? (Share this with your students when you pull them together. It is important that they understand why they are meeting with you.)

2. How might I design a group where students can learn from one another through discussion, peer modeling, targeted activities, and additional support from me? What students would work well together in this group?

3. What will my instruction look like in the small group? How will it be different than what we've done in class? What types of student-led activities, teacher-led discussion, and modeling needs to happen to reach our learning outcome?

4. What type of targeted feedback does this particular group of students need from me? (For additional support, see chapter 6, "Motivating with feedback.")

5. How might I structure the group to maintain a balance between teacher-led and student-directed, with the goal of having the students continue to support one another after the group has been disbanded?

6. How often/long will we meet before I reassess the learning outcome? (Share this with your students when you pull them together. It is important that they understand the duration of the group.)

When to do it: Learning cycle groups can take place throughout the year. Start by creating one group and meet with them three times in total. This is a form of short-term flexible grouping.

While doing it: Notice the learning that happens in a short amount of time. The most successful groups often meet less than five times. Why is this?

Assess and analyze your impact: Transfer the vision

At this point in your journey, your vision is becoming clearer, and your reflections on your practice are deepening and becoming more frequent, leading you to really think the way experts think. You're relying on your knowledge of effective cooperative learning strategies to support group processing and deep learning among your students. And now, as you assess and analyze the impact of your actions up to this point, we remind you to keep your guiding question in mind: *How do I match cooperative groups to individual needs?*

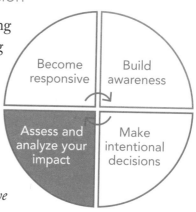

Seems a little oxymoronic, doesn't it, to hit individual students' needs within dynamic group settings? File that away for the coffee-table book you author as a retiree. In the meantime, your tendency to explore the effectiveness of your approaches is spot-on. As you well know, experts don't go it alone; indeed, they consult with one another to diagnose and solve problems. With a "critical friend," use the following reflective questions (and then create your own to add to the list) to help you to develop your expert mental models and challenge each other's thinking:

Reflect on Teaching	Reflect on Learning
• What data are you using to assign students to groups? If you have multiple structures, how do you determine which data are most useful for the most appropriate groupings? • When you provide small group instruction to students, how is your instructional delivery different? How do you determine which strategies to use with which groups? • How can you ensure that all group members are fully engaged and committed to each other's learning and success throughout this process?	• As you implement various grouping structures, what do you notice about student learning outcomes? As a whole? In particular groups? For individual students? What changes do you see across each standard, from unit to unit, or over time? • As you examine student work and evidence of learning, to what extent do you see your various grouping configurations influencing student learning outcomes? How do you draw these conclusions? • When students struggle with learning even after working and connecting with their groups, what's next?

Become responsive: Respond in the moment

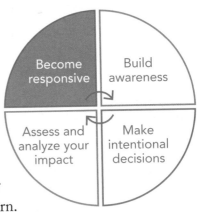

The third phase in this pathway marks a seismic shift in your thinking, as well as your actions. As you've pursued the question that launched this pathway—*How do I match cooperative groups to individual needs?*—you're transitioning from engaging students in cooperative tasks to considering how to use cooperative learning with more precision to help every student move toward mastery. Hopefully, you've also seen new *student behaviors* taking root, like encouraging and helping each other learn. You may have seen some new ways of teaching (and thinking about teaching) emerging in yourself, including an ability to "let go" of the classroom a bit, trusting that with direction and practice, students can engage in productive group work even with your back turned. Still, you may see room for you (and your students) to grow. Take a moment and reflect on your professional growth from the beginning of this pathway until now, and challenge yourself (and a trusted colleague, instructional coach, or administrator) with a few bonus reflective questions:

❖ When your students are all settled and working in their cooperative groups, where does your focus go? What thoughts dominate your mind? What decisions does this compel you to make?

❖ Are students becoming more self-directed? How so, or why not? How is this impacting your class during lesson segments in which you're not set up to engage cooperatively—say, whole class or independent work time?

❖ Do you ever notice if your groups are getting "stale"—that they've fallen into unproductive habits, the passion to meet is waning, the learning is falling by the wayside? How (and how quickly) will you respond?

Overall, your awareness of your students' needs has compelled you to take action, and as you've implemented various student groupings, your attention has turned to the effectiveness of those choices. All your reflections, of course, may surface new professional challenges and questions for you. For example, you may wonder how to provide students with opportunities to work in groups that engage in complex problem solving and deep learning. If so, you may wish to turn to the next page to consider, *How do I create opportunities for students to support one another in deep learning?*

 Or, if you find yourself with another nagging question, turn to the grid on p. 16, find that question, and turn to the page where we help you address it.

How do I create opportunities for students to support one another in deep learning?

Be consistent *Teacher-owned, Student-experienced*	Be connected *Teacher-directed, Student-connected*	Differentiate *Student-engaged, Teacher-facilitated*	**Empower** *Student-owned, Teacher-guided*

Welcome to the fourth phase of the "Creating dynamic group learning" pathway. Here, you'll begin to *empower* students to collaborate authentically in a *student-owned, teacher-guided* environment. This is no subtle shift, either. Building your students' capacity to work interdependently requires steady, significant development of your own capacity—both as a master of the technical elements of teaching and as a reflective practitioner. Getting to this point requires building on the foundation of everything you've learned, the acute awareness you've built, the many steps you've taken with great intentionality, and your ability to gauge your impact and make midcourse corrections as necessary.

 If you're joining us from another pathway, we encourage you to review the previous three phases in this pathway to ensure you're ready to address this challenge.

Build awareness: Bring the variables together

How do I create opportunities for students to support one another in deep learning? As your practices have become more sophisticated, and your students more frequently engaged in cooperative group learning, you may find yourself wondering what it would take for them to go one step further—namely, helping them to become self-directed learning groups. After all, employers often say one of the key traits they look for in employees is people who function well on teams. So, what would it look like for you to help students engage in group projects that tackle complex challenges? Let's explore some big ideas from research that offer some guiding principles for helping students use group learning to support one another with deep learning.

Actively teach social skills. Here, we return to the research of Roger and David Johnson (1999), who, in addition to positive interdependence and individual responsibility, identified three additional traits of effective cooperative groups:

- ❖ **face-to-face promotive interaction** (supporting learning by celebrating success and effort)
- ❖ **interpersonal skills** (developing communication, trust, decision making, and conflict resolution skills)

❖ **group processing** (reflecting on how effectively the team is functioning and might function better)

The basic idea here is that we cannot expect students to develop group interaction skills by chance or osmosis. Rather, we must actively teach and give students opportunities to practice such skills, like taking turns when speaking, engaging in active listening, clarifying and checking for understanding, and encouraging one another to take intellectual risks and share creative ideas.

Design group work to encourage deep learning. Actively teaching social skills creates the right conditions for cooperative groups to engage in deeper, more complex learning. In the previous phases along this pathway, your students likely engaged in cooperative learning activities that helped them to process new ideas or make sense of their learning. In this phase, you'll develop and guide even more-sophisticated cooperative learning activities that will help students tackle complex challenges together to extend and apply their learning. As Kathleen Cushman (2010) discovered when she interviewed several dozen students who had developed a deep passion for learning, they often said that peer learning helps to stoke their curiosity and encourage them to take intellectual risks. That said, peer learning activities must be well designed. Research shows, in fact, that group projects are most effective when they *build on foundational knowledge* and *encourage critical thinking*. A meta-analysis of 35 studies of inquiry-based science projects (e.g., posing problems and asking students to conduct scientific experiments to resolve the problem) reported only modest gains in student achievement compared with conventional methods, yet much larger effects for developing students' critical thinking skills (Smith, 1996). This finding leads us to our next guiding principle.

Frame group projects around a driving question. A major shortcoming of many student projects, according to researchers at Stanford and Vanderbilt universities, is that they tend to become "doing for the sake of doing" (Barron et al., 1998, p. 274). To wit: A model rocket building project initially resulted in very little student understanding about "what made a better or worse rocket" or how to "evaluate the effectiveness of their rocket in any way" (p. 274). One student, for example, saw the purpose of the project as simply, "You know, to build them and see how high they will go" (p. 274). Yet after revising the project around a "driving question"—a request for rocket designs from NASA, which would select the best design for use in other classrooms—students explored whether the rocket would go higher if it was painted or left unfinished, equipped with three fins or four, or fitted with a rounded or pointed nose. Students demonstrated much better content knowledge and ability to think like scientists.

Engage student groups in solving complex challenges. According to business researchers and consultants McKinsey and Company, increasing automation and artificial intelligence is apt to displace millions of workers and eliminate many job categories over the next decade or two—especially jobs that entail routine or repetitive work (Manyika et al.,

2017). Meanwhile, jobs that require creative thinking, complex problem solving, and social-emotional and communication skills, will be on the rise. Studies of U.S. classrooms have shown, however, that teachers often downgrade complex problems to simple, step-by-step procedures (Stigler & Hiebert, 2004). Not surprisingly, the longer U.S. students stay in school, the more they fall behind students in other developed nations on tests of basic skills and their ability to solve complex problems (Richland, Stigler, Holyoak, 2012).

A National Research Council study noted that one of the best predictors of whether high school students will enter STEM fields in college was having "research experiences in high school," namely "scientific investigations and engineering design projects." Yet this same study found that "this type of STEM instruction remains the exception in U.S. schools"—even in STEM-focused schools (Subotnik, Tai, & Almarode, 2011, p. 19). Students can work independently on complex challenges, so the point here isn't that group projects are the only way to engage students in deep learning. Yet group projects can and should provide students with an opportunity to grapple with big ideas and compelling questions that both challenge and motivate them.

Make intentional decisions: Move beyond strategy to design

So, how do you bring all of these ideas together in your classroom? The ability to do this—both consistently and consistently *well*—is often referred to as the art of teaching. You're way past the focus on *what* you are going to do to address this challenge; indeed, you're now thinking about *how* all of these strategies and approaches blend together to create an assessment design. *Empowering* students in such a classroom environment does not happen by accident, and it's no coincidence that your growth as a reflective practitioner has accompanied—in fact preceded—this shift in practice. Because of the complexity and uniqueness of your situation (no one has ever faced exactly what you're facing before, with exactly the students you have), you're in uncharted territory, as it were. How cool is that? But it also means there's no step-by-step guide that we (nor anyone) can offer. Instead, we can offer guiding principles designed to support students' metacognition (thinking about their own learning) and help them become increasingly independent in self-assessing and self-correcting their learning. The following two tools— "Group Reflection Protocol" and "Collaborative Inquiry"—can help you to continue this journey with confidence.

Group Reflection Protocol

Why do it: To develop effective group skills, students need to practice and reflect on what worked and did not work in their group. This helps them form new understandings of teamwork based on that experience, which then informs their actions and commitment in the future.

How to do it: Use the protocol below to guide reflective dialogue within a group. Team members complete their self-reflection using guided questions before coming together and sharing with the group.

Student exercise:

- What I liked most about our group was _____.
- What I struggled with in our group was _____.
- Our group was effective because _____.
- The least effective thing about our group was _____.
- The things I did that helped the group the most were _____.
- The things I did that helped the group the least were _____.
- The characteristics I feel make a good group are _____.
- The roles I'd like to play in the group are _____.
- Next time I wish we _____.
- We could be more effective if we _____.

Protocol:

Students sit in a circle and identify a facilitator/timekeeper.

The first person (presenter) begins by reading his/her answers from their reflection exercise in complete sentence form. The initial time limit is 3 minutes.

Continuing around the circle, each person briefly responds to the presenter and what the presenter has said in less than a minute. The timekeeper monitors. The purposes of the responses are:

- To affirm or acknowledge the speaker's thinking,
- To express confusion about something the presenter may have said (although at this time there is no response *from* the presenter), and
- To question the presenter's assumptions about the issue raised.

After going around the circle with each person having responded for less than one minute, the person that began (the presenter) has the "final word." In no more than one minute, the presenter may respond to what has been said. Now what is his/her thinking? What is his/her reaction to what has been shared?

The next person in the circle then becomes the *new* presenter and begins by sharing his/her reflection. Proceed around the circle, responding in the same way. This process continues until each person has had an opportunity to share and have the "final word."

The facilitator leads the group in a 5-minute debrief where the group determines if group norms need to be revisited and revised based upon the groups' reflection.

When to do it: This tool works well after any group has come together to learn, whether teacher-driven or not. It is best facilitated by a teacher at first, and employing the gradual-release of responsibility approach, will eventually reach the point where group members take turns as facilitator.

While doing it: Pay close attention to the thinking exhibited by students. How accurate is their self-reflection? What type of feedback might you provide that directs their thinking down a particular path (seeking improvement, altering interactions, focusing on outcomes, etc.).

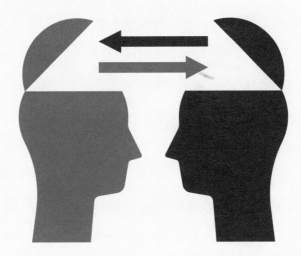

Collaborative Inquiry

Why do it: A growing body of research demonstrates that students learn more deeply if they are engaged in activities that require applying classroom-gathered knowledge to real-world problems. Problem-based learning approaches are similar in nature to project learning, in which students use complex problems and cases to actively build their knowledge.

How to do it: Place students into heterogeneous teams of 3–4. Using the form below, guide groups through the inquiry process. After one complete cycle, groups may be reorganized, and a new cycle started. Use the chart below to get started.

Pose real questions and identify a driving question	Investigate	Create, reflect, and discuss	Conclude findings
Determine what is to be investigated and formulate a question or hypothesis.	How will we seek answers or solutions to our question? Gather information about the topic, including learning that has been done in class. Seek additional sources.	Create by experiment and examination. Discuss the findings and provide explanations or bring clarity to others' learning. Reflect on outcomes. Do they make sense?	Rethink and draw conclusions. Determine solutions.
What have we learned so far about this topic?	What do we know so far?	What information did we gather? How is it relevant to our question?	What did we learn?
What questions do we still have?	How do we know it? What evidence do we have?	What parts support an answer? What does the information suggest?	What did the evidence say?
What do we wonder?	What other resources might help?	What parts do not support our answer?	How might we share this with others?
What problems in the world are related to our learning?	How will we know the information is valid?	Does it raise new questions?	What action needs to be taken?

When to do it: This activity is best done at the end of learning. However, there are instances when the inquiry process can support learning throughout a unit.

While doing it: Observe the types of inquiry paths that students take. What does this tell you about their thinking and understanding? How might you use that information to craft differentiated feedback for each group?

Assess and analyze the impact of your actions: Assess with purpose

At this phase in the pathway, you're using your deep knowledge and skills to help students take ownership of their learning journeys. Some may observe your collaborative structures and consider such *empowerment* in your classroom to be innovative and creative divergence. As a committed, reflective practitioner, you're well aware that you've reached a place in your professional development that is only possible because of your consistent, intentional focus on growing, learning, gauging, and tinkering with your practices to better meet 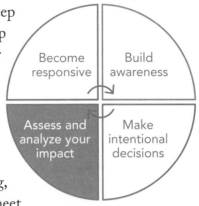 individual students' needs. You know the most important part of any classroom isn't what you're doing as a teacher, but rather, what's going on in students' minds; thus, you want to design group learning experiences that add real value to student learning—helping them to learn and do things together they couldn't do independently. Your initial question is truly guiding your inquiry: *How do I create opportunities for students to support one another in deep learning?* Do the learning experiences you've designed for student groups support deep learning? Are they truly working interdependently? With that in mind, gather some colleagues, administrators, coaches, and your teammates and lead a discussion based on the following questions (and feel free to add your own):

Reflect on Teaching	Reflect on Learning
• How often is a truly collaborative, inquiry-based project appropriate for your class? How do you know when to engage students in such an activity? • What, precisely, are the behaviors, comments, and actions you're looking for when students work in collaborative groups? Have you identified them for yourself? Have you asked your students for input? Do they have clarity of these skills? • What other factors are you bringing into the equation that contribute to deep learning and growing interpersonal skills? How do you consider all the other elements of your classroom (clear targets, individual goals, assessment strategies, etc.) in designing projects, groupings, and learning progressions?	• How does students' performance reflect deep learning? How is that different than simply mastering a learning target or meeting a standard consistently? • As you have built interdependent cooperative groups and orchestrated collaborative inquiry-based projects, are students demonstrating the "soft skills" of cooperation, problem-solving, investment in others' success, grit, and empathy more frequently or less? How so? • How might you engage students in self-reflections and self-assessments of their collaborative skills? If these are indeed employability markers, do they know where they stand? What are they doing to improve themselves as teammates and potential coworkers?

Become responsive: Trust your intuition

Things are happening in your classroom, aren't they? Good things. Cooperative, collaborative projects. Interdependent teams. Self-driven individuals. No, it's not all rainbows and unicorns—in fact, there may be times that you find you've gotten ahead of your students. You may question your own actions or motives. Perhaps you've designed some group projects that were too challenging, prompting students to revert to freeloading behaviors of expecting one or two of their peers to carry the load. Or maybe you realize you asked students to

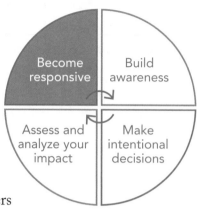

do group work they could have just as easily (or more effectively) have done independently. That's OK. No doubt, you'll make adjustments and design better learning opportunities next time. Trust your inner voice. At this point, your reflective capacity has developed to a point where you're attuned to your students' needs and how to address them, both in the moment and from a grander perspective. And if you'd like to couple your inner voice with that of your trusted colleagues, we invite you to reflect on the following questions together, challenging each other's thinking to continue to refine your practice:

- ❖ How can you continue to monitor student growth to determine the best structures and activities that lead to deep learning—and build critical interpersonal skills at the same time?

- ❖ How will you determine what's working, and to what extent? Which of your collaborative projects truly leads to deep learning in a causative (direct) way, as opposed to a correlative (indirect) way?

- ❖ What adjustments do you need to make in your class? Why are those adjustments necessary? How will you go about it? How will you help students commit to the changes?

You're probably wishing there were more phases in this pathway, right? Well, we agree, and we want to acknowledge a couple of realities: First, you've really grown as a thinker and a practitioner as you've established interdependent collaborative relationships as the cornerstone of your classroom environment. Second, though you've progressed through this chapter, there really is no end to this work. You can always grow, you can always improve, and you can always learn and refine your approaches. Yes, there's a lot to celebrate, and yes, there's still a lot on the horizon.

Final thoughts on creating dynamic group learning

As you've come to the end of the "Creating dynamic group learning" pathway, it's important to take stock of your journey, appreciate the phases you've mastered, and note the growth you've made. In short, this is a wonderful time to appraise your professional development.

First, let's look at the pathway from the 10,000-foot level:

Be consistent *Teacher-owned, Student-experienced*	Be connected *Teacher-directed, Student-connected*	Differentiate *Student-engaged, Teacher-facilitated*	Empower *Student-owned, Teacher-guided*

You've made significant strides in transforming your classroom from one that's inherently *teacher-owned* (and student-experienced) to one that is becoming more *student-owned* (and teacher-guided). Through a systematic process of identifying key questions that either confound or interest you (or both), you've investigated and addressed four critical problems of practice all related to the "Creating dynamic group learning" pathway. Along the way, you repeated a very predictable, very deliberate pattern of reflective steps that a) built your self-reflective capacity and b) enhanced your professional acumen. That pattern, the Reflective Cycle, really ought to be second nature to you by now:

❖ Build awareness about the problem of practice by asking key questions and conducting research to learn more.

❖ Make intentional decisions about implementing strategies, based on the research and your desired goal.

❖ Assess and analyze the impact of your actions to determine the effectiveness of particular strategies over a period of time.

❖ Become responsive to the changing needs you notice to better meet your (and, more specifically, your *students'*) needs.

❖ Repeat, repeat, repeat, and repeat again and again and again.

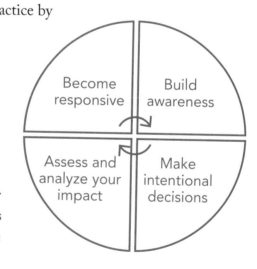

Remember the Theory of Action that drives this combination of approaches:

Theory of Action	IF we start with key problems of practice, use research-based best practices to solve them, and reflect on our practice as teachers, THEN we will become more expert in our practice, better able to meet our students' needs, and engaged in career-long professional growth that will allow us to become amazing, unstoppable teachers in whose classrooms learning will flourish.

Though you've come to the end of this particular pathway, you're far too astute to believe the journey is over. Learning is cyclical—a progression that leads you ever upwards, not unlike a spiral staircase—and you realize there will be times that you need to backtrack, regroup, and revisit some of the foundational elements of this pathway to solidify and enhance your effectiveness. And of course there's more yet to learn, different approaches to implement, and all sorts of new ways of looking at—and solving—your newfound problems of practice. Indeed, the growth you've made is more than just about helping students to work together and support each other's learning; in addition, you're becoming masterful at the art of growing as a reflective practitioner and transferring your learning into the classroom.

And as you've certainly noticed, attending to the social nature of learning and building interdependent groups is just part of a robust, powerful, successful schooling experience for students. Now your task is to weave the other refinement pathways into your work in a seamless expression of excellence, ensuring that all students thrive and flourish.

Or, if you find yourself with another nagging question, turn to the grid on p. 16, find that question, and turn to the page where we help you address it.

Epilogue
Spinning the flywheel ever more

The time has come to tackle the most important problem of practice of them all.

Yours.

Whether you used our book to tackle one big problem of practice or to take a stab at all 24, you likely came to the realization that this is a journey with no finish line. Striving for greatness in teaching is about the pursuit of knowledge and skills, yes, but it's way more than that too. It's about knowing yourself as a learner—understanding how you can channel your self-reflective energies into ongoing development as a professional.

Before plunging into a problem of practice that you'll define yourself, let's recap just a bit to synthesize your learning journey up to this point.

We began by positioning our approach in a Theory of Action that compels each of us—each of you—to pursue professional growth with this delightful mix of curiosity, zeal, passion, and intentionality. It's pretty straightforward:

Theory of Action	IF we start with key problems of practice, use research-based best practices to solve them, and reflect on our practice as teachers, THEN we will become more expert in our practice, better able to meet our students' needs, and engaged in career-long professional growth that will allow us to become amazing, unstoppable teachers in whose classrooms learning will flourish.

To address that Theory of Action, we offered a developmentally progressive list of problems of practice, which we define as a particular element of your classroom responsibilities that nags at you, confounds you, and provides a challenge that you haven't yet been able to overcome.

We extracted our list from the highest-leverage, highest-impact teaching approaches, and blended the problems into six pathways that characterize what the best of the best teachers do really well:

1. Nurturing a positive learning environment.
2. Challenging students to commit to mastery.
3. Designing engaging learning.
4. Motivating with feedback.
5. Assessing for learning.
6. Creating dynamic group learning.

And then you set to work on them. Or, rather, you set about building your awareness about one problem of practice at a time, thinking intentionally about implementing variously more complex strategies, assessing the impact of those actions with acuity, and adapting and adjusting as necessary. Our hope is that you'll repeat that cycle—*the Reflective Cycle*—ad infinitum as your skills and reflective capacity grow and strengthen.

As you learned, you became more consistent with the fundamental building blocks of the approaches you were pursuing. Then you shifted your focus onto how students were responding to your efforts. Onward and upward, your next phase included an emphasis on differentiating the learning experience for each and every student. Finally, tapping into your reservoir of creativity and innovation, you carefully crafted and began to nurture an environment in which the students truly own their learning trajectories.

And now look at you and your practices. You've made it!

We almost caught you, didn't we? You saw those laurels and considered resting on them. Lest you get too comfortable with your own growth, remember the paradigm: There is no finish line. As co-author Pete is so fond of saying, "Beware the traveler who believes he has arrived." After all, what do we always tell our kids when they tell us they're finished? When you think you're done, you've just begun.

That said, what have you really accomplished, no matter which problems of practice you attacked and which pathways you traveled? You've developed replicable patterns of thought. It's those self-reflective habits that will propel you ever faster, ever farther, and ever more confidently in the direction of your choosing. You are, as a professional, unstoppable.

Knowledge is only useful when it's put into place. So what are you going to do with the gains you've made in self-awareness? Now that you understand how you change and grow—how people change and grow—how can you share that information? Are your colleagues coming to you, asking for tips and strategies to build their own self-reflective repertoire? Have you reached out to your teaching compatriots to share the nuggets you've collected along the journey, comparing them and testing each other's ideas out to achieve outrageous success in your classrooms together?

And here's yet another question to drive your mental engine toward another gear: How have you internalized the process? Can you translate this to a new, as-yet-unsolved (and perhaps undefined) problem of practice? Can you apply your learning to unique and diverse situations that will truly require your exquisite focus and reflective-cycle processing skills?

Please join us at **mcrel.org/pursuinggreatness** where a microsite dedicated to readers of *Pursuing Greatness* will walk you through identifying and solving a 25th problem of practice that's unique to you and your current needs as a reflective practitioner. We'll follow the same process you've learned about in this book, but the entire exercise will be totally personalized.

See you online . . . and in empowered classrooms everywhere!

mcrel.org/pursuinggreatness

References

Alter, A. L., Aronson, J., Darley, J. M., Rodriguez, C., & Ruble, D. N. (2010). Rising to the threat: Reducing stereotype threat by reframing the threat as a challenge. *Journal of Experimental Social Psychology, 46*(1), 166–171. https://doi.org/10.1016/j.jesp.2009.09.014

Bailey, F., & Pransky, K. (2014). *Memory at work in the classroom: Strategies to help underachieving students.* Alexandria, VA: ASCD.

Bangert-Drowns, R. L., Kulik, C. C., Kulik, J. A., & Morgan, M. T. (1991). The instructional effect of feedback in test-like events. *Review of Educational Research, 61*(2), 213–238.

Barron, B. J. S., Schwartz, D. L., Vye, N. J., Moore, A., Petrosino, A., Zech, L., & Bransford, J. D. (1998). Doing with understanding: Lessons from research on problem- and project-based learning. *Journal of the Learning Sciences, 7*(3–4), 271–311. https://doi.org/10.1080/10508406.1998.9672056

Batson, C. D. (2009). These things called empathy: Eight related but distinct phenomena. In J. Decety & W. Ickes (Eds.), *Social neuroscience. The social neuroscience of empathy* (pp. 3–15). Cambridge, MA: MIT Press. https://psycnet.apa.org/doi/10.7551/mitpress/9780262012973.003.0002

Beesley, A. D., & Apthorp, H. S. (Eds.) (2010). *Classroom instruction that works* (2nd ed.) [Research report]. Denver, CO: Mid-continent Research for Education and Learning. Retrieved from https://files.eric.ed.gov/fulltext/ED543521.pdf

Benjamin, A. S., & Bjork, R. A. (2000). On the relationship between recognition speed and accuracy for words rehearsed via rote versus elaborative rehearsal. *Journal of Experimental Psychology: Learning, Memory, and Cognition, 26*(3), 638–648. https://psycnet.apa.org/doi/10.1037/0278-7393.26.3.638

Bethell, C. D., Newacheck, P., Hawes, E., & Halfon, N. (2014). Adverse childhood experiences: Assessing the impact on health and school engagement and the mitigating role of resilience. *Health Affairs, 33*(12), 2106–2115. https://doi.org/10.1377/hlthaff.2014.0914

Bill & Melinda Gates Foundation. (2014). *Teachers know best: Teachers' views on professional development.* Retrieved from http://k12education.gatesfoundation.org/download/?Num=2336&filename=Gates-PDMarketResearch-Dec5.pdf

Bloom, B. S. (Ed.). (1985). *Developing talent in young people.* New York, NY: Ballantine Books.

Bremner, J. D. (2006). Traumatic stress: Effects on the brain. *Dialogues in clinical neuroscience, 8*(4), 445–461.

Cohen, B. L., Garcia, J., Apfel, N., & Master, A. (2006) Reducing the racial achievement gap: A social psychological intervention. *Science, 313*, 1307–1310.

Comer, J. (1995). Lecture given at Education Service Center, Region IV. Houston, TX.

Cornelius-White, J. (2007). Learner-centered teacher-student relationships are effective: A meta-analysis. *Review of Educational Research, 77*(1), 113–143. https://doi.org/10.3102/003465430298563

Cushman, K. (2010, September). Show us what homework's for. *Educational Leadership, 68*(1), 74–78. Retrieved from http://www.ascd.org/publications/educational-leadership/sept10/vol68/num01/Show-Us-What-Homework's-For.aspx

Dean, C. B., Hubbell, E. R., Pitler, H., & Stone, B. (2012). *Classroom instruction that works: Research-based strategies for increasing student achievement* (2nd ed). Alexandria, VA: ASCD.

Deci, E. L., Koestner, R., & Ryan, R. M. (1999). A meta-analytic review of experiments examining the effects of extrinsic rewards on intrinsic motivation. *Psychological Bulletin, 126*(6), 627–668. Retrieved from http://citeseerx.ist.psu.edu/viewdoc/download?doi=10.1.1.588.5821&rep=rep1&type=pdf

Dewey, J. (1933). *How we think* (rev. ed.). Boston, MA: D. C. Heath & Co.

Dinham, S. (2005). Principal leadership for outstanding educational outcomes. *Journal of Educational Administration, 43*(4), 338–356. https://doi.org/10.1108/09578230510605405

Dinham, S. (2007a). The dynamics of creating and sustaining learning communities. *Unicorn Online Refereed Article No. 43.* Australian College of Educators.

Dinham, S. (2007b). The waves of leadership. *The Australian Educational Leader, 29*(3), 20–21, 27.

Durlak, J. A., Weissberg, R. P., Dymnicki, A. B., Taylor, R. D., & Schellinger, K. B. (2011). The impact of enhancing students' social and emotional learning: A meta-analysis of school-based universal interventions. *Child Development, (82)*1, 405–432. https://doi.org/10.1111/j.1467-8624.2010.01564.x

Dweck, C. S. (2000). *Self-theories: Their role in motivation, personality, and development.* London: Psychology Press.

Dweck, C. S. (2006). *Mindset: The New Psychology of Success.* New York, NY: Random House.

Dweck, C. S., & Leggett, E. L. (1988). A social-cognitive approach to motivation and personality. *Psychological Review, 95*(2), 256–273. https://psycnet.apa.org/doi/10.1037/0033-295X.95.2.256

Eagleman, D. (2015). *The brain: The story of you.* Edinburgh, Scotland: Canongate Books.

Elliott, E. S., & Dweck, C. S. (1988). Goals: An approach to motivation and achievement. *Journal of Personality and Social Psychology, 54*(1), 5–12. https://psycnet.apa.org/doi/10.1037/0022-3514.54.1.5

Ericsson, A., & Pool, R. (2016). *Peak: Secrets from the new science of expertise.* Boston, MA: Houghton Mifflin Harcourt.

Fisher, D., & Frey, N. (2013). *Better learning through structured teaching: A framework for the gradual release of responsibility* (2nd ed.). Alexandria, VA: ASCD.

Frayer, D., Frederick, W. C., & Klausmeier, H. J. (1969). *A schema for testing the level of cognitive mastery*. Madison, WI: Wisconsin Center for Education Research.

Frey, N., Fisher, D., & Everlove, S. (2009). *Productive group work: How to engage students, build teamwork, and promote understanding*. Alexandria, VA: ASCD.

Fry, S. W. (2007). First-year teachers and induction support: Ups, downs, and in-betweens. *The Qualitative Report, 12*(2), 216–237. Retrieved from https://nsuworks.nova.edu/tqr/vol12/iss2/6

Goodwin, B. (2015). *The road less traveled*. Denver, CO: McREL International.

Goodwin, B. (2018). *Student learning that works*. Denver, CO: McREL International.

Goodwin, B., & Hein, H. (2016). The X factor in college success. *Educational Leadership, 73*(6), 77–78.

Goodwin, B., & Hubbell, E. R. (2013). *The 12 touchstones of good teaching: A checklist for staying focused every day*. Alexandria, VA: ASCD.

Goodwin, B., & Slotnik, W. J. (2019, March 25). Debunking the myth of the teacher performance plateau. *Phi Delta Kappan*. Retrieved from https://www.kappanonline.org/teacher-performance-plateau-slotnik-goodwin/

Haberman, M. (1991). The pedagogy of poverty versus good teaching. *Phi Delta Kappan, 73*(4), 290–294.

Hall, P., Childs-Bowen, D., Cunningham-Morris, A., Pajardo, P., & Simeral, A. (2016). *The principal influence: A framework for developing leadership capacity in principals*. Alexandria, VA: ASCD.

Hall, P., & Simeral, A. (2008). *Building teachers' capacity for success: A collaborative approach for coaches and school leaders*. Alexandria, VA: ASCD.

Hall, P., & Simeral, A. (2015). *Teach, reflect, learn: Building your capacity for success in the classroom*. Alexandria, VA: ASCD.

Hall, P., & Simeral, A. (2017). *Creating a culture of reflective practice: Capacity-building for schoolwide success*. Alexandria, VA: ASCD.

Halverson, R., Barnicle, A., Hackett, S., Rawat, T., Rutledge, J., Kallio, J., Mould, C., & Mertes, J. (2015). *Personalization in practice: Observations from the field* (WCER Working Paper 2015–8). Retrieved from http://www.wcer.wisc.edu/publications/workingPapers/papers.php

Hamre, B. K., & Pianta, R. C. (2005). Can instructional and emotional support in the first grade classroom make a difference for children at risk of school failure? *Child Development, 76*(5), 949–967. https://doi.org/10.1111/j.1467-8624.2005.00889.x

Hattie, J. (2009). *Visible learning: A synthesis of over 800 meta-analyses relating to achievement.* New York: Routledge.

Howell, R. J. (2011). Exploring the impact of grading rubrics on academic performance: Findings from a quasi-experimental, pre-post evaluation. *Journal on Excellence in College Teaching, 22*(2), 31–49. Retrieved from http://citeseerx.ist.psu.edu/viewdoc/download?doi=10.1.1.457.8218&rep=rep1&type=pdf

Jackson, R. R. (2018). *Never work harder than your students & other principles of great teaching* (2nd ed.). Alexandria, VA: ASCD.

Johnson, D. W., Maruyama, G., Johnson, R. T., Nelson, D., & Skon, L. (1981). Effects of cooperative, competitive, and individualistic goal structures on achievement: A meta-analysis. *Psychological Bulletin, 89*, 47–62.

Johnson, R., & Johnson, D. (1999). Making cooperative learning work. *Theory Into Practice, 38*(2), 67–73. https://doi.org/10.1080/00405849909543834

Jones, M. G. (1990). Action zone theory, target students and science classroom interactions. *Journal of Research in Science Teaching, 27*(7), 651–660. https://doi.org/10.1002/tea.3660270705

Jonsson, A., & Svingby, G. (2007). The use of scoring rubrics: Reliability, validity and educational consequences. *Educational Research Review, 2*(2), 130–144. https://doi.org/10.1016/j.edurev.2007.05.002

Josephson Institute. (2010). *Josephson Institute's 2010 report card on the ethics of American youth.* Los Angeles: Author.

Joyce, B., & Showers, B. (2002). *Student achievement through staff development* (3rd ed.). Alexandria, VA: ASCD.

Joyce, J. (1922). *Ulysses.* New York: Simon & Brown.

Juvonen, J., Wang, Y., & Espinoza, G. (2010). Bullying experiences and compromised academic performance across middle school grades. *The Journal of Early Adolescence, 31*(1), 152–173. https://doi.org/10.1177/0272431610379415

Kagan, S. (1989, December). The structural approach to cooperative learning. *Educational Leadership, 47*(4), 12–15.

King, A. (1991). Effects of training in strategic questioning on children's problem-solving performance. *Journal of Educational Psychology, 83*(3), 307–317.

Klem, A. M., & Connell, J. P. (2004). Relationships matter: Linking teacher support to student engagement and achievement. *The Journal of School Health, 74*(7), 262–273. https://doi.org/10.1111/j.1746-1561.2004.tb08283.x

Kohn, A. (1999). *Punished by rewards: The trouble with gold stars, incentive plans, A's, praise, and other bribes.* New York, NY: Houghton Mifflin.

Langley, A. K., Gonzalez, A., Sugar, C. A., Solis, D., & Jaycox, L. (2015). Bounce back: Effectiveness of an elementary school-based intervention for multicultural children exposed to traumatic events. *Journal of Consulting and Clinical Psychology, 83*(5) 853–865. https://psycnet.apa.org/doi/10.1037/ccp0000051

Locke, E. A., & Latham, G. P. (2006). New directions in goal-setting theory. *Current Directions in Psychological Science, 15*(5), 265–268. https://doi.org/10.1111/j.1467-8721.2006.00449.x

Manyika, J., Lund, S., Chui, M., Bughin, J., Woetzel, J., Batra, P., . . . Sanghri, S. (2017, December). *Jobs lost, jobs gained: What the future of work will mean for jobs, skills, and wages.* McKinsey & Company.

Marsh, H. (2012). Relationships for learning: Using pupil voice to define teacher-pupil relationships that enhance pupil engagement. *Management in Education, 26*(3), 161–163. https://doi.org/10.1177/0892020612445702

Marzano, R. (1998). *A theory-based meta-analysis of research on instruction.* Aurora, CO: Mid-continent Regional Educational Laboratory.

Marzano, R. J., Pickering, D., & Pollock, J. E. (2001). *Classroom instruction that works: Research-based strategies for increasing student achievement.* Alexandria, VA: Association for Supervision and Curriculum Development.

Maslow, A. (1954). *Motivation and Personality.* New York: Harper.

Medina, J. (2008). *Brain rules: 12 principles for surviving and thriving at work, home, and school.* Fall River, MA: Pear Tree Press.

Meiklejohn, J., Phillips, C., Freedman, M. L., Griffin, M. L., Biegel, G., Roach, A., . . . Saltzman, A. (2012). Integrating mindfulness training into K–12 education: Fostering the resilience of teachers and students. *Mindfulness, 3*(4), 291–307. https://doi.org/10.1007/s12671-012-0094-5

Melnick, S. A., & Meister, D. G. (2008). A comparison of beginning and experienced teachers' concerns. *Educational Research Quarterly, 31*(3), 39–56. Retrieved from https://files.eric.ed.gov/fulltext/EJ788428.pdf

Neumann, M., Edelhäuser, F., Tauschel, D., Fischer, M. R., Wirtz, M., Woopen, C., . . . Scheffer, C. (2011). Empathy decline and its reasons: A systematic review of studies with medical students and residents. *Academic Medicine, 86*(8), 996–1009. doi: 10.1097/ACM.0b013e318221e615

OECD. (2012). *Equity and quality in education: Supporting disadvantaged students and schools.* Paris: OECD Publishing.

Okeke, N. A., Howard, L. C., Kurtz-Costes, B., & Rowley, S. J. (2009). Academic race stereotypes, academic self-concept, and racial centrality in African American youth. *Journal of Black Psychology, 35*(3), 366–387. https://doi.org/10.1177/0095798409333615

Patall, E., Cooper, H., & Robinson, J. C. (2008). The effects of choice on intrinsic motivation and related outcomes: A meta-analysis of research findings. *Psychological Bulletin, 134*(2), 270–300. https://psycnet.apa.org/doi/10.1037/0033-2909.134.2.270

Pierson, R. (2013, May). *Rita Pierson: Every kid needs a champion* [Video file]. Retrieved from https://www.ted.com/talks/rita_pierson_every_kid_needs_a_champion?language=en

Pink, D. H. (2011). *Drive: The surprising truth about what motivates us.* New York, NY: Riverhead Books.

Powell, S., & Nelson, B. (1997). Effects of choosing academic assignments on a student with attention deficit hyperactivity disorder. *Journal of Applied Behavior Analysis, 30*(1), 181–183. https://doi.org/10.1901/jaba.1997.30-181

Quaglia Institute (2011). *My voice national student report (grades 6–12) 2011.* Retrieved from http://quagliainstitute.org/dmsView/MyVoiceNationalStudentReport(Grades6-12)2011

Rawson, K. A., & Kintsch, W. (2005). Rereading effects depend on time of test. *Journal of Educational Psychology, 97*(1), 70–80. https://psycnet.apa.org/doi/10.1037/0022-0663.97.1.70

Richland, L. E., Stigler, J. W., & Holyoak, K. J. (2012). Teaching the conceptual structure of mathematics. *Educational Psychologist, 47*(3), 189–203. https://doi.org/10.1080/00461520.2012.667065

Ritchhart, R., Church, M., & Morrison, K. (2011). *Making thinking visible: How to promote engagement, understanding, and independence for all learners.* San Francisco: Wiley.

Ritchhart, R., Palmer, P., Church, M., & Tishman, S. (2006). *Thinking routines: Establishing patterns of thinking in the classroom.* Paper prepared for the AERA Conference, April 2006.

Roediger, H. L., III, & Pyc, M. A. (2012). Inexpensive techniques to improve education: Applying cognitive psychology to enhance educational practice. *Journal of Applied Research in Memory and Cognition, 1*(4), 242–248. https://doi.org/10.1016/j.jarmac.2012.09.002

Rosenthal, R., & Jacobson, L. (1992). *Pygmalion in the classroom.* Expanded edition. New York, NY: Irvington.

Sapolsky, R. M. (2017). *Behave: The biology of humans at our best and worst.* New York, NY: Penguin Books.

Schmidt, W., McKnight, C. C., & Raizen, S. A. (1997). *A splintered vision: An investigation of U.S. science and mathematics education.* Hingham, MA: Kluwer Academic Publishers.

Schön, D. (1983). *The reflective practitioner: How professionals think in action.* New York, NY: Basic Books.

Shute, V. J. (2008). Focus on formative feedback. *Review of Educational Research, 78*(1), 153–189. https://doi.org/10.3102%2F0034654307313795

Singer, T., & Klimecki, O. M. (2014). Empathy and compassion. *Current Biology, 24*(18), R875–R878. https://doi.org/10.1016/j.cub.2014.06.054

Smith, D. A. (1996). *A meta-analysis of student outcomes attributable to the teaching of science as inquiry as compared to traditional methodology* (Unpublished doctoral dissertation). Temple University, Pennsylvania.

Souers, K., & Hall, P. (2016). *Fostering resilient learners: Strategies for creating a trauma-sensitive classroom.* Alexandria, VA: ASCD.

Souers, K., & Hall, P. (2018). *Relationship, responsibility, and regulation: Trauma-invested strategies for fostering resilient learners.* Alexandria, VA: ASCD.

Souza, D. A. (2011). *How the brain learns* (4th ed.). Thousand Oaks, CA: Corwin.

Sparks, S. D. (2018, August 26). Are classroom reading groups the best way to teach reading? Maybe not. *Education Week.* Retrieved from https://www.edweek.org/ew/articles/2018/08/29/are-classroom-reading-groups-the-best-way.html

Stevens, R. J., Slavin, R. E., & Farnish, A. M. (1991). The effects of cooperative learning and direct instruction in reading comprehension strategies on main idea identification. *Journal of Educational Psychology, 83*(1), 8–16.

Stigler, J. W., & Hiebert, J. (2004). Improving mathematics teaching. *Educational Leadership, 61*(5), 12–17. Retrieved from https://www.researchgate.net/profile/James_Stigler/publication/228731157_Improving_mathematics_teaching/links/02e7e529e9b1081f6f000000/Improving-mathematics-teaching.pdf

Streeck-Fischer, A., & van der Kolk, V. A. (2000). Down will come baby, cradle and all: Diagnostic and therapeutic implications of chronic trauma on child development. *Australian and New Zealand Journal of Psychiatry, 34*(6), 903–918.

Subotnik, R. F., Tai, R. H., & Almarode, J. (2011). *Study of the impact of selective SMT high schools: Reflections on learners gifted and motivated in science and mathematics.* Paper prepared for the workshop of the Committee on Highly Successful Schools or Programs for K–12 STEM Education, National Research Council, Washington, DC, May 10–12, 2011.

TNTP (2015). *The mirage: Confronting the hard truth about our quest for teacher development.* New York, NY: Author. Retrieved from https://tntp.org/publications/view/the-mirage-confronting-the-truth-about-our-quest-for-teacher-development

Torrance, E. P. (1967). *Understanding the fourth grade slump in creative thinking* (Cooperative Research Project No. 994). Washington, DC: U.S. Department of Health, Education, and Welfare, Office of Education, Bureau of Research. Retrieved from https://files.eric.ed.gov/fulltext/ED018273.pdf

U.S. Department of Education, National Center for Education Evaluation and Regional Assistance, Institute of Education Sciences. (2009). *Assisting students struggling with reading: Response to intervention (RtI) and multi-tier intervention in the primary grades*. Washington, DC: Author. Retrieved from https://ies.ed.gov/ncee/wwc/Docs/PracticeGuide/rti_reading_pg_021809.pdf

U.S. Department of Health and Human Services, Public Health Service, National Institutes of Health, National Institute of Child Health and Human Development, National Reading Panel. (2000). *Teaching children to read: An evidence-based assessment of the scientific research literature on reading and its implications for reading instruction* (NIH Publication No. 00-4769). Retrieved from https://www.nichd.nih.gov/publications/pubs/nrp/smallbook

Wadlington, E., & Wadlington, P. (2011). Teacher dispositions: Implications for teacher education. *Childhood Education, 87*(5), 323–326. https://doi.org/10.1080/00094056.2011.10523206

Wang, M. C., & Stiles, B. (1976). An investigation of children's concept of self-responsibility for their school learning. *American Educational Research Journal, 13*(3), 159–179. https://doi.org/10.3102/00028312013003159

Wanzek, J., Wexler, J., Vaughn, S., & Ciullo, S. (2010). Reading interventions for struggling readers in the upper elementary grades: A synthesis of 20 years of research. *Reading and Writing, 23*(8), 889–912. https://doi.org/10.1007/s11145-009-9179-5

Wiggins, G., & McTighe, J. (2005). *Understanding by Design* (2nd ed.). Alexandria, VA: ASCD.

Wiliam, D. (2007). Keeping learning on track: Classroom assessment and the regulation of learning. In F. K. Lester (Ed.), *Second handbook of mathematics teaching and learning*. Greenwich, CT: Information Age Publishing.

Wiliam, D. (2011). *Embedded formative assessment*. Bloomington, IN: Solution Tree.

Wormeli, R. (2011, November). Redos and retakes done right. *Educational Leadership, 69*(3), 22–26.

Yeager, D. S., & Walton, G. M. (2011). Social-psychological interventions in education: They're not magic. *Review of Educational Research, 81*(2), 267–301. https://doi.org/10.3102%2F0034654311405999

About the Authors

Pete Hall is a veteran school administrator, keynote speaker, and professional development agent who has dedicated his career to supporting the improvement of our education systems. This is his ninth book—and his fifth collaboration with Alisa Simeral, including *Creating a Culture of Reflective Practice: Capacity-Building for Schoolwide Success* (ASCD, 2017). He also authored *Lead On! Motivational Lessons for School Leaders* (Eye on Education, 2011) and over 20 articles on school leadership. A passionate advocate for Whole Child/Whole Adult approaches, Pete provides support to leaders, schools, and organizations across the globe. You can contact him via email at PeteHall@EducationHall.com or catch his Twitter feeds at @EducationHall.

Author and consultant Alisa Simeral has guided reform efforts as a teacher, instructional coach, administrator, professional developer, and leadership mentor in K–12 and adult education settings. Her focus is empowering educators to take charge of their professional learning by developing and refining the metacognitive habits famously identified by John Dewey. She is a co-author of numerous publications, including the best sellers *Creating a Culture of Reflective Practice: Capacity-Building for Schoolwide Success* (ASCD, 2017), *Building Teachers' Capacity for Success: A Collaborative Approach for Coaches and School Leaders* (ASCD, 2008), and *Teach, Reflect, Learn: Building Your Capacity for Success in the Classroom* (ASCD, 2015). She works as a consultant and professional speaker at schools, districts, and education organizations worldwide, supporting their work to cultivate reflective practice and shift from cultures of compliance to cultures of commitment. Alisa's mantra is "When our teachers succeed, our students succeed."

Bryan Goodwin is president and CEO of McREL International. For more than 20 years at McREL, he has translated research into practice, scanning the world for new insights and best practices on teaching and leading, and helping educators everywhere adapt them to address their own challenges. A frequent conference presenter, he is the author of *Out of Curiosity: Restoring the Power of Hungry Minds for Better Schools, Workplaces, and Lives* (McREL, 2018) and *Simply Better: Doing What Matters Most to Change the*

Odds for Student Success (ASCD, 2011). He also is a co-author of *Instructional Models: How to Choose One and How to Use One* (McREL, 2019), *Curiosity Works: A Guidebook for Moving Your School From Improvement to Innovation* (McREL, 2018), *Unstuck: How Curiosity, Peer Coaching, and Teaming Can Change Your School* (ASCD, 2018), *Balanced Leadership for Powerful Learning: Tools for Achieving Success in Your School* (ASCD, 2015), and *The 12 Touchstones of Good Teaching: A Checklist for Staying Focused Every Day* (ASCD, 2013). Bryan also writes for ASCD's *Educational Leadership* magazine. Before joining McREL in 1998, Bryan was a college instructor, a high school teacher, and a business journalist.

Bj Stone, Ed.D., is a co-author of *Classroom Instruction That Works* (ASCD, 2012) and *A Handbook for Classroom Instruction That Works* (ASCD, 2012), and is the author of the *Facilitator's Manual for Classroom Instruction That Works* (McREL, 2012). Bj is a former middle and high school science teacher, university instructor, and central office administrator. She has a B.S. in biology, an M.S. in science education, and an Ed.D. in educational leadership and policy study from the University of Northern Colorado. She served as a consulting director at McREL International for 12 years, working internationally and nationally with K–12 teachers and administrators. Bj is currently an independent consultant and owner of Advantage Learning and Leading, coaching teachers and administrators and facilitating learning related to curriculum and instruction.

Bess Scott, Ph.D., is an associate professor of educational leadership at Doane University in Lincoln, Nebraska. She spent her 36-year public school career in Omaha and Lincoln, teaching French, English, PE, and health, and serving in multiple leadership roles culminating with director of continuous improvement for Lincoln Public Schools. Bess has also been a managing consultant for McREL International. She is a national training associate for Thinking Collaborative as well as an MBTI Certified Practitioner. Bess has presented at multiple national conferences including AASPA, Learning Forward, NSDC, ASCD, NASSP, NAESP, NMSA, and AMLE, with an emphasis on effective instruction, continuous school improvement, and leadership.